CARVED ON THE PALM OF HIS HAND

BONNIE LOUISE NEWHOUSE

PRESS

www.xulonpress.com

CONTENTS

INTRODUCTION

I first titled the book *A Time for Searching*. Halfway through the years of working on it, I realized the title referred to only one chapter. Then one day, I saw a plaque on a table at a garage sale. Immediately I realized the title should be changed to *Carved on the Palm of His Hand,* as close to a telegram from God that I had ever received.

> See! I will not forget you . . .
> I have carved you on the palm of my hand.
> (Isaiah 49:15)

Now, I could see! I had thought God had forgotten me. All the while, God was carving me on the palm of His hand. As a potter with a piece of clay, working and molding it to match the vision he had for it and keeping it in His shop until ready for use, so God had kept me hidden in the palm of His hand. He may have even put me on the shelf for years—or so it seems, "For I am His workmanship, created in Christ Jesus for good works, which God prepared beforehand that I should walk in them" (Ephesians 2:9).

The Potter knew what He purposed for this piece of clay, how He wanted to use me, and which tools would be required to mold me into that vessel for His purpose. Sometimes the tool was heavy and came close to breaking me. Sometimes the fire was so hot, it seemed to consume me. Yet the Potter knew exactly the needed process to mold me to match the vision He always had for my life. As Paul told the

Corinthians, "We have this treasure in earthen vessels, that the excellence of the power may be of God and not of us" (II Corinthians 4:7).

I discovered my life mirrored those seasons listed in Ecclesiastes, chapter 3, although not the same order. "Crossing a Threshold" with the scripture from Ecclesiastes: a time for loving and a time for dancing was my first chapter. Some seasons would be a surprise and come too soon. We are never ready for chapters that involve war, death, and dying, but they, too, are part of life. For others, we would have to wait many years. The chapters entitled "Waiting on the Lord," "Miracles," and "Unfinished Business" reveal that God's pace is unhurried. He will accomplish His mission in His timing. It takes a lot longer with matters of the heart and soul than the outside appearances. God had a plan. Some seasons were paused or interrupted, such as my college years, only to be resumed later. The years of raising children would be spaced.

As God's vessel, I never knew when He would choose to take me from hiding and thrust me to the front lines to be part of a larger plan. In the chapters, "School Studies," "In The Midst of the Years," and "Warfare in the Valley," I found myself thrust to the front line of different battles. I learned that whatever God's assignment was, I never felt ready in my own power but had to rely on God's power. That is the way He planned it. When I was my weakest, He was strongest!

In "Tested by Fire," "Where Are You, God?" "Vicarage," and "Pandora's Box Is Opened," I would experience the refining fire of God so He could mold me into just the shape he needed for the work He planned for me to do. In the chapters "Our Last Year," "Deploying My Spiritual Gifts," and "In the Trenches," God would reveal to me the gifts He had given me and the purpose for which He created me. He created the works. My assignment was to walk through them.

My friend Judith gave me a copy of the book, *The Weight of Your Words,* (1) in which author Joseph M. Stowell writes about "The Provision of God":

> God provides all we need to go through circumstances
> that would normally defeat us with fear. He supplies
> us with His Word, which assures us of the fullness
> of His character and gives us instructions that really

work. He provides the support of fellow believers who pray for us and with us. We also have access to His indwelling Spirit, who prays for us, guides us, teaches us, and provides the assurances that He will meet all of our needs.

DEDICATION

This book is dedicated to my husband of fifty-one years, Arthur, and our children: Benjamin, Danielle, Matthew, and Traci whose lives will be introduced to the readers.

ACKNOWLEDGMENTS

wish to express my appreciation to my husband, Arthur M. Newhouse, who has supported me while we lived each season and then relived each of them again as I captured the memories in writing; our daughter Danielle Newhouse Rice, who painstakingly retyped the entire manuscript into computer format; to our children, Benjamin, Matthew, and Traci who have agreed to let me share some of their life experiences while growing up; to my siblings, Wayne, Richard, Barbara, Marion, Connie, and cousin Marilyn, who will find some of our family experiences among the pages; to Art's siblings, Robert, Thomas, Barbara, and Bernard, who will read some of the family experiences we shared after I joined their family in marriage; to my friend Judith Danford, who for many years has shared the vision of what this book would look like and then assisted me in meticulous editing; to my lifelong friend Dee Ann DuBois, whose ideas as a reader helped make it easier reading; and to my friends and extended family, who have been a part of my life and have been willing to have our shared personal experiences written in this story.

Chapter 1

CROSSING A THRESHOLD

"A time for dancing . . . A time for loving"
Ecclesiastes 3:8, 4 (JB)

One Sunday afternoon in early November of 1963, my friend Mary and I drove to an apartment in downtown Lansing, Michigan to visit some friends. When we arrived, we found them in the midst of painting the bedrooms of their bachelor pad. Feeling a bit mischievous, I picked up a paintbrush and began brushing it on the wall, to the dismay of our friends.

Seeing the impending disaster, one of the fellows quickly grabbed the brush from my hand, "Why don't you come see the other room—the one we've already finished?"

I followed him down the hall to the other bedroom and pretended to inspect the paint job. Looking around the room, I noticed a picture of a girl on the dresser and paused wondering who she was. I was still gazing at it when an unfamiliar fellow stepped into the doorway, "I'm Art, and this is my room. What are you doing here?"

For a moment I stood speechless, my eyes fixed upon the tall, handsome blond fellow, "Oh, I'm just . . . looking at the paint job." Then, pointing to the picture, I asked, "Who is she?"

"My girlfriend," he answered coldly. "Listen, you two are going to have to leave. We're going out to get something to eat."

Somewhat embarrassed at the sudden request to leave, Mary and I quickly said goodbye to our friends and left. I could not stop thinking about the tall, handsome blond-haired stranger. His face seemed frozen in my memory. What was it about him? I could not explain the moment our eyes met.

The following week Mary and I went to a dance at the "Ponytail," a new teenage dance club south of Lansing. Dancing was a favorite hobby and the activity I most enjoyed on the weekends. As usual, my spirits were high as I sat at the table listening to the music and watching the doorway, waiting for John to arrive. It was my intention to invite him to the bank's upcoming Christmas party. Instead, I recognized Art's face and found myself calling out, rather loudly, across the crowded dance floor, "Hey Art, remember me?"

Recognizing me, he came over to our table and sat down. We talked and danced together for the remainder of the evening. I suddenly realized I had been so enamored with Art, I never noticed if John had arrived. I still needed a date for the bank's Christmas Party. *The Christmas party*, I thought to myself, *the perfect opportunity to ask him for a date*.

"Would you like to come to my Christmas party?" I asked, giving him the date and time, "The bank where I work always has it at Walnut Hills Country Club," I added rather proudly as if to give him further incentive.

"Gee, I can't," he said shaking his head. "I have to work that night."

Seeing my disappointed look, he further explained, "I work the night shift at Oldsmobile and have to work that night."

"Well, if you can't come, I'll invite someone else." Although I liked him very much I did not want to miss the party.

Art thought about it for a moment, then reconsidered and promised to attend with me. Afterward, I learned how he had managed to get the time off. He gave me his copy of the reprimand he had received after his unexcused absence from work.

We dated steadily after the dance. John and the girl in the picture became ghosts, and two weeks later, Art asked me to wear his class ring. At first, I would not accept the ring. I explained I had gone steady several times before and each time resented being bound to one person and the restrictions it placed on my social life. It ruined an otherwise good relationship.

Art was not to be easily discouraged and pursued the issue again several weeks later. I had given a great deal of thought to the idea of going steady with this person. Truthfully, I had spent considerable time reflecting on the events of the past six months.

"Maybe this time it will work out," I rationalized to myself as I contemplated the idea of going steady again. "Aside from the relationship, there are some obvious advantages in going steady. I have to admit it is fun to flash around an oversized class ring. I could wrap it in bright angora to fit my finger, and everyone would know that I am special. There is a sense of security in having a boyfriend and a sure date for the weekend. Actually, it would give me a measure of stability; a constant in my otherwise changing world." Stability and changed world—yes, stability was something I longed for. As I thought back over the last six months, I understood why.

Only a few weeks before, the nation had been rocked to the core with the news that President Kennedy had been shot. I was at work when the secretary to the personnel director came into our department with the shocking news. Initially, there was an attitude of disbelief. After all, how could something like this happen in America? Throughout the afternoon, the story unfolded. It was true. It had happened in America. He had been fatally shot during his visit to Dallas with Mrs. Kennedy. Before I left work, we knew the shots had been fatal.

Two days later, I remember standing in the family room of my home watching the evening news. Lee Harvey Oswald, accused assassin of the President was in handcuffs. Suddenly, we heard the sound of gunshots! Oswald collapsed. Chaos filled the television screen as people scrambled to catch his shooter. We stood speechless. It had happened so quickly and while we watched the evening news.

An underlying blanket of depression enveloped the country. It was as though the ground was no longer solid. It seemed the entire country was mourning: Democrats and Republicans. We had watched the funeral procession, the horse without its rider, the flag-draped casket, and Jacqueline Kennedy and her children. There was no escaping the tragedy for months: the news reports, the endless investigation, the sadness. Every nightly national newscast brought a reminder of that terrible day.

Yet, even before these national events occurred, I had sensed my world had turned upside down. So much had changed since my high-school graduation. Like most high-school graduates, I was optimistic about my future. I was on a high like a bird that had been training to fly for eighteen years. I had enrolled for fall term at Lansing Community College. I hoped to complete a two-year business degree and learn bookkeeping. My friend's grandmother, who headed the proof department at a Lansing bank, had encouraged me to apply for a job in the check-paying department at the main branch downtown only a few blocks from the college.

By the end of that summer, I concluded that my preconceived notion about the outside world was not nearly as rosy as I had once thought. In three short months, I had been exposed to a side of the world that I had not known, shattering my fantasies of the storybook romance. Riding the city bus to work opened my eyes.

The bus stop where I waited was across the street from a house whose occupants were of questionable repute. Every morning there was a different man and a different car in the driveway. The children seemed to roam about unsupervised. I wondered what their life was like behind those doors. If that was not enough, the bus driver who was married had a girlfriend who rode the route with him, sitting directly behind him chatting all the while. I had observed other promiscuous activities in the outside world. Suddenly I felt bombarded with the negative side of life. I did not like what I saw and found it unsettling.

As fall approached, I had looked forward to getting my mind off the world and all its problems and concentrating on something positive, something uplifting. Yes, making new friends and going to college would be a wonderful change of atmosphere. The bank adjusted my work schedule to fit my new college schedule. I would attend classes in the morning, work from noon until seven, and return to the campus for evening classes most days.

All the reports I had heard about the difference between high school and college proved accurate. There was no homeroom teacher to supervise us or keep us on schedule and no one to guide us to our classes or even cared if we attended. That responsibility rested on our shoulders. I was very grateful that somehow in my training thus far, I had developed the necessary self-discipline to adjust. With my busy schedule, there was no way I could get all the work done if I didn't use my time wisely. To have paid my tuition with money I earned was an added incentive.

I will never forget that first term, which proved crucial for many. Everyone soon discovered that the popular places to congregate were the cafeteria or the commons, a room smaller than the cafeteria that had vending machines for food and snacks. Some students would sit and socialize for hours. On those occasions I did sit down briefly, I envied them their freedom and the fun they seemed to be having. By midterm, some realized there was more to college than the glamorous social life and adjusted accordingly. Others, though, continued to idle away their time and by second term had disappeared from the campus.

Yes, life was very different now. Things were not the same as they had been in high school. It was a large dose of reality. At times, the responsibility seemed overwhelming as I faced the outside world. My thoughts having returned to Art's question: "Will you go steady?" Yes, the security of having a steady boyfriend and being special to someone felt very secure. Although our first meeting did not reveal it, in time I sensed something special about Art. In the following months, I discovered he possessed many tangible qualities that I looked for: He possessed manliness balanced by tenderness. He was sincere, considerate, and thoughtful in little ways. Until now, I had doubted the person who had been long in my dreams really existed in the world. Would I ever be able to find the right balance of these qualities in any man? I knew I had found a prize.

Although we were both busy working and attending college, I knew I was experiencing some of the happiest moments in my life. During the week, we saw each other for only a few minutes or an hour squeezed into a hectic day. Much of our communication was in notes and letters, each of us tucking them away to reread on occasion.

As our relationship deepened and we began to talk seriously of a future together, I again found myself plagued with negative thoughts about marriage. I saw unfaithfulness and failed marriages everywhere. These relationships must have started out positive and loving, just as ours was. What happened? Were there any marriages where genuine love and trust could be found five, ten, or twenty years down the road? More important, would our love stand the pressures of change and time?

One Sunday, during a period of despondency, I accompanied Art to visit his parents in nearby St. Johns. We attended church and stayed for dinner. After the meal, Art was outdoors with his father, and I found myself alone in the living room. I glanced around the room looking for something interesting to read when I caught sight of a bookcase. Glancing through the books, one book title caught my attention: *The Power of Positive Thinking,* (1) by Norman Vincent Peale. That afternoon I read as much as possible and then purchased one for myself the following week.

Slowly I read it, devouring its contents. I was fascinated with the new information and its potential to improve the way I coped with life. Gradually, I realized that I had allowed the negative things in my life to dominate my thinking and clutter my mind. I had come to a tunnel filled with darkness.

I began to implement Dr. Peale's method of replacing each negative thought with a positive thought—namely a Bible verse. First I had to become consciously aware of my thought pattern. Every time a negative thought came floating into my mind, I immediately had to replace it with a Bible verse—one with a positive thought. I felt an intense battle going on within me—a spiritual tug of war—over the control of my mind. By turning to Scripture, God was fighting the battle for me. I began to see a glimpse of light in that dark tunnel.

"What would you think about going to Zale's Jewelry after work on Saturday?" Art casually mentioned after picking me up from work one day in early June.

I looked at him in surprise, "Zale's Jewelry Store?"

"Yeah, they're having a sale on diamond rings."

"Well . . . I guess so." My thoughts suddenly were in a flurry. He wants to look at rings: engagement rings? The ball was rolling faster than I had anticipated. I reminded myself an engagement can last for several months or maybe a year. There would be plenty of time to adjust and plenty of time to plan. Yes, marriage was a long way off.

That brief conversation was Art's marriage proposal. Later, when I teased, "You never asked me to marry you," he replied, "Well, I figured if you didn't want to get married, you wouldn't have agreed to go look at wedding rings."

We went to Zale's on Saturday as planned and picked out the rings with the understanding we wait a few months to announce our engagement. Art would keep them at his apartment until the time seemed right.

"Maybe you can save it for a Christmas present or my birthday in late August," I suggested. That would buy me a little more time. Buying the rings was a big enough step for now and took all the courage I could muster. Engagement was serious business.

Art kept the rings at his apartment for almost a month before I agreed to accept the engagement ring. June 28 was no ordinary day but a day our family always celebrated—the birthday my father shared with my younger brother, Richard. Art had joined our family celebration by going to a nearby lake for swimming and a picnic. When I emerged from the lake, dripping wet, straight hair, and no makeup, it suddenly occurred to me that if Art could accept me looking like that, it must be love!

After we left the lake, we stopped by Art's apartment to pick up the ring and rejoined my parents at home. Dad seemed to share our joy, but Mother's reaction was subdued. "I hope you're going to wait a while," she said frowning, "after all, you're only eighteen!"

"Don't worry, Mom," I reassured, giving her a hug. "We aren't getting married for at least a year."

Becoming engaged was a major decision for both of us. Six months before, when we exchanged class rings, we had mutually agreed not to use them as weapons to toss back and forth whenever disagreements arose. The commitment to be married was far more serious. Once more, we renewed our mutual promise to resolve any future differences.

During our courtship, I discovered what made Art so special and unlike any other fellow I had dated: in one letter he wrote: "We must have faith in each other and above all, faith in the Lord, honey. He knows what is best for us, and if we let Him do the driving, we can't go wrong."

Although Art could not understand my periods of depression, he was a constant source of strength. His faith was much stronger than mine was, and he believed God could make our marriage different. To him, God was a real and personal part of his everyday life. I was a Christian but had never taken God at His word in this way. I trusted Art, and because his faith was strong, I trusted what he was telling me was true. That thread of faith sustained me and gave me the courage to trust my future to him. I was about to take that leap of faith, blindly trusting that our marriage would not be another "statistic."

Feeling relieved that our future was in God's hands, I proceeded with the wedding preparations. We talked to our pastor and arranged a wedding date in August of 1965. I will always remember our first premarital meeting with Reverend Woldt.

"Would you like a message or talk about marriage?" he asked, looking at me. "It's the custom in our church."

I hesitated for a moment, "Well, I'll think about it and let you know at our next meeting."

For the next several weeks, I was in a quandary, having interpreted Reverend Woldt as meaning I would have to give the talk. Petrified at the thought of delivering a speech in front of everyone on my wedding day was out of the question!

When our next appointment arrived, I explained to him that I hated giving speeches and just could not do it on my wedding day. Reverend Woldt burst into laughter, "No, Bonnie, you won't be giving the talk. I'll be giving the talk!" Feeling very foolish and embarrassed and at the same time relieved, my eyes filled with tears. Reverend Woldt later told us he had shared the incident with many other couples during premarital sessions.

Six weeks before our wedding, I began to feel apprehensive about the commitment and fearful that I was about to make the mistake of a lifetime. "Oh Mom," I sobbed, "What am I going to do? The wedding invitations have to go out next week. I'm just not sure."

"Well, Honey," she said wrapping her arms tightly around me, "It's not too late to call it off. I think you need a little time apart from Art to think about it and to pray about it . . . I think it would be a good idea not to talk to him or see him for a week."

When Art called our house and learned of my emotional quandary, he did not push the issue but agreed to give me some space. Upset by the turn of events and unsure of the outcome, he sought advice from an older man he worked with.

"Oh, don't worry," he encouraged, "It's probably just wedding jitters. That happens sometimes."

During my week apart from Art, neither Mother nor any member of my family pressured me but let me work through my thoughts in solitude. I sought only God's counsel as I asked the questions: Why was I feeling so overwhelmed? Did I not love this man? Answers came into clear focus as I reflected on my thoughts. I loved Art. Fear had come as I tried to peer too far down the road. Yes, marriage is for a lifetime, yet each day must be lived one day at a time. God's peace gradually quelled my anxious heart as He assured me He would walk with us. My faith restored, I was able to resume wedding plans.

My melancholy spirit soared to new heights as our wedding day approached. Caught up in a frenzy of wedding preparations and bridal showers was an exhilarating time. I loved being the center of attention at work, at home, and with family and friends. Having come from a family of four children, I could not ever remember receiving so much attention and so many presents.

Our wedding was seven-thirty in the evening of August 28, 1965. The day passed quickly with endless last-minute tasks to be completed. Finally, we arrived at the church late in the afternoon where everyone was bustling with activity. My attendants were scurrying around getting dressed while Mother helped me get into my wedding gown. It was a beautiful white floor-length gown of Chantilly lace, trimmed with a fitted bodice and long sleeves. The moment I had seen it in the department store, I had recognized it as the one pictured in my mind for years. No sooner were we dressed than there seemed a steady stream of people dashing in and out of the dressing room to pick up corsages and take pictures.

"The floor-length turquoise gowns look very becoming with the girls' dark hair," I thought proudly as I surveyed my attendants. I had chosen my close friend Dee Ann as maid of honor. We had shared so many good times together, and it was important that she should share this happy occasion. Art's sister Barbara was a bridesmaid, having become good friends during our courtship. My thirteen-year-old sister, Barbara, served as junior bridesmaid and seemed to have grown up overnight from a little girl to a lovely young lady. Art's four-year-old niece, Cindy was the flower girl, and although she had the reputation of being a "tomboy," her long dress transformed her into a delightful little girl. Suddenly, the commotion ended as my attendants left to begin their walk down the aisle. I stood alone with my father in the stairway leading up to the sanctuary.

Giving me away in marriage was a very emotional experience for Dad. His face was white, and his hands were trembling. Rather than being strong for me to lean on, it was the opposite. He was not his usual self, making smart remarks or finding humor. There was no humor in his demeanor this day. He was worried about his role in the ceremony.

"Is it, 'Her mother and I'?" he repeatedly asked.

"Yes, Dad, that's right," I gently reassured, squeezing the hand that held mine. We were two solemn faces as we slowly began the long walk down the aisle of Christ Lutheran Church. Both of us were concentrating on only one task; that of walking arm in arm and yet far enough away so as not to cause Dad to trip on my full wedding gown with the chapel train.

I was glad when the ceremony ended, and we walked down the aisle together. Standing in the receiving line was the most relaxing part of our wedding. All the formality was over, and everything had gone perfectly. I was filled with joy as we greeted all those who had come to share the ceremony and knew this mountain-top experience would remain outstanding in our memories. The day was over all too soon, and I was thankful for the pictures taken capturing that momentous occasion.

When the time came to move my belongings into the mobile home we had purchased, I realized leaving the nest completely would have to be a gradual process for me. No one seemed to notice I had purposely left some clothes in the closet of the bedroom I had shared with my sister. We had always been a close family, and I was the first of four children to leave home. I was aware of the importance of my role in the family as the eldest daughter of a working mother; being her substitute had given me a sense of self-importance and fulfill-ment, although at times, I had resented all the responsibility.

My father and younger brother seemed the most affected by my absence. Sometimes Dad would call to say that he was cooking something special and invite us for dinner, other times he would drop by unexpectedly simply to say hello. My brother, Rich on the other hand, did not express his sentiments until years later when he told me he felt as though I had abandoned him. In time, the family adjusted to my absence. In fact, I was surprised how quickly they adjusted and learned to manage without me. Yet, I reminded myself Art needed me now, and my need to be needed was transferred to my husband.

As a romantic person, I felt a couple could be as starry-eyed after their marriage as they had been during their courtship—holding hands, sitting close to one another in the car, or kissing goodbye in front of the office. I told myself I would not let our marriage change us as it seemed to change everyone else. I had talked to many others about my feelings, always getting the same response. "It isn't that you don't love the person as you once did, it is just that your young love matures into something even better." It took a long time before I understood what they meant. Accepting this inevitable change was undoubtedly the greatest adjustment for me as a young bride.

Trying to juggle all the new responsibilities, in addition to my job and school, was overwhelming. Where do I find time to keep a tidy house, prepare meals, and do laundry? Clearly, I could not reduce my hours at work, but I would have to spend less time on my schoolwork. Deciding to prove myself a capable wife, I gave highest priority to my domestic role. When the first quarter was over, however, and the grades came out, I sorely regretted my decision. My score in wifely duties did not matter when compared to the terrible disappointment I felt when I received a "C" in my accounting class—the class in which I had always excelled. Determined to prove I could maintain my good grades, I vowed to take the class over the next quarter and relax my own expectations on domestic matters. My studies took precedence over any of the other roles throughout the remainder of my college years.

Shortly after we married, we began to think seriously about our religious life and church commitment. During our courtship, we attended both the Lutheran Church, where my family held membership and the Episcopal Church in nearby St. Johns with the Newhouse family. While we did not discuss it often together, we both realized this arrangement could not continue indefinitely. The time had come to choose one or the other. I assumed I would change for no reason other than my preconceived notion that the wife should change to the husband's denomination as Mother had done.

Meanwhile, Art had been giving considerable thought to this decision. Unbeknown to me, he had been inwardly searching for years. As an infant, he had been baptized into the Catholic faith and later, when the family left the Catholic Church, they had become Episcopalians. I was quite surprised when he told me of his decision to begin instructions in the Lutheran Church. He was confirmed at the same altar where we married, the day after Christmas.

Our country was heavily involved in the Viet Nam War; in the fall of 1965 Congress had passed a new draft status law to close what they viewed as a loophole for many of the nation's male students. The new law required male students to carry twelve or more credits to qualify for military deferment. With a full-time job, Art was carrying less than twelve credits. We knew he could not handle a heavier class schedule and maintain passing grades while working full time. He must make the choice between attending college or be drafted.

Art's college education was important to both of us and affected our future. Being drafted and going to war might mean no future; the risks were too high. The decision to quit his job at the factory and enroll as a full-time student was one we made together. With the loss of Art's full-time income, we could not survive financially on my income from the bank. I would have to find a better paying, full-time job and continue my education in the evenings.

As I mentally prepared for job interviews, my first task was to fend off the negative thoughts barraging me. "You can't apply for an accounting job," the voice chided. "You're too young. You haven't finished school yet."

I knew that in order to sell myself for the position for which I was applying, I first must believe in me and be confident. I must focus on the knowledge I had already learned and the valuable job experience I had acquired while working at the bank. A scripture verse quoted in Norman Vincent Peale's book, *The Power of Positive Thinking*, came to mind: "I can do all things through Christ who strengthens me." (2)

"I am capable of handling a job with more responsibility," I found myself retorting boldly, "I can refer to myself as a bookkeeper."

26

The morning of my interview, I took special care in dressing, knowing regardless of how I felt inside, I must give the impression that I was a mature, capable young woman. As I set out for my interview, I glanced one more time in the mirror. The young woman I saw appeared grown up and confident with the mink-trimmed coat and new matching shoes and purse. One would never suspect that just a few months before, she had been a frightened teenager facing an unknown world.

The owner of the Certified Public Accounting firm frowned as he looked over my application, while I sat quietly in the chair opposite him.

"I'm reluctant to hire you because of your lack of experience in the field of bookkeeping," he said, as if thinking aloud. "But, I will give you that chance to prove yourself. How soon could you start?"

I looked at him and smiled. "I will need to give two weeks' notice at the bank. I will be available on December 1."

Chapter 2

ME, A PASTOR'S WIFE?

"A time for knocking down"
Ecclesiastes 3:3 (JB)

*I*t was an ordinary February day in 1966 when Art drove me to the small office where I worked as a bookkeeper before going on to his classes at nearby Lansing Community College. Except for a brief call in the afternoon, I would not hear from him again until he picked me up after work. Midway through the morning on this particular day, however, I was surprised to hear Art's voice on the telephone. "Can you go to lunch with me today?"

"Yes, sure," I said wondering what his reason was for the sudden luncheon date.

"Great, I'll pick you up in front of the office at noon."

"Okay, see you then." I stared at the receiver as I hung up. "Wonder what's on his mind?" With my curiosity aroused, I anxiously watched the clock for the remainder of the morning. At noon, I grabbed my coat and hurried down the stairway of the old house now serving as an office building. Through the door window, I could see our yellow convertible waiting for me in front. Scarcely had I closed the car door when Art blurted out, "How would you feel about being a pastor's wife?"

I looked at him in dismay. "You've got to be kidding!"

"Nope, I've been thinking about this for a long time," he said excitedly.

"You never told me," I said, trying to hide the hurt I felt.

"I never told anyone."

I sat back in the seat. "But, I'm not just anyone," I thought to myself, "I'm your wife."

"Listen, let me explain. This morning I was sitting in the cafeteria talking to my cousin, Bill. He was telling me he has decided to go into the ministry, when I heard that Voice again. 'Art, I want *you* to be a minister.' I know it sounds crazy, but that's just the way it happened."

I struggled to keep from laughing. "Me, a pastor's wife?" I thought, "This sounds like a joke." I looked up at him. The expression on his face told me it was no joke. No, something had happened to him in the cafeteria; his face was radiant and his speech exhilarated. I had never seen Art this excited.

He went on to explain how God had been calling him to the ministry since his early teens. "In sermons I would hear God telling me to go into the ministry. He seemed to be constantly bugging me," he continued. "Whenever I read my Bible, certain verses seemed to jump out at me."

I nodded, beginning to believe his strange story. "Why didn't you?"

"I didn't want to be a minister," he confessed. "I thought the ministry was for sissies. I wanted to be a doctor. I wanted to make money and have material things. I didn't want God to control my life. I wanted to control my own life."

Suddenly the picture was clear: his indecision about his future, failing at Michigan State, dissatisfaction with working in the factory, enrolling at Lansing Community College. Art had changed his major so many times no one believed him: Pre-Med, Pre-Law, Accounting, and Marketing. It had become a joke among family and friends. All that time he fought what he knew God wanted him to do with his life. Now, I could see Art was at peace within himself.

Quietly listening, my own mood changed from one of laughter to a new seriousness. "What made you change your mind today?"

"I told God I was tired of fighting. If He wanted me to be a minister, I would do it. I was tired of fighting against His will. Strangely enough, as soon as I gave in, God gave me the desire to be a minister. Now, more than anything, I want to be a minister."

Art's excitement and radiance mysteriously transferred to me. Suddenly, my spirit became exuberant, and a warm glow came over me deep inside. I, too, felt called. I felt special. God's hand of favor had fallen upon me, singling me out to be a pastor's wife. More than anything, I wanted to be a pastor's wife.

Art peered, searching my eyes for an answer. "Well, what do you think about being married to a pastor?"

"I guess that would be okay with me," I responded as casually as I could muster. I was too embarrassed to share my secret feelings and purposely held back the pride and joy I felt deep in my heart.

Concentration seemed futile when I returned to work that afternoon, with my thoughts continually wandering back to Art's startling news. My stomach was queasy as I pondered the new turn my life had taken. Lost in my own world, I shared none of my exciting news with the others in the office. "If only I could be alone to think about this in private," I thought.

My mind was still preoccupied after dinner when Art dropped me off at the college before going to meet with our pastor. My pencil seemed to tingle as I sat in my accounting class practicing writing, "Rev. and Mrs. Arthur Newhouse" and thinking to myself. "*Certainly there will be some changes necessary.* After all, I know I'm far from perfect." I glanced around the room and saw only two other girls in my class. I had become friends with several of the male students. "Now that I'm going to be a pastor's wife, I probably shouldn't talk to them," I concluded.

Art's announcement of his decision to enter the ministry came as a relief and a surprise to our pastor. When Art called the church earlier in the day requesting an appointment, Reverend Woldt had mistakenly guessed he was coming in for marital counseling and was greatly relieved to learn the reason for Art's visit. He was surprised because prior to our marriage, Art had been Episcopalian and had only recently been received into membership of our church. Having spent considerable time instructing him in the doctrine of the Lutheran Church, Art had given no indication he was contemplating the ministry.

The prospect of another "son of the congregation" entering the ministry was cause for great rejoicing for Reverend Woldt. In the thirty years he had served as pastor of Christ Lutheran Church, the only other young man to enter the ministry from our congregation had been his son, Bill. Heartily supporting Art's decision, he promised to help him achieve the goal set before him.

Art's visit with our pastor also revealed the disappointing news that admission to either of the two synodical seminaries required a bachelor's degree. It would be two years before Art would earn his bachelor's degree. Two years was a long time to wait. We were both so excited and enthusiastic about the future, we were prepared to pack and leave immediately.

Although Art could not officially begin his studies at the seminary for two years, the impact of his decision immediately affected our lives. We did not fit the expectations everyone, including ourselves, had of what a pastor and his wife should be. Clergy families were devout Christians, without sin and always busy doing the work of the church.

One look at our lives told us we did not fit the description. We did not attend church every week nor were we involved in the life of our congregation. We did not even pray together or have family devotions. Far from perfect, we were uncomfortable in our new roles.

A poor example of a Christian family, much less a pastor's family, we made a conscious effort to conform to the image. We began to attend church on a regular basis and became involved in some church activities. Singing in the choir was one activity we felt comfortable doing and enjoyed. We were less enthusiastic and did not feel at ease participating in other activities. Art consented to become the Assistant Sunday School Superintendent. I reluctantly attended several of the women's meetings.

Step two on our agenda was making an effort to transform into devout Christians. To begin, we attempted to integrate family devotions into our life. Art picked up one of the daily devotional guides from church one Sunday morning and later that evening, we adjourned to our living room sofa for family devotions.

I felt like an actress as I sat motionless beside Art, while he read the day's devotion. Part of me wanted to be serious and lose myself in the role of a devout Christian wife while another part of me wanted to run from the script.

When the telephone rang midway through the devotion, I welcomed the interruption and jumped up to answer it. I could feel Art eyes glaring at me from the sofa during the entire conversation.

"Why didn't you let it ring," he scolded after I hung up.

"Well . . . I . . . We . . . always answer the phone," I answered sheepishly.

"They would have called back," he said sternly.

Getting angry myself, I retorted, "Aren't we carrying this thing just a little too far?"

He hesitated for a moment and then the stern look on his face began to fade as his muscles relaxed. "Maybe you're right," he said softly. "I suppose it wouldn't hurt to be a little more flexible."

Art's decision to become a pastor had a significant effect on our relationships with a majority of our friends and relatives. Although many were not critical, we began to notice a change. Seeking to relate to our new identity, some were ill at ease and unnatural. There were hesitations in conversations and uncomfortable moments of silence between sentences while their minds carefully censored their thoughts before daring to speak. Believing that Christians could not have fun together and remain Christian, they gradually drew away.

Some reverted to the other extreme in their efforts to identify with us. They felt compelled to talk about religious matters: their church, the Bible, Sunday school classes they taught, Bible studies they attended, church activities they participated in, and so forth. "See how much like you we are," they seemed to be saying. "We do all these religious things, too." They did not understand this was not a natural part of our lives. Our entire life was not God-centered and religious activities. They assumed we must know all about the Bible if Art was going to be a pastor. This simply was not the case. Their language was foreign to us. Because they made us feel uneasy, we avoided them. For most, the identity of a pastor and wife constantly overshadowed the two individuals we were.

We realized we did not conform to the image some had of a pastor and his wife, when we began to notice some previously accepted behaviors were no longer acceptable. Some of the criticism came in subtle remarks while others were quite bold and direct. Usually the sharpest criticism came from within our own families, oftentimes at family gatherings. When relaxing with our families, we felt we could be ourselves and were most apt to be unguarded.

Art joined the other relatives who had gone outside the house to smoke a cigarette after my Aunt Beatrice's funeral one afternoon. While mingling with the others, my Great Aunt Cora tapped him on the shoulder. "Are you still going into the ministry?"

"Yes," he responded, wondering why she was inquiring.

"Are you sure you're going into the ministry?"

"She's really impressed with the idea," Art thought to himself, "She must intend to leave me some money in her will."

Art smiled proudly, "Yes, I'm still planning to be a minister."

Directing him away from the others to the shade of a nearby tree, Great Aunt Cora looked him straight in the eye, "Can you imagine Christ walking on the Sea of Galilee with a cigarette in His mouth?"

We responded to the critics differently. While Art was confident and quick to defend his actions, I became intimidated. I had no defense, no weapons of authority, with which to fight back. "Are these legitimate complaints," I continually asked myself, "or merely attempts to force us into a mold to satisfy their expectations?"

The people I reacted most negatively to were those who held the office of pastor high on a pedestal, above others and above me. To them, being a pastor was an awesome position—next in line to God. It was not difficult for me to spot them. When we were together, their eyes fixed on Art. When he spoke, they listened attentively, embracing every word. Their preoccupation with him told me they were far more interested in what Art was doing or saying than in anything I had to say. To know some of my friends and relatives no longer valued my opinion or respected me as a person as they had once hurt me deeply. Feeling rejected, I drew away from those who had proven themselves disloyal.

The pain I felt slowly began to turn to anger and resentment inside. "If only I could get it out and talk to someone," I thought. "But I can't. No one would understand. I can't tell anyone what I'm feeling. I shouldn't feel this way. Christians shouldn't feel this way. Why am I so sensitive? Isn't all this a natural happening? Isn't it natural for people to look up to a pastor with respect? All the other pastors' wives in the world don't seem to be bothered when people make over their husbands. They don't seem to mind continually taking second place. They just accept it graciously. It's no problem for them, so why is it a problem for me? Why can't I be like the others? Why do I have to feel this way?"

I did not share what I was thinking with anyone—not even my husband because I didn't trust the feelings I had. Yet, concealing my angry feelings was no easy task. Not only were they not going away, they were growing. They were festering inside me like an ugly cancer spreading until they began to bubble over and become outwardly visible. When the anger and resentment came out, however, I found myself turning my hostility instead toward Art. He was the cause for this turmoil in my life.

It was not intentional. I did not decide one day to get even. It manifested itself slowly in subtle, barbed remarks and unnecessary sarcasm directed toward Art. They were tiny arrows shot from my mouth whenever the opportunity arose. I did not like myself for doing it. It was not like me to talk to my husband that way. I knew I was not fighting fair because Art was not aware of the war. The mounting tension was causing a strained relationship.

When I could no longer contain my angry feelings, they came bursting forth in a flood of tears in the midst of what began as an unrelated argument.

"Don't you notice how people treat you differently now that you're going into the ministry? They don't even care what I think anymore. How would you feel if you were me?" I shouted angrily. It all came out so quickly, I did not have time to worry about what Art would think. It was not a matter of trusting my feelings or risking them to be wrong. I had no choice.

Art did not return my anger but spoke quietly. "Yes, I've noticed."

I looked at him in disbelief. "You noticed?" I breathed a sigh of relief as the tremendous burden I had carried lifted. All those secret fears I harbored deep inside vanished. I wanted to shout with joy. "These things aren't a figment of my imagination! They are real! I'm not losing my mind!" He would not have had to say another word.

Chapter 3

TESTED BY FIRE

"A time for losing"
Ecclesiastes 3:6 (JB)

By the fall of 1966, we had completed our two-year courses at Lansing Community College and transferred to Michigan State University. We viewed Michigan State as a stepping stone to seminary: a necessary evil to tolerate until we got to the place we really wanted to be. To God, our time there provided the ideal setting for the next phase of His agenda.

The transition from a small community college to a large university brought unanticipated adjustments. I felt a sense of lost identity standing in a long line to register for classes and then being asked for my student ID number rather than my name. That experience reinforced the fact that now I was only a minute fraction of thousands of students. The larger my world, the smaller and unimportant I felt.

Academic requirements were more rigid and competition much tougher at MSU. Unlike my classrooms at Lansing Community College, my humanities classroom was the size of a small auditorium. Distractions in a room that size made concentration on the lecture a difficult chore. Living off campus and commuting to our classes in East Lansing proved time-consuming and expensive. More important was the feeling of detachment from the college community. It became apparent as the term progressed that we were living in two different worlds far removed from one another.

One January night as we lay in bed reflecting on the transition, we began sharing our feelings. I was surprised to hear Art express feelings similar to mine. He, too, did not feel a part of campus life. Living off campus made it difficult to socialize with other students or be involved in campus activities. With the exception of a few students who lived in our mobile home park, most of our neighbors were much older. Could it be that the home so ideal for us as newlyweds, no longer suited our needs? Was it time for us to consider selling our mobile home and move into married housing?

"Oh, I hate to think about having to sell our home," I said mournfully, sensing the direction this conversation was leading us.

"I know, Wife, I feel the same way."

"I mean . . . it's our first home. It's so much a part of us. . . . all the memories. How can we even think about selling it?"

Art reached for my hand and squeezed it tightly. "It's hard for me, too."

Knowing he shared my sentimental feelings made it easier for me to face. I had not realized how important it was to me. "Just thinking about leaving here gives me a sick feeling. I feel like a traitor, discarding an old friend no longer useful to me. It scares me to think about moving. I feel secure here—safe from the outside world." Suddenly I became aware of the importance of having arrived at this point together and being in one accord about our decision. *"This is not something I would want to be pushed into,"* I thought.

As our conversation continued in the stillness of the night, we concurred that our changing needs outweighed our sentimental feelings. Not only did we share a common desire to live in married housing, we shared a readiness to move forward and a willingness to risk the unknown. With our minds clearly settled on these important issues, the next step seemed obvious. Tomorrow we would place an ad in the newspaper. If selling our mobile home and moving on campus was also God's will for us, we were certain a buyer would come forth. In the meantime, Art would stop by the University apartments' office and check into the details of renting an apartment in Spartan Village.

Had we any second thoughts about our hasty decision, there was little time to change our minds because within two weeks, our mobile home sold for the full asking price. We placed our name on a waiting list for married housing and moved our belongings into a small apartment in Lansing until an apartment became available. The only disadvantage in making the change was the "no pet" policy strictly enforced on campus. Moving there would necessitate giving up our Siamese cat.

We loved Tiki, given to us the previous year by Art's younger brother Bernard after our first kitten died of distemper. When he, too, contracted the disease soon after he came to us, we had lovingly nursed him back to health despite the veterinarian's poor prognosis. During the past year, he had become an important member of our family, a favorite topic of conversation between us, and a common denominator in our busy lives. Parting with the pet we had grown to love would be a painful experience. We had no peace until David, Art's sister's fiancé, agreed to give him a good home and allow us frequent visits.

We were elated when the married housing office notified us that an apartment in Spartan Village would be available in April. After driving past acre after acre of married housing units on our way to and from class, it seemed impossible to believe one of them would be our home. According to the map given us, an apartment at the end of the second floor of one of the L-shaped brick complexes would be our home.

As soon as we walked through the door, we fell in love with our new apartment. The carpeted living room and neatly upholstered furniture gave a cozy appearance and an instant feeling of warmth. The sturdy wooden desk, prominently placed in the living room to the left of the front door, reminded us that studies were a high priority in this place. Although we did not often talk about it, we knew Art's grades these next two terms were crucial to our future.

When Art applied to transfer to Michigan State, we had been surprised to learn that the poor grades earned as a freshman were a permanent blemish on his record. The fact that he had reckoned with the folly of his past and had begun anew had little bearing on the situation. Regardless of the grade-point average he earned at Lansing

Community College, he would begin at Michigan State carrying the burden of the past with him. His readmittance stipulation was to bring his old GPA up to a "C" within three terms.

By the fall of 1967, the distant lurking shadow was becoming a dark cloud hovering over our future. Although he had steadily improved his grade-point average, difficulty with learning German, a seminary requirement, impeded his progress. We prayed night after night, but our prayers seemed futile.

I felt helpless as day after day I watched Art struggle. The only thing I knew to do to help was listen to him recite vocabulary words, or type up lists of new words to memorize. As the situation worsened, and I could see he was becoming very discouraged and depressed, I found some inspirational Bible verses, wrote them on small index cards, and gave them to him for encouragement.

Finals week came, and the pressure mounted with my humanities final scheduled for the same day Art took his German final. I hurried home after work, anxious to hear how he had done on his final and eager to review my notes once more. The moment I walked through the door, I sensed the final had not gone well. His face was drawn and his blue eyes appeared pained.

"Well, how did it go?" I questioned, trying to be optimistic.

He looked down and his voice trembled, on the brink of tears. "I flunked it. There's no use in even taking the rest of my finals."

I stared at him in disbelief, a flurry of thoughts racing through my head. "How can this be? How can God let this happen? Why didn't He help Art?" We had been praying for months. This final was so important. "Doesn't God care? Where is He?" I could not accept the fact this was the end of the road.

Refusing to let his negative spirit drag me down, I persisted in questioning him. "How do you know you flunked? You can't be sure."

"I'm sure I did. It was really tough." There seemed no doubt in his mind as to the outcome.

"You don't know you flunked it."

"Wife, I know I didn't do well. I might as well just give up."

Putting my arms around him, I hugged him tightly. "You can't give up now," I pleaded. "You have to take your other finals. I can't believe it's that bad."

44

Moments later, I realized my own final was less than an hour away. "I don't have time to stand here any longer trying to cheer him up," I thought. "Obviously I haven't succeeded in changing his mood or his mind."

"Well, I think you should study and take your other finals. I can't talk anymore." With those parting words, I grabbed a sandwich and retreated to my quiet study corner at the end of the couch. Burying my head in my notebook, I tried to ignore my husband and shut out the previous scene.

Inside, a raging tug of war was tearing me apart. "I have to get a good grade on this final. I won't let this interfere with my grades. I'm a student, too. My grades are important, too. It's his problem." Another voice reminded me, "Yes, but you are also a wife. Your husband needs you. He needs your encouragement. You're letting him down. Which is most important?" I tried to study but found concentration impossible. Anger welled up inside—anger because I had to make a choice.

Feeling guilty, I gathered up my notes and prepared to leave. Art hadn't said a word and the forlorn look remained. I was not encouraged. "I'll see you later," I called out. "I'll be a little late. I promised Mom I'd return her shoes after class tonight. She has to have them tomorrow." I started out the door and then looked back. "I'll pray for you." As I drove off to class, I was unable to dispel the picture of my deserted husband.

Once the final was distributed, my mind was preoccupied. As soon as I handed in my paper, thoughts of the evening's event returned. "Why did I ever promise to take Mom her shoes tonight, of all nights?" I knew tonight was not a good night to show my face at home. "I'll run in and give her the shoes and come right home," I promised myself determinedly. "This is no time for conversation."

My plan would have worked well had my father not walked into the kitchen as soon as I closed the door. "How's it going, Honey?"

All the pent-up emotion burst forth, and I sobbed uncontrollably. Dad looked on in dismay. "What's the matter, Honey? Did Art beat you?"

"Oh no, Dad, It's nothing like that."

I felt like a little girl again with my parents hugging and reassuring me, telling me everything would be all right. Finally, I gained enough composure to tell them what was happening and to ease their worried minds.

Driving home a few minutes later, in quiet desperation, I sought to bargain with God. "God, I don't ever want to have to make that choice again. If You will get us out of this mess, I promise I'll drop out of school until Art is finished. I can't be a good wife to him if I'm not able to help him when he needs me the most." No answer came, but an inner peace came over me. When I returned home, Art was sitting at his desk studying for his other finals. God had lifted him up.

Grades for fall quarter arrived in the mail the week after Christmas, confirming Art's suspicions. His poor performance on his German final had lowered his grade in that class to unsatisfactory, hindering further progress in raising his overall GPA. A letter soon followed notifying him that his probationary period had ended and having failed to comply with the terms of his probation, he was suspended.

Realizing the seriousness of our predicament, our future at seminary now in jeopardy, we exhausted every option open to us to remedy the situation. First, Art consulted with our pastor to see if the possibility existed whereby he could bypass the seminary requirement of a Bachelor's Degree. Reverend Woldt immediately sent a letter to the seminary, explaining Art's present circumstances and requesting their help. A letter addressed to Art arrived within a few days, expressing sincere sympathy for his situation, stating only in special instances, of which this did not qualify, could this requirement be waived. They advised him to do his best to resolve the situation where he was.

Hoping he might be able to complete his undergraduate work elsewhere, he inquired at nearby colleges. There was little chance of transferring with his GPA so low. Left with no alternative other than to follow the seminary's advice, we would have to work through the problem at MSU. Depressed and losing faith, we cried out to God. "God, why are You allowing this to happen? What are Your reasons for all of this? Can't You do something? After all, putting Art in the ministry was Your idea. Why are You suddenly closing the doors now, after bringing us this far?"

One afternoon a few days later, Art shared our plight with Israel, our Jewish neighbor with whom we were casually acquainted. Hearing

Art's story, Israel offered his assistance. A graduate assistant at the university, he was more familiar with administration policies and knew of the recently created position at Michigan State to resolve such problems. Israel recommended Art take his case to the ombudsman who served as a mediator between the students and administration.

After hearing Art's case and reviewing his records, the ombudsman concluded Art's steady progress in raising his GPA already established he had both the ability and desire to meet the requirements. He was successful in obtaining an extension for him, confident Art would bring his average up to an acceptable level if given additional time. The University revoked Art's suspension, allowing him to register for winter quarter classes on schedule. We thanked God for marvelously bringing us through the crisis.

I had just begun to settle down from the turmoil when Art called me at work one afternoon. "You won't believe this."

"Won't believe what?"

"You'll never believe what came in the mail today."

Settling back in my chair, I took a deep breath, "Now what?"

"I've been drafted."

"What?"

"I just got a letter from the Selective Service saying I have to report for duty on February 11." He sounded too calm for the news he was bearing.

"They can't do that," I retorted. "You're a full-time student. It must be a mistake."

"Oh, I'm sure it's nothing to worry about. It's not the first time they've messed up. I'll go to St. Johns tomorrow and get it straightened out. It seems a couple of times a year I have to go there to straighten out something. I wish they'd get their act together."

Inquiring at the Selective Service Office the next day, Art learned they had on file a copy of his termination notice from Michigan State. They had not received notification of the revocation. Second, the Army physical examination he had been ordered to undergo in December, thought at the time to be routine procedure, coupled with the termination notice, had immediately qualified him for the draft.

"I'll see that you receive a copy of my reinstatement," Art reassured the woman before leaving. On the way home, he stopped by the university to notify them of their error and requested they send a copy of his reinstatement to his draft board at once.

A few days later, Art called the Selective Service Office to verify that they had received the information.

"Yes, we have received a notice of your reinstatement," the woman answered coldly. "I'm afraid it's too late."

"Too late; it must be a mistake!" Rising anger had replaced the once calm voice.

"I'm sorry, Mr. Newhouse. Once the red tape is in motion in official matters, there is very little that can be done."

Art hung up the receiver in a state of disbelief and dialed my number at work.

Recognizing his voice, I asked anxiously, "Did they get your reinstatement notice?"

He paused, "They said it doesn't matter."

"What do you mean, it doesn't matter?"

"They told me even though they've received the notice, once the red tape is in motion, there is little, if anything, that can be done now." For the first time since this latest episode began, Art's voice was clearly distressed.

Official or not, it was impossible for me to believe any mistake could not be rectified. "That doesn't make sense," I snapped angrily, wanting to go there myself and tell them what I thought.

"Well, maybe if I go and personally talk to them again, it'll do some good." The fact he was unwilling to let the matter drop gave me hope.

I returned to my work and tried to push out the negative thoughts creeping closer to the surface of my mind, "What if it was too late to do anything? What if Art did have to go to war?" The country was involved in a rapidly escalating war in Viet Nam. He could be sent to the war zone. It could mean a lengthy separation and perhaps . . ." I did not even want to think about it.

In a final effort to nullify the induction notice, Art went to the Selective Service Office the following day and for the second time explained his situation to the woman in charge.

"I'm sorry, Mr. Newhouse, at this point there is only one form that could cancel the official induction notice you have received. We don't tell people about this form, but if they come in and ask and we find it in their file, they are exempt from the draft. I will tell you the chances of it being in your file, however, are very remote. But, if you like, I will check your file one more time."

Going back to the files, she carefully searched through all the papers accumulated in his file. A few minutes later, she returned carrying a piece of paper.

"I found it!" She exclaimed looking surprised. "I can't tell you what it is, only that some time ago you must have come in and signed it."

To witness once again God's hand at work greatly strengthened our faith. He had provided a way out of our problem months ago. He knew the form was in Art's file because the previous mix-up had been part of His plan. He had used this situation to test our faith and prove He could be trusted even for complex problems. From that point on, we knew we were completely in God's care. If God could bring us through all of this, we had faith to believe we could trust Him to bring us through any future obstacles.

Israel living next door and Art confiding in him that afternoon was not coincidental. God had placed him there. Having lived much of his life in Germany, Israel spoke the German language fluently. Art's struggle with German became a personal challenge for Israel, and he was relentless in giving his time and efforts to help Art master it. A rare combination of friend and tutor, Israel respected Art, yet did not hesitate to scold if he felt Art was not putting forth his best efforts. Together, they became a winning team and close friends.

Seeking release from the pressures of school, Art bought an inexpensive guitar and taught himself to play in his spare time. His natural musical abilities blossomed, and soon he was writing his own music and lyrics. When word of his talent spread among family and friends, he frequently was asked to play. Entertaining with his music gave him a new sense of satisfaction and boosted his self-esteem. He was happy, enjoying life, and had a very positive attitude about himself.

Chapter 4

WHERE ARE YOU, GOD?

"A time for tears"
Ecclesiastes 3:4 (JB)

*W*ith life going smoothly for Art, I should have been at peace and happy, too. Yet, I was miserable. I dreaded those small gatherings when Art entertained our family and friends. The more I sat and watched him glow in the limelight, the more my self-esteem diminished. I had no idea my decision to drop out of school would have a deep traumatic effect on my life. It propelled me into an identity crisis, causing me to feel inferior in the college environment. I had not realized how important it had been for me to continue my education, even if only one class a term. Apart from being a student, I had no strong sense of self-identity or self-worth.

Fighting depression, I reminded myself, "No one made you leave. It was your own choice. You know you're intelligent enough to go on." Convincing me was difficult when the actions of others told me otherwise. Conversations with our college friends conveyed that identity had little to do with grades or level of intelligence. The most important thing was whether you were a student with a degree.

The wives in the couples closest to us were teachers, with the exception of Israel's wife, who was a surgical nurse. Most were working toward their master's degree. Without a degree and without a goal deemed worthwhile, I felt looked down on. Obviously, there was no status as an office worker. No one seemed interested in what I was doing. "It doesn't matter what they think," I told myself. "You know you have a responsible job. You know your employers and your fellow employees respect you and the work you're doing." Yet, each night when I left the office and returned home, my self-esteem evaporated, reminding me it did matter.

When home with Art, my anxiety increased. Whenever I thought about his identity and his new hobby, anger welled up. "Where are my hobbies?" I had not realized until now that somehow my hobbies had fallen by the wayside. Textbooks, work, and household chores had replaced time spent reading. When we started going together, I had given up dancing, which had been an important part of my identity in my late teen years. Never having replaced those hobbies, I sensed a tremendous void in my life. I had lost something very important to me. I had invested my total being into my husband and his identity.

"How ironic," I thought to myself. "I gave up my education so I'd be available when Art needed me, and a month later the crisis is over and he doesn't need me at all. He has Israel to help him. Look at me! I'm trapped! I promised God I'd drop out of school until Art finished if He'd get us out of the predicament we were in. I can't retract my vow, regardless of the consequences." I was angry with myself for having been so foolish, angry with God for not having met my own needs, and angry with Art for no longer needing me.

Even more intense was the terrible hurt I felt inside; my heart was broken. "He doesn't appreciate the sacrifice I made for him. He actually seems proud of the fact he doesn't need me now." Thinking about it gave me a queasy feeling in the pit of my stomach. "What had happened to the considerate, loving person I married and to our marriage? Almost overnight, he seemed self-centered, arrogant, and insensitive to my needs, not caring that I'm so unhappy. He's aloof and unaffectionate unlike before. He must have found someone else," I surmised.

One day I summoned the courage to ask. "What's the matter with you anyway? Have you found a girlfriend?" The words seemed to stick in my throat. Just hearing them spoken made me nauseous.

Art glared angrily at me. "No, I *haven't* found someone else! There *isn't* anything wrong!" Empty of compassion, his words did little to rest my fears and suspicions.

Feeling unfulfilled as a person and detached from my husband, I became very threatened and jealous of those people who remained in his world. Not only did he have Israel and the other fellows in our apartment complex, he had other friends at school.

I answered the phone one day and was surprised to hear a feminine voice on the other end ask, "Is Art there?"

Startled for a moment, I paused. . . . "Yes. . . . I'll get him." Immediately, jealous feelings surfaced.

"It's for you. . . . a girl. "I said, covering the mouthpiece with my hand.

Listening from the kitchen, I could hear the conversation related to one of Art's classes. As soon as he hung up the receiver, I began to interrogate him. "Who is *she*?"

"Oh, she is just a girl in one of my classes, asking about an assignment."

"Why'd she have to call you?" I snapped accusingly. "Why didn't she call another girl in the class?"

"I don't know why she called me," Art said innocently.

"Doesn't she know you're married?"

Sensing my jealousy, he tried to quiet my suspicions, "Oh, Wife, it's no big deal. She's just a friend. If you saw her, you'd know that. She's not even good looking; she's fat."

Girlfriend or not, I came to painful conclusions about the state of our marriage. First, I must face the fact that our marriage had undergone a major shakeup from the roots; it would never be the same. Second, I must accept the fact the man I live with has changed. Circumstances have changed. I hated to admit, I was not sure if I liked this new person, much less loved him.

Searching for answers, God opened my eyes to see an important, unrevealed truth about our marriage. The dependent relationship that had been comfortable for me and had worked thus far would no longer work. During the previous months, Art had come to realize how dependent he had been. God had shown him he did not need me that way now. Proud and happy to be independent and standing on his own, he did not intend to return to our dependent relationship.

I knew if our marriage was to survive this crisis, our whole relationship must change; how, I did not know. I could see no solutions, no light, only darkness; I was spent. As the gap widened, I sank into the depths of depression, and the void growing larger seemed to swallow me up. I was sick inside, bitter, angry, and felt betrayed, wanting to run but without a place to go.

Ignoring the unhappiness was impossible. Although I could successfully conceal my emotions from others, it became increasingly difficult to conceal them from myself. Oftentimes during quiet moments while sitting in church or at my desk at work, my emotions would creep to the surface and tears would well. I knew there was a lake of tears deep inside but was afraid I would lose control of them if I ever let them begin.

One day, my feelings dangerously close to the surface, I shared my jealousy and angry feelings toward Art with a Christian friend at work.

When I finished my confession, Carol looked at me in amazement. "You shouldn't feel like that," she scolded. "Don't you know the Bible says love is always patient; love is not jealous . . . ?"

I fought back tears as she continued. "You should count your blessings and stop being so selfish."

The stinging words of her reprimand echoed in my mind all afternoon, leaving me more depressed. Now, I had to claim the negative feeling of guilt to the lengthy list of feelings a Christian should not have.

"That'll be the last time I ever bare my feelings to her or anyone else again," I vowed, "From now on, I'll keep them to myself! I'll bury them so deep no one will ever get near them again."

I thought a lot about what Carol had said, yes it was true. Love is that; God's love is, anyway. "I may be married," I thought to myself, "but I don't feel loved, and I certainly don't feel secure in this marriage." Carol would never understand, "She is single and would love to be married. In her fantasy, she believes marriage will bring her happiness and solve all her problems and should have done the same for me."

"Maybe Carol is right. Maybe I should stop being selfish and count my blessings. Art assured me there is no one else. The problem is so vague and intangible; maybe I have no problem. If there isn't a problem, why am I so unhappy? I feel like crying all the time. What happened to me? Why do I feel so insecure and jealous of all Art's friends? Why do I feel so threatened by all these changes? Why can't I be happy Art has gained confidence in himself? Where is the person who only a few years ago felt the Lord's hand of favor upon her? Where are You, God? Once You seemed to be so close; now You seem so far away. Don't You care about my unhappiness?"

As I surveyed a seemingly hopeless situation, God's answer began to come in unmistakably clear thoughts. "Stop focusing on the negative. Your situation is not hopeless. Yes it is true; some things cannot be changed. You cannot change Art. You cannot go back to school because of your vow. You cannot change the attitude of the college community, including your friends. You cannot change jobs. You cannot change anyone but yourself."

A ray of hope suddenly shone through the dark clouds quickening my heart. I repeated the last sentence in my mind. "You cannot change anyone but yourself." I cannot change anyone but myself. *Myself! I can change Myself!* I can take control of my life again!

I listened attentively as God continued to reveal new thoughts. "You can begin by changing your attitude. Don't look at education as the only means to improve yourself. Other things in life are equally important to gain self-confidence. Begin to look for other ways to increase your self-esteem."

Acting on God's direction, the wheels of my mind began turning, opening up a new world. Dreams once far off in the future, suddenly became realities for the present. Just as swiftly as the dreams, a plan for financing those dreams came into focus. Immediately, I knew what I would do and how to do it.

Until now, there hadn't been money to pay for the expensive dental work I needed. The dentist had warned me gaps would occur in time unless I replaced the extracted molars. I had already noticed myself self-consciously avoiding a full smile because of the gaps, even though I knew it was one of my greatest assets. "Now is the time to take care of my teeth. They can't wait until Art is finished with school."

"And when I finish paying for the necessity," I thought excitedly, "I'll reward myself with a luxury. I'll buy some contact lenses to boost my morale! I know I should wear my glasses more, but I've always believed they detracted from my appearance. I don't care if other people think it's vain and extravagant." My spirits soared as I envisioned new contacts. "How exciting it will be to see clearly all the time!"

"Look at the positive aspects of your situation," God went on. "You have some genuine desires for yourself, and now you have some extra time to do some things for you. A part-time job is unnecessary as I have already made a provision for you."

God showed me the uniqueness of the office where I worked. In addition to salaried employees, the company offered an incentive plan, believing people strive harder when working for themselves. Employees earned an hourly wage and encouraged to work as many hours as they wished, as long as there was work. Wages, placed in a draw account, could be drawn on any payday. "Now, I can take advantage of this plan."

With Art's approval and anxious to begin, I approached the managing partner the next day and requested to be placed on the incentive plan. Pleased with my decision, he assigned two monthly bookkeeping accounts for me to do at home on the weekends. Within the week, I also made the dentist appointment. If my plans worked out, the dental work would be complete by spring, and in the summer I could be fitted for contacts.

While waiting for my long-term goals, I focused on a short-term goal—my outdated wardrobe. In light of my changed perspective, I realized my wardrobe could be updated with a small amount of money to purchase two new pairs of shoes and some sewing supplies. An investment of my time would go a long way toward brightening up my wardrobe. I was sure Mother would be happy to give me a few instructions and let me use her sewing machine.

During the following months, I kept myself busy to avoid thinking about the void in my life. I declined invitations to join classes offered for student wives by Michigan State in golf, handicrafts, and so forth, failing to see their importance. Instead, I chose to spend my free time in familiar surroundings with those closest to me; those who loved and supported me. In addition to singing in the church choir, I often visited my family and occasionally a friend. While all these activities were satisfying to a point and filled empty hours, none filled my deep void.

Eventually, I learned God had heard and understood my angry cries. He had not forgotten me nor would He take me out of the situation. He would walk through it with me. In the midst of my suffering, personal special blessings came, blessings I would not have enjoyed had I been unwilling to be obedient. He was not punishing me for the vow I made. Perhaps in making that vow and voluntarily removing myself from the worldly, academic ladder to success, I had taken the first step up an invisible ladder, a ladder to spiritual maturity. God was my Teacher and Mentor. He would do for me what Israel was doing for Art in German; always pushing me to a higher level, sometimes reprimanding me, but always with love.

Chapter 5

DRAWN TOGETHER

"A time for war"
Ecclesiastes 3:8 (JB)

Although during this time we were traveling parallel paths, there was one point when our paths touched, drawn by the common bond of love — mutual love and concern for Art's youngest brother. Bernard was a year younger than me and like his twin sister, Barbara, had stayed with us for a short while before enlisting in the Navy and becoming a hospital corpsman. Bernard's assignment to active duty in Viet Nam with the 1st Marine Division in February, 1968, brought us face-to-face with the reality of the war and served as a catalyst for communication between us. When we were unable to talk about ourselves, we were able to communicate about the war in Viet Nam.

Bernard came to see us the night before he left. We sat up until the early morning hours, listening as he shared his feelings and fears about his future. We recognized our time together was precious, so there were no wasted words, no idle chatter. His words were disturbing, yet we listened, sensing his need to express them as though he was on a mission to cover specific topics. Military statistics were his introduction. "The fatality rate for medics is fairly high," he joked, "somewhere in the neighborhood of 85 percent. We've been told they're on the lookout for medics. I guess they get special points and privileges for hitting them."

"We'll pray that God will keep you safe," Art said confidently while I nodded my head in agreement.

Seeing his information had not alarmed us, Bernard continued in a more serious tone. "I had the strangest dream a while back. I dreamed that on April 23 of 1968, I would take a long trip away from the family. I don't know what it means," he said searching our eyes for an interpretation.

Curious and intrigued by the significance of the dream, Art and I exchanged puzzled glances. "Could it be there is prophetic validity to his dream, a message from God," I wondered. "Or is it insignificant?"

A few moments later Bernard took a piece of paper from his pocket and unfolding it, handed it to Art. "I've been writing some poetry the past few weeks. Would you like to read this one?

Art read the poem quietly and then passed it to me. Silence filled the room as I began to read.

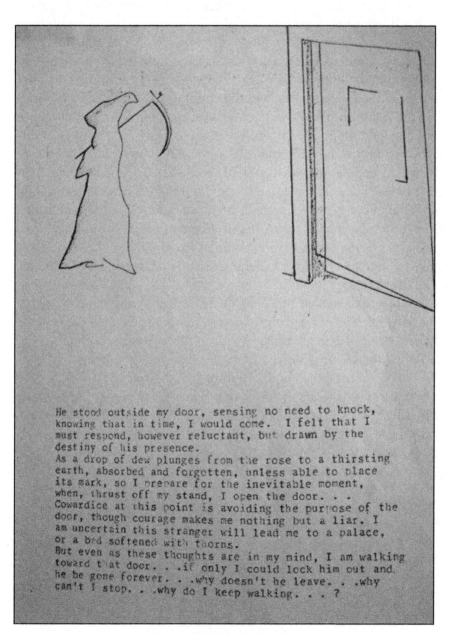

He stood outside my door, sensing no need to knock,
knowing that in time, I would come. I felt that I
must respond, however reluctant, but drawn by the
destiny of his presence.
As a drop of dew plunges from the rose to a thirsting
earth, absorbed and forgotten, unless able to place
its mark, so I prepare for the inevitable moment,
when, thrust off my stand, I open the door. . .
Cowardice at this point is avoiding the purpose of the
door, though courage makes me nothing but a liar. I
am uncertain this stranger will lead me to a palace,
or a bed softened with thorns.
But even as these thoughts are in my mind, I am walking
toward that door. . .if only I could lock him out and
he be gone forever. . .why doesn't he leave. . .why
can't I stop. . .why do I keep walking. . .?

Bernard's Poem "Death"

An eerie feeling swept over me as I read the poem and gazed at his illustration. I, too, sensed the uneasy presence of death hovering overhead. I wanted to ignore this unpleasant confrontation with death, yet Bernard's words and vivid description made it impossible. Suddenly death seemed too real, too close. Art's reaction was similar to mine. Neither of us had the courage to ask further questions but did our best to make light of the conversation from that point on.

The next morning, Art and I joined other family members at the Lansing airport to bid Bernard farewell. "No one would ever guess we were sending him off to war," I thought as we stood at the departure gate. "The way we're acting, you'd think we're sending him off on a vacation. If only we could be more honest and show Bernard how much he means to us. If only we could hug him tightly and tell him we love him before kissing him goodbye." Instead, each person kept his emotions locked tightly inside, seemingly bound by an unspoken agreement to be brave.

Art posted a map of Viet Nam on the wall above his desk, carefully marking each location according to Bernard's letters and date where he had been. While he moved about in the war zone, we attentively watched the evening news reports to see where the heavy fighting had been taking place and listening for familiar locations. Every night we prayed together for God to watch over Bernard and return him safely to us. Every week we wrote to him, sharing our news and offering words of encouragement. We awaited his letters anxiously.

Our spirits were buoyant when we received a letter dated March 7, 1968, written on the backside of a map.

> Received your letter last week when mail was dropped in with supplies by helicopter. You see, I'm on this mountain about thirty-five miles north of Da Nang and being 4000 feet up, a helicopter is about the only way to get things in. There is no ice or snow on this mount, but it is completely covered with thick, hot jungle terrain. With temps up in the 90s, it can really get hot humping these hills. Luckily we've only encountered the enemy twice up here and suffered few and minor casualties. Yesterday three of my

people had heat exhaustion and, believe me, I was one fast moving and tired corpsman. The last one I reached was dead from cardiac arrest, so I administered external cardiac massage and mouth-to-mouth resuscitation, and he finally came around. He was medivac'd this morning after a relapse last night. It makes me feel good that I'm able to save a man's life, and I feel that my part over here is worthwhile. No longer do I worry about anything because the gooks have tried twice and missed, so they are out of the game. Nobody gets a third chance to strike me out. I know that your prayers are helping, too. They must be; I've come close and yet came out without a scratch. Take care of yourselves and keep praying because it's working. Thanks for what you have done already. See you next Feb. (1969)

In a letter dated April 11, 1968, Bernard wrote:

We have been in the tail end, mostly, of this op. and have set up a semi-permanent camp on the top of some hill overlooking Hwy. 9, which is the road to Khe Sanh. There is a river at its base, and we usually go swimming every day. In fact, we're leading quite a life of leisure, if you can call it that.

Every now and then a priest comes out and gives Mass, and we always have a big turnout. The altar usually consists of the hood of a Jeep, but the thought and meaning is still there. I have a Sunday Missal and I read it quite a lot, and it seems to help. If a person ever came over here not knowing God, it doesn't take him long to find him. Spiritual consolation and reliance is one of the most important things over here to keep a person going, believe me.

On Saturday afternoon, April 27, 1968, Art answered the telephone and recognized the voice of his older brother, Tom.

"Where've you been?" Tom scolded. "I've been trying to reach you."

"Trying to take a nap," Art snapped, "what's up?"

Tom hesitated for a moment and then his voice dropped. "We've just received word that Bernard's been killed."

"What!" Art suddenly turned pale. "How can that be? We just got a letter from him."

"Apparently he was killed the 21st, last Sunday," Tom went on. "They notified the folks this afternoon."

Art turned to me, his face pale. "Bernard's been killed!" I had heard enough of the conversation to know this was the telephone call we had been dreading.

"I don't understand," Art said, shaking his head after hanging up the receiver. "I was so sure our prayers were working."

"Me too," I sobbed. "I mean . . . we just got that letter from him today. He said our prayers were working."

We were stunned. It was unbelievable. Bernard just told us God was taking care of him. His letters confirmed that. What had happened to our communication with God? Where was God when Bernard died? Had he turned His head the other way?

Furious with God, we lashed out. "Every night we pleaded with You for Bernard's safe return and trusted You to honor our prayers. Not only did we believe, we constantly encouraged Bernard through our letters to believe You would protect him from harm. We had faith to believe, regardless of the statistics, that Bernard would be spared, and he would return home safely. We were faithful in keeping our part of the bargain, God. We did all we could do. You didn't live up to Your part. You didn't honor all those prayers. You took Bernard away! You've betrayed our trust!"

"Why, God? Why did You allow this to happen? Why would You allow his life to be snuffed out like this? You knew how much he meant to us. Why did You take him? Why would You take someone only twenty-one years old in the prime of his life? You had given him so many gifts and talents to help his fellow man. He had so much potential. Oh God, such a waste of a life, and for what great cause did he die? Oh God, surely You have made a great mistake."

Bernard's death had a major impact in many areas of our lives. Comparable to an earthquake's effect on the foundation of a house, so was our faith in God shaken. We had entrusted God with our future when Art committed himself to the ministry. Now, it seemed God had lost control of His world. It was inconceivable to us that Bernard's death could be His will. With God's credibility now in question, we began to entertain serious doubts about His character. "If God is able to be everywhere at once, why didn't He see? If God is all-powerful, why didn't He stop it? Isn't He more powerful than our enemy as we have been led to believe? How can we continue to trust someone whose ways aren't flawless, someone who isn't always in charge?"

We could not get beyond the fact that all our prayers had been in vain—or that God had said "No." Filled with anger and wavering in our trust, we ceased praying about anything. "Why should we pray?" we asked ourselves. "We've no reason to believe praying is effective. Either God wasn't hearing our prayers, or somehow they weren't good enough to change the circumstances."

Looking through angry eyes, we could not see that Bernard's message to us the night before he left was God's gentle and loving attempt to prepare us for Bernard's death. Rather than confront reality as Bernard had done, and use these last few months looking to the Lord to prepare us spiritually to face the days ahead, we chose to ignore the message and persisted in praying for Bernard's safe return. We did not trust that somehow even this was part of God's plan for *all* of us.

Initially, the gap of communication between us widened as Art, feeling alone in his grief, withdrew into himself.

"No one knows how I feel," he shared with me one day. "I not only lost my brother; I lost my best friend as well."

"You're right," I agreed, "I don't understand what you're going through. There's no way I can know how you feel inside. No one close to me has ever died before."

When he began to emerge from his depression and verbalize his feelings, though, there was a familiar ring to what he was saying, "Something I treasured has been taken from me. There's a void in my life that can't be filled by anything or anyone. I know I'm not supposed to feel this way, but I'm very angry with God."

Now, Art shared my disillusionment with being a Christian and walking with God. The truth was evident. Being a Christian does not mean you will never again have a problem or never have to suffer pain. You will not always feel the way a Christian should feel. You may feel anger again. Your prayers may not be answered the way you desire, nor will you always understand the God you serve.

Healing for both of us began with the arrival of summer. The bright summer sun beckoned us to leave the darkness and the dreary winter behind. We needed to get out of ourselves and out of doors like two butterflies emerging from tightly wrapped cocoons. We needed the sunshine to warm our hearts and appreciate once more the beauty in God's creation. We needed to see the birds and hear their melodies and to feel the softness of the grass beneath our bare feet. We needed to smell the sweet fragrance of the flowers. We needed people.

Once outdoors, we were pushed to interact with our neighbors, who like us, had left their quiet study corners to bask in the warm sun. Soon, it was impossible to dwell on our problems; there was no time for solitude. The upstairs wing of our building became a community of its own with everyone participating, whether relaxing in the sunshine together, cooking a meal outside, or having a party.

God used our neighbors to bring balance into our lives. We needed to learn to let up on the serious, and rest in our faith. God's message was clear. "You need to take time out for laughter and fun along life's way. It's okay to socialize with friends and sometimes do foolish things like stomping on grapes for homemade wine or hosing down the roof of the building to cool your apartments." What a refreshing experience it was to be carefree once again.

When classes resumed in the fall, football games provided the avenue for group entertainment and release of pent-up energy. Unlike previous years when we had considered season tickets to the games a luxury, we now knew they were a necessity for us and for our marriage. Although not a student, I joined the others in eagerly anticipating the weekend games. A lively spirit and fervent desire for a victory united us as we walked in the brisk fall air with blankets, thermos bottles, and cushions tucked under our arms to Spartan stadium.

With fall term ending, we began our final preparations to leave Michigan State. Rather than delay our departure until Art completed his final quarter of German, MSU allowed him to complete his last quarter of German at seminary and transfer the grade back to MSU to complete his formal degree. MSU approved Art's request to take his finals early to enable us to move to Springfield, Illinois in time to begin the winter quarter on schedule at Concordia Theological Seminary.

Twinges of guilt were among my feelings as I thought about the future and reviewed the past with quiet reflection. "I should feel sad at the prospect of leaving family and friends behind," I mused. "But, I don't. Frankly, I look forward to moving and beginning a new life in Illinois. There it'll be just the two of us; no family, no friends. I won't have to compete for Art's attention any longer. We'll be able to recapture the closeness we once enjoyed, and life will be just like it used to be. Art will need me now. I can put this part of my life behind me and pretend it was just a bad dream."

Deep inside, though, closer to my heart lay the truth. The busy schedule of the last few months had succeeded in keeping my mind off self, but I made no real progress. My identity crisis had not been resolved; it had only been shelved for another time. I feared the inevitable day when I'd have to face the unfinished business. "Maybe next time it'll be easier," I told myself hopefully. "Maybe when we're in new surroundings by ourselves; the answers will be more evident. Maybe then I'll find my place in the world and once more feel a sense of self-worth."

Chapter 6

SEMINARY LIFE BEGINS: NOVEMBER 1968

"A time for uprooting what has been planted"
Ecclesiastes 3:2 (JB)

strange feeling enveloped me as I peered at the small U-Haul trailer following behind our car. I looked at Art, his eyes fixed on the road ahead.

"Doesn't it give you a funny feeling to know that everything we own is in that little trailer back there?"

Art glanced in the rear view mirror, "Yeah, it is kind of strange, I guess."

My thoughts lingered on the trailer behind us. The importance of its contents had suddenly taken on an entirely new meaning, having nothing to do with monetary value. "That tiny trailer contains our only visible link with the life we're leaving behind and the new life before us. Every item there is a permanent part of our life, both present and past. Now that our lives are uprooted, these treasures are the only stabilizing factors left." For a moment, fearful thoughts crept in. I reminded myself, "I have to believe it will all work out. We've done everything possible to prepare for this day."

Subscribing to a Springfield newspaper the month prior to our move had been helpful in familiarizing us with the new surroundings and giving me an idea of the job market there. From it, I had obtained the names of several employment agencies to whom I had sent introductory letters and resumes. All had responded suggesting I call and arrange for an interview upon our arrival.

At Art's request, the seminary had supplied us with a list of available apartments near the campus. From the list we had chosen, and subsequently arranged via mail, to rent a two-bedroom, furnished apartment. In addition to the security of knowing our apartment awaited us, God had provided one couple who had extended the hand of friendship to us. We had been thrilled when Art received a letter from a fourth-year student offering to be Art's "big brother." Art's name and address in the list of incoming students had caught his attention as a Michigan native. Marty and his wife Mary and their three children expected us for dinner this evening, after which Marty would go with us to our apartment and help move in our belongings.

We arrived in Springfield in the late afternoon and, curious about our new apartment, immediately set out with map in hand to find it. The street address led us to a drab old two-story building directly across from the seminary grounds.

"This must be it," Art said bringing the car to a stop in front of the old building.

"Our apartment is above a pool hall?" I shrieked, pointing to a sign on the adjacent building.

"Looks like it is," Art grinned.

"Nobody said anything about this in the letter."

"Well, at least we have a place to live."

The landlord occupied one of the two downstairs apartments and directed us to an outside stairway leading to the two upstairs apartments. "Yours is on the right at the top of the stairs," he said, handing Art the key.

I looked around suspiciously as we climbed the stairs. Art unlocked the door, and we stepped in, closing the door behind us. I stood motionless for a moment, staring at the room around me. My heart sank.

"This is the most uninviting apartment I've ever seen," I moaned, fighting back tears.

"Oh, it'll be better after we get our things moved in," Art reassured.

"I doubt if anything can make this room cozy," I grumbled under my breath, looking at the old, hard studio couch at one end of the large, dreary room. A counter divided the living room from the kitchen with the only natural light in the entire room coming from two long kitchen windows, covered with bare, faded window shades.

Further inspection did nothing to lift my spirits. One bedroom was sparsely furnished with outdated furniture while the other bedroom had no furniture at all. I walked slowly back to the living room, muttering to myself, "How can I ever make this ugly, cold place into a home for us?"

My eyes were drawn to the two long kitchen windows, a glimmer of hope broke. I envisioned them dressed with sheer, frilly, white curtains to soften the effect of the room's harshness, yet still allow ample sunlight. "Maybe Art's right, maybe after we're settled in and have added a touch of our own personalities, the room won't seem so cold," I thought.

Having satisfied our curiosity, Art unhitched the trailer and once more we set out, map in hand, in search of our new friends and the meal that awaited us. Marty greeted us at the door and introduced us to his wife and three children. After visiting briefly, Mary returned to the kitchen to add the final touches to the meal. I remained in the living room, listening quietly while the two seminarians engaged in theological chatter, and then I, too, excused myself and joined Mary in the kitchen.

"You'll enjoy the Seminary Wives Study Program," Mary said enthusiastically. Classes meet on Tuesday nights. If you'd like, I'll pick you up next week. You can register for your class then."

"Gee, that sounds great," I said appreciatively. "It'll help me to get acquainted with some of the other wives and give me something to do when Art is studying."

During dinner, Marty shared how God had called him into the ministry and some of their experiences since that time. "It doesn't seem possible we'll be going on our final call this spring," he reminisced, glancing at Mary with a loving twinkle in his eye. "You'll be surprised how quickly the time will pass."

After dinner, Marty followed us back to our apartment and stayed until the trailer was empty. Alone again, we sat down overwhelmed by the magnitude of the task before us. Thoughts of waking up to this upheaval on Sunday morning motivated us to ignore our body's fatigue and slowly to push ourselves to begin unpacking the boxes. It was nearly midnight when the last box had finally been unpacked and we stood back, proudly surveying our accomplishment.

The apartment looked remarkably better than when we had first walked through the door. The family pictures were in their usual place on the chest of drawers in the bedroom. The Early American cedar chest, a wedding gift from Art, stood nearby adding a touch of elegance to the room. The brightly colored afghan from Great Aunt Cora lay tossed over the old studio couch with the lamp my parents had given us now shining beside it. The familiar movement of the pendulum and the rhythmic ticking of the treasured cuckoo clock Art's parents had brought us from Germany gave new life to the once lifeless apartment. "I'll never love this place," I thought, "but I think I can tolerate living here for a while."

We invited our neighbor from the adjoining apartment for dinner on Friday. While preparing to set the table, I opened the silverware drawer and noticed a flash of movement inside. Quickly, I slammed the drawer shut. When I recovered from my fright, I cautiously opened the drawer a second time.

"Eek!" I squealed, "There's a bug in the drawer!"

Hearing my cry, Art dropped the paper he was reading and hurried into the kitchen. "What's the matter with you?"

"There's . . . there's a bug in that drawer," I said squeamishly, pointing to the drawer.

Art pulled the drawer open just in time to see the long bug scurry around among the silverware. "It's a cockroach," he said helpfully.

"*Cockroach*!" I exclaimed in horror. "But . . . I thought cockroaches were only found in dirty, filthy places; you know — like the slums."

"Well not always. They live in damp, hot places. I'll bet they thrive in these old buildings," he said calmly.

"Cockroaches, in *my* kitchen!" The mere thought ruined my appetite for the evening. Not only was this a personal affront on my kitchen, it was a reflection on me. What'll we do?"

"Oh, I'll talk to the landlord and get some spray to get rid of them."

The landlord denied ever having a problem with them, forcing us to fight the battle of the bugs on our own. We removed everything from the cupboards, scrubbed them thoroughly, and sprayed with insect spray. A careful examination of the premises a few days later revealed not only the presence of cockroaches but silverfish as well. Once again, we cleared the cupboards, scrubbed, and sprayed a second time, all to no avail. By this time, we had found evidence of the bugs under the kitchen sink and in the bathroom as well.

"That does it!" I told Art firmly. "I am not going to live with these bugs any longer. If the landlord won't do anything about them, he can find himself some new tenants!"

"Okay, but let's wait until after Christmas. As soon as we come back from Christmas break, we'll begin looking for another apartment."

"Let's not say anything to anyone about the cockroaches," I cautioned. "I don't even want our parents to find out. We'll just tell them we didn't like the apartment."

Setting aside my contempt for the apartment and the bugs, I plunged into holiday preparations. "Christmas is the same everywhere," I reminded myself, "even in Springfield."

"It's funny how our experiences of the past year sound much more exciting to read about than live through," I remarked to Art one afternoon as I sat at the kitchen table writing letters to tuck inside Christmas cards. After mailing the cards, I made Christmas cookies and fudge to take home to our families. Together we shopped for gifts and a Christmas tree.

Twinges of excitement encompassed me as we shared in the fun of decorating the Christmas tree. When we were satisfied with the placement of all the lights and ornaments, I turned off the living room lights and waited expectantly as Art reached over to plug in the tree lights. The moment the plug touched the electrical outlet, we saw a bright flash of light followed by a loud popping noise and then the room darkened. We looked at each other in astonishment. Every strand of lights had burned out.

"This old building isn't wired to accommodate the heavy electrical load at Christmastime," the landlady told Art sternly upon hearing his story, "Weren't you aware of our rule prohibiting Christmas lights in the building?"

For a moment Art was speechless and then quietly replied, "We didn't know anything about that rule."

By the time he had returned upstairs and reported to me the landlady's response, I was close to tears about the whole situation—the apartment, Springfield, and Christmas. "Who ever heard of a Christmas tree with no colored lights, anyway?" I snapped, "Everyone knows the lights give it that special touch. They . . . they give it life." Under my breath I added, "And if there's one thing this place needs it's a little life!" My only consolation was that in a week we would be going home for the holidays; home where life had not changed.

After the holidays, we wasted no time in our search for a new apartment and found a furnished apartment several miles from the seminary, on the west side. Although not as old as the previous building, our new apartment was on the second floor of an older home now converted into a two-family dwelling. Walking into the warm and friendly apartment was a welcome contrast to our previous experience. The small rooms had old, cozy furniture and the carpeted living room and bedroom created an atmosphere of warmth. The kitchen was light and cheery, with two large windows overlooking a sprawling oak tree. The front porch was ideally suited for storage, while another small room at the top of the stairway would be Art's study.

"What we need now is a pet to add a little bit of life to our new apartment," Art casually suggested one day while we were busy packing boxes in preparation for our move. "Why don't we get a kitten?"

I frowned, looking at the disarray of boxes, "A pet now?" I turned to Art, ready to protest and then stopped. His blue eyes were bright in anticipation of a cuddly little kitten.

"Well, maybe you're right. Maybe it would be fun to have a little kitten to keep us company."

The next night I came home from work to find not a kitten as I expected, but a half-grown black cat slinking around in the middle of all the moving boxes. The frightened cat, who Art named Moses, seemed terrified of his new home and the confusion he found. Seeking refuge under the couch or bed, Art was an arm's length away on the floor repeatedly trying to coax him out. Sensing my hostility toward him, Moses set out to win me as his friend. Night and day, he followed at my heels, meowing loudly until I would stop to pet him or pick him up.

Moses was the lucky one to find the first cockroach in our new apartment. Evidence of the after-hours battle between our cat and the cockroach would be four cockroach legs on the bathroom floor. After a while, Moses could not stomach eating any part of it, instead choosing to disable the nighttime intruder with a few gentle swats of his paw. Again, we got out the bug spray and continued our "battle of the bugs," resolved this annoyance was just a part of our new life in Springfield.

Settled and at peace in our new home, we turned our attention next to another area in our lives, which remained unsettled. We never dreamed making friends at seminary would be so difficult. Certainly one might expect to find students in a secular school to be cliquish, but at a seminary? Disillusioned at our findings, we did our best to make excuses.

Arriving mid-year with only four other students put us at a disadvantage. Orientation for mid-winter arrivals consisted of a small "get acquainted" tea at the home of the Dean of Students. That welcome was a sharp contrast to the weeklong orientation activities to acquaint September arrivals and their families with one another. Since then, many of our classmates had developed close friendships with other seminary couples, who had no need to cultivate new friendships. Just as understandable were the close bonds between students who had come through synodical schools together prior to entering the seminary. Then, too, it was a natural tendency to interact socially with those who shared your immediate year of seminary experience.

It was becoming apparent that the one friendship was in trouble. I sensed an uneasy feeling about our friendship with the newlywed couple we met at the get-acquainted tea. Since that first meeting, we had spent many hours together, lunch several times a week, meeting one another at the laundromat on Saturday and sharing dinner every Saturday night. I tried to brush off the negative feelings that haunted me, but they persisted. "Why do I have to feel this way?" I asked myself. "What's wrong with me anyway?"

Finally, I broached Art on the subject. I'm feeling smothered by their friendship," I confessed. "I think we're spending too much time together."

"Yeah, I feel the same way," he answered without hesitation.

Amazed, I never guessed he shared my secret feelings. "You do?"

Art nodded in agreement.

"Well, what are we going to do about it?" I probed, hoping he might come up with a painless solution. "I . . . I don't want to hurt their feelings."

At first Art was silent then said, "I don't know what to do about it."

Fearful that confrontation would cost us their friendship, we chose to ignore the danger signals. Unknown to us, our friends obviously felt the same as we did. They resolved the conflict simply by not reciprocating the Saturday dinner invitation one weekend. We never socialized again.

Deeply hurt by the abrupt loss of their friendship, we felt rejected. "There must be something wrong with us," we concluded. Fearful of experiencing the pain and rejection, we cautiously avoided any close relationships. We lacked the insight to see the detachment as a positive growing experience—a sign of emotional and spiritual maturity. We learned that in His wisdom and perfect timing, God had gently and painfully directed us away from depending on others to a relationship of dependence on Him, a necessity if we were to progress in our walk with Him.

That lesson had been reinforced in another area of my life. Neither my accounting classes nor my previous work experience had adequately prepared me for my job as a bookkeeper and junior accountant, thrust in the middle of the busiest season of the year in a certified public accounting firm. Daily, tension filled the air as employers and employees frantically scurried to keep pace with the increased workload. The gradual introduction to each new set of books became a luxury of times past as a variety of clients, whose bookkeeping methods varied, found their way to my desk. Before long, I was caught up in the office frenzy with the balancing scale of speed and accuracy hanging from my neck like a millstone.

I felt my chest tighten in panic as I stared at the paperwork. "Lord, I don't know where to begin. This is like a giant puzzle. I'll have to unscramble the pieces before I can do anything. But Lord, I can't keep running to the other bookkeepers when I have a question. They've got their own work to get out."

A solution came to mind. "You could find many of the answers yourself by referring back to the previous months' work."

"I can't do that. That will take too much time, and You know I have to account for every minute."

"Don't worry. The important thing is to do as much as you can by yourself." Taking God's direction as my authority, I set aside my preoccupation with speed and focused on becoming self-reliant. I learned to exhaust my own resources before turning to others for guidance.

Tax season ended, and with the slower pace, I relaxed and enjoyed, for the first time, keeping a neat set of books for my regular clients. That respite was short. My superiors, realizing I had time to spare, began to supplement my work schedule with assignments out of the office. On those occasions, a senior accountant would drive me to a client's office, give general instructions, and leave me to complete the assignment with a minimum of supervision. Challenged to my limits and frustrated beyond measure, I had to rely on God for step-by-step direction.

"You wouldn't believe the things they expect of me," I complained to Art after an especially exhausting afternoon. "I can't imagine what I ever said in my interview that gave them the idea I could do all this. Somehow, I must have misled them."

Art listened sympathetically but offered few words of advice while I continued to ramble on.

"Maybe I should quit and look for another job," I said halfheartedly. Seconds later, I discounted the idea, "No, I doubt I'd be able to find another job here that pays as well." Deep inside though, I knew that was not the reason. The truth was my pride would keep me there, despite the problems. I was not a quitter.

"No," I announced determinedly. "I won't admit defeat. I'm going to stay and work through this. If they don't feel I'm doing a good job, they'll just have to fire me."

Art looked up from his book and flashed a supportive smile. I had the impression he knew I would arrive at this conclusion.

My decision to stay and make the best of the situation meant I had to confront the issue of my identity as a pastor's wife and its effect on my relationship with the other employees. For most, I had come through the trial period and now accepted me as a human being quite like them in many ways. Those who at first avoided me, fearing I might preach to them or pass judgment, now seemed more relaxed. Conversations had become more spontaneous with others who once felt compelled to discuss religious topics, but now knew I could converse about many other subjects.

There remained a small group of critical Christians, however, with whom my trial had not ended. Among them were the two female book-keepers with whom I worked closely. Over time, my relationship with them had become more strained as they became more acquainted with me. Outwardly, they appeared friendly, yet I had grown to distrust them. Although subtle and indirect, the message they conveyed was clear. "You do not meet our standards for a pastor's wife. We don't approve of your makeup, your clothes, or your actions."

"You should be careful you don't become a stumbling block," one of them awkwardly interjected into a conversation one morning while standing in their office. I looked at her in astonishment, baffled by her bold remark, yet unable to utter a single word of response. Like the prick of a pin on a buoyant balloon, my spirits plummeted. Quickly, I finished my business and returned to my desk in the staff room. I tried to shrug off her comment but could not and mulled the incident over in my mind.

"What in the world did she mean by that remark? Stumbling block for who? Stumbling block for Art? Did I say something she felt would somehow hurt him or might hurt his ministry? What was it that could be viewed as a stumbling block? Was it my conversation with one of the accountants this morning? Maybe she overheard me laughing and joking with him. Could she have meant I am a stumbling block for him? Am I wrong in being friends with him and the other accountants? Am I a stumbling block for someone else? What am I doing so wrong as to warrant this criticism? I suppose I could ask her what she meant. No, I am not that crazy. I'm not about to ask for more trouble."

That was only the beginning. The seed of mistrust had taken root. I found it impossible to ignore the hum of their constant whispering I could hear from my desk when the office was quiet; the whispering ceased when I entered the room. "They must be talking about me," I concluded. "Why don't they like me? Are they jealous that I'm younger and do the same work? Short of confrontation, there was no way to know.

Unable to escape their watchful eyes and judgment, my defense was to shield myself by constructing a high solid wall of aloofness around me. No longer self-assured and confident, I began withdrawing from everyone in the office rather than risk saying or doing anything that might be open to criticism. "From now on, I'll stay clear of them," I vowed. "I won't give them another chance to criticize me. I'll give nothing more of myself than is absolutely necessary to do my job. I'm going to quit trying to win them for my friends." Only one trusting confidant remained.

"Oh Lord, if only the office wasn't so quiet today. If only there was more noise, I wouldn't hear them whispering. If only my desk was at the other end of the office. I can't understand how they get their work done or why the bosses don't do something? Surely, I'm not the only one who hears what goes on in there. Oh Lord, I can't stand it. Sometimes I think I'm going to go crazy."

The whispering didn't stop. The bosses never moved their desks or mine. I continued to withdraw deeper and deeper into my shell. In the midst of my suffering and loneliness, I could hear the still, small voice of God, "Building walls and running from critics are only temporary solutions to your problem. Neither serves any useful purpose or leads to spiritual growth for either of you. There is no point in running away because wherever you go in life there will always be someone critical of you. Your only real defense is in knowing the Truth."

"All right," I reluctantly conceded, "I accept the fact that being judged is inevitable. I can see that what You are saying is true. But I'll not trust that verdict to come from ordinary people, people with their own weaknesses and self-interests to contend with. You're the only one I trust enough to be my judge and lead me to the Truth. I know You love me and will judge me fairly. What do You require of me as a pastor's wife?"

Still pondering these thoughts while wandering downtown during my lunch hour one day, I noticed a large old building on the opposite side of the street. Curiosity led me to cross the street and investigate further.

I read the sign in front of the building that said LIBRARY. Of course—the library," I mumbled to myself excitedly, "Why didn't I think of that?" My heart raced as I quickly mounted the steps of the old stone building. A warm feeling came over me at the rediscovery of my long-lost friend. It had been years since I had allowed myself the luxury of browsing through the library just for fun.

"Where do I begin?" I asked myself, staring at the shelves and shelves of books from floor to ceiling. Slowly I ambled back and forth among the aisles. Past the mysteries that had been my escape as a child, past the romance titles that had been my refuge as an early teen. My eyes caught sight of the sign overhead that said INSPIRATIONAL. I stopped abruptly. I knew God had directed me here. No longer would I wander aimlessly downtown during the lunch hour. I had found my refuge.

Like a thirsty plant eagerly devouring a drink of water, I soaked up and inwardly digested the food I found. *Woman to Woman* (1) by Eugenia Price, and several books by Dale Evans were among the first treasures God led me to read. Their honesty overwhelmed me; the experiences they shared were like offerings of purest gold. Nowhere among the pages did I read of perfection at last obtained or holy lives now lived for the world to see. I read humbling accounts; stories of growing pains and constant struggles to live lives pleasing to God. How encouraging to read God was with them in their struggles and answered their prayers.

Through my reading and quiet meditation, God continued to teach me His truths. "Idolatry is the root of your problem. Focusing on others and their opinions is sinful. It will only bring you unhappiness. It is impossible to meet their demands for each is imperfect like you. Not only are your attempts to please them futile, your attempts to please them are binding them to you. You become a slave to them. I am the one you must seek to please; not those around you. I will give you the approval you need. I will bring to your awareness everything you need to know."

"Forget about being a good pastor's wife. Concentrate your efforts on becoming a good Christian wife. That will in no way conflict with your becoming a good pastor's wife. You are free from that label. I, myself have set you free. Now, you are on the same level as everyone else. You no longer have to accept their unfair expectations. I have set you free!"

More answers came from God through my Seminary Wives' class. "Don't try to be something you're not. Be yourself." The words echoed in my mind like the ringing of a golden bell. "Don't try to be something I'm not! Be myself!" The weight of the responsibility immediately lifted from my shoulders, and the tenseness began to melt away. At last, an attainable goal: being myself. The once-fuzzy picture of the stereotype came clearly into view revealing the Truth. The neat little package labeled "Ideal Pastor's Wife" was nonexistent. God had made each pastor's wife a unique creation for His own special purpose.

Chapter 7

NO LONGER ALIENS

"A time for sewing"
Ecclesiastes 3:7 (JB)

*B*y the summer of 1969, we no longer felt like aliens in a strange world as we took the first steps to adapt to our new environment. The change of seasons symbolized our gradual internal transformation. Just as it had been necessary to shed our winter coats for summer jackets, the new life would not fit comfortably until we released the old. We would not find carbon copies of old friendships. Strong family ties had been broken. Life away from home and families was different. Our lives would never be the same.

Daring to reach out to new friends, we learned the comforting news that our experiences had not been unique nor had lessons learned been in vain. Others, like us, had made the same mistake as they groped for security in the unfamiliar seminary setting. As we shared our experiences with one another, a sense of protectiveness preserving new-found relationships developed. Determined not to fall into the same trap, we moved forward cautiously making a conscious effort to allow ample space.

With our self-confidence as a couple restored, we became involved in extracurricular seminary activities. Art joined the softball team. In September, we joined the seminary bowling league. We also accepted the invitation to serve on the Orientation Committee for the new class of seminarians. Working on the committee gave us an opportunity to find out first-hand just how much we had missed and to play a small part in helping others make the transition to seminary life.

Another important step was our fieldwork experience. At the end of fall quarter, in addition to required academic courses, Art was assigned to join three other seminarians doing a year of fieldwork at Concordia Lutheran Church in Decatur, Illinois, forty miles east of Springfield. Under the supervision of Pastor Jim Hawley, he would gain valuable practical experience in a congregational setting. Responsibilities were rotated, allowing each seminarian to experience teaching confirmation, Bible classes, helping with youth programs, assisting with communion, reading the liturgy, and preaching.

Concordia became a home away from home. We looked forward to our Sunday morning drive to be a part of their church family. The worship services were spiritually uplifting. How refreshing to hear sermons not aimed at the theological intellect but on a personal level everyone could understand. There was an eagerness to learn more about Christ's teachings in the Bible classes with nearly everyone taking an active part in the discussions. Yes, something special was happening there; something we had not seen in every congregation. There was an excitement and enthusiasm among the people. We saw many interacting with one another, showing genuine love and concern as one might expect to see in a large family. Although we, like foster children, were to be part of their church family for only a short while, that same love and warmth was extended to the seminarians and their families.

Love and acceptance was also evident from the parsonage, where once a month, Pastor and Mrs. Hawley entertained the field workers and their spouses for Sunday dinner. What a welcome surprise to find no fanfare and no pretense or religious piety to impress us. Instead, we saw their humanness. Perhaps that was what impressed me most, reaffirming what God had recently shown me. Sometimes our discussions focused on the challenges; other times we talked about the joys. I listened intently, knowing the picture they were painting was accurate. "Never forget," Pastor Hawley advised one afternoon, "Your parishioners aren't God, and neither are you."

Struck by that gem of wisdom, I leaned closer so as not to miss any of the discussion. "Wow!" I thought to myself. I sensed the importance of these round-table discussions. Surely, they were as important as any-thing we might learn in the classroom. This was quality time, a time to treasure, and a precious gift from God. Like a sponge soaking up water, my mind absorbed all that I heard, so I would be prepared when the day came for us to serve a congregation.

Because of the love we felt toward the people there, Concordia was an ideal setting for something as special to us as Art's first sermon. Each of us in our own way had made specific preparations for that milestone in our lives. For days, I had spent my spare time meticulously sewing a new white surplice for Art to wear for the occasion. We made plans to share our day of celebration with seminary friends, John and Sharlee. They would travel to Decatur with us that Sunday and join us for dinner after the service. To capture the excitement of the day for members of our families, John had agreed to take snapshots of Art in the pulpit after the service.

Alone in my thoughts, I sat quietly in the pew beside Sharlee, waiting for the service to begin. I chuckled to myself as I looked around at the people in the rows ahead of me. They had no idea what had transpired behind the scene in preparation for this day. Art had spent hours painstakingly writing his sermon, utilizing all the techniques and knowledge taught him. Proud of his accomplishment, he submitted it to his instructor. His Homiletics professor did not share his satisfaction. "You've only mentioned the name of Jesus twice," he had scribbled at the top of his paper. "You'll have to rewrite it." Not until it had passed all criteria: correct doctrine, absence of heresy, and sufficient mention of the name of Jesus, had it been approved to preach.

I thought about those first practice sessions in our living room to prepare Art for speaking before a congregation. Smiling, I recalled the night he handed me a hymnal and asked me to play the part of the parishioners. I had struggled to keep from giggling as I sat on the living room sofa holding our cat in my lap, while Art solemnly stood reading from a hymnal propped up on the ironing board serving as his lectern. He had not seen the humor that I saw but had become quite provoked at my lack of sensitivity.

Memories of those practice sessions faded when Art processed down the aisle. The new white surplice symbolized to me a change in his roles; no longer that of my husband but now a minister of God. The reality of the past few years took hold, "My husband is a minister!" A tremendous surge of pride and joy engulfed me followed by a warm blush of embarrassment.

"You're not supposed to feel this way," a voice within me scolded. "These feelings are inappropriate for a pastor's wife. You are supposed to project an image of nonchalance and maturity and act as if there is nothing extraordinary about the events of the day."

"But how can I?" another part of me protested. "Anyone can see the joy bursting forth inside of me. It's written all over my face!"

"But, it's immature to show these emotions. You need to hide them and pretend to feel the proper way."

There was only one sure way to conceal the emotions. Reluctantly, the muscles of my face tightened as I listened carefully as Art read the sermon text from Matthew 6:24–34:

> No man can serve two masters: for either he will hate the one, and love the other; or else he will be loyal to the one, and despise the other. You cannot serve God and mammon.
>
> Therefore I say to you, do not worry about your life, what you will eat, or what you will drink; nor about your body, what you will put on. Is not life more than food and the body more than clothing?
>
> Look at the birds of the air, for they neither sow nor reap, nor gather into barns; yet your heavenly Father feeds them. Are you not of more value than they?
>
> Which of you by worrying can add one cubit to his stature?
>
> So why do you worry about clothing? Consider the lilies of the field, how they grow; they neither toil nor spin, and yet I say to you, that even Solomon in all his glory was not arrayed like one of these.
>
> Now, if God so clothes the grass of the field, which today is, and tomorrow is thrown into the oven, will He not much more clothe you, O you of little faith?

Therefore do not worry saying, What shall we eat? Or, What shall we drink? Or, What shall we wear? (For after all these things the Gentiles seek:)

For your heavenly Father knows that you need all these things. But seek first the kingdom of God, and His righteousness, and all these things shall be added to you.

Therefore do not worry about tomorrow: for tomorrow will worry about its own things. Sufficient for the day is its own trouble." (1)

I sat in quiet wonderment, awestruck by the power in Art's message. God was speaking to me again; this time through my husband. Curious whether anyone else had been as inspired, I searched the faces of others around me before returning to God's message for me.

"No man can serve two masters. . . . That's what God told me a few months ago!" I thought excitedly. "This is the scripture to support it. And here He is repeating the same message to me again."

There was eeriness about God's second message. Could it be my secret thoughts and fears about the future had already found their way to His Throne Room? "Don't worry about your bodily needs: food, clothing and drink. I know what you need, and what's more, I am quite capable of caring for you. Trust me. If you will make seeking me your first priority, I will provide for all of your needs." Yes, God knew me well. With the vicarage year rapidly approaching, my mind had already become preoccupied with fluttering thoughts of another move, another city, another home, another church, new friends, and more adjustments. I would need to draw on these words of encouragement in the coming months.

Vicarage represented the first time for many couples when husbands would be earning a small but adequate salary and assume the role of primary breadwinner for a year. Vicarage preparation for a number of couples included plans to have their first child. After five years of marriage, I was more than ready to start raising a family. I was even willing to relinquish tight control of the family finances and be willing to trust God to provide for our needs. We hoped for a pregnancy in the spring or early summer and deliver sometime in the early months of vicarage.

I could devote my time and energy to caring for our new baby while Art was busy tending to his duties as vicar.

For those of us who entertained these plans, excitement filled the air at monthly Seminettes meetings, as one-by-one, the news spread that another seminary couple was expecting a baby. "Did you hear the news? The Smiths are expecting in September. I wonder which couple will be next?"

"Next month . . . maybe next month will be my turn," I told myself confidently, "Maybe next month we'll be the lucky ones to make the proud announcement."

As the months passed, however, it became more difficult to rejoice with my seminary sisters. Instead, ugly feelings of envy crept to the surface whenever I heard of another pregnancy confirmed or saw another seminary wife proudly donning maternity clothes. "Why, God? Why are their plans progressing so smoothly while mine remain incomplete? Why are you showering the blessing of motherhood on them and ignoring my cries?" No answer came. With each passing month, my disappointment grew and my faith dimmed a little more.

"I'll be so glad when summer gets here," I blurted out tearfully, plunking down on the sofa beside Art after class one night.

Startled at my sudden outburst, he stared at me in speechless bewilderment.

"Then I won't have to face the girls," I continued, "and be reminded every week that I'm not pregnant yet. By then most of them will be gone on vicarage. There will be no more meetings or classes until September."

Art's blue eyes revealed his own pain. Reaching over, he gave me a sympathetic hug. "Who knows, Wife, maybe by then you'll be pregnant, too," he said hopefully.

By September, I was coming to grips with the fact that, contrary to my preconceived notion, planning for a baby was not something over which we had control. It was useless and emotionally draining to continue agonizing over the issue. I was worn out from the pain and weary of thinking about it. I had come to a crossroad.

"I refuse to let this ruin my life," I told Art determinedly. "Even if I never get pregnant, I don't want to become a bitter, unhappy person like _____. I'm not going to wait a lifetime for a baby that may never come."

Art seemed relieved at my change of attitude. "We can always adopt," he said matter-of-factly. "There's really no difference."

"I know," I agreed, feeling the pressure slowly lift from my shoulders. "Besides, maybe God does know best. Maybe he wanted us to save some money first. If I'm not pregnant by the time we leave for vicarage, I'll look for a job. With both of us working, we should be able to save some."

"I'll be starting pre-vicarage interviews this month," Art announced a few days later. "What do you think we should put down as our first choice?"

"You mean we get a choice?" I asked in surprise.

"Well, I don't know how much weight it carries, but they do ask us to fill out a questionnaire listing our first, second, and third choices."

My ears perked up with renewed interest at the thought that our opinion might carry any weight at all. "Like what? What kinds of questions?"

"Oh you know. What part of the country would we like to go? Do we prefer a small town or big city, large or small congregation?"

I pondered his questions thoughtfully. The size of congregation did not matter much to me. Nor did I harbor strong feelings about the type of community. I did care about location. My eyes brightened as I gazed off dreamily. "Wouldn't it be neat to go someplace really different—someplace we've never been before?"

"Yeah," he grinned. "Like California."

Then, as though simultaneously stricken with the same negative thought, we plunged back down to earth, "You're being selfish; what about your parent's feelings? You can only go home twice a year as it is. How would they feel if you couldn't go home for a year? How would you handle being so far away from your families for that long?"

With our joy of adventure now hampered by guilt feelings neither of us willing to own, the discussion ended abruptly. Ultimately, Art requested a small congregation in the Midwest or North as his first choice, with the last three months to include clinical pastoral education training. The final decision lay in the hands of the Seminary Placement Committee, who had the responsibility to match eligible students with congregations who had requested a vicar. They would announce their decision during the joint Call Day and Reformation Service on October 29, 1970.

By the time Call Day had arrived, the excitement and anticipation had mounted to such a high level, I felt as though I would burst at any moment. Efforts to concentrate on the sermon were futile. Sitting in the gymnasium beside Art's parents, I thought, "Next month we'll be moving somewhere in the United States to live for a whole year. . . . Oh, I wish he'd hurry up. . . . I can't bear the suspense."

The sermon ended, and the distribution of calls began. I instinctively reached over for my mother-in-law's hand, listening for Art's name to be read. I squeezed it tightly when I heard his name called and watched as he rose from his seat behind the podium and walked forward to accept the call.

"Arthur Newhouse . . . Redeemer Lutheran Church, Denver, Colorado."

My heart leaped for joy! *Denver, Colorado*! Had it not been for the austere atmosphere and the seriousness of the moment, I might have run up to the platform and hugged him. Going to the beautiful state of Colorado sounded too good to be true. How could we be so fortunate to be sent to a place everyone raved about, a place we had never been?

Beaming with joy, I turned to Art's mother, sitting quietly beside me. "Isn't it exciting?" I squealed.

"Oh, that's . . . that's so far away," she whispered faintly, on the verge of tears.

"I know, Mom," I said sympathetically. "But now you and Dad can come and visit us and see Colorado, too!"

By the end of the day, the details of the call were firmly fixed in my mind. Art's vicarage would officially begin December 1, serving the large metropolitan congregation of 1,015 communicant members in southwest Denver. Two full-time pastors had served the congregation until recently; the eldest of whom now on extended leave of absence, suffering from emphysema. As the senior pastor planned to retire soon, the congregation needed a vicar to assist Pastor Reetz in carrying out the pastoral responsibilities.

Not only was Art ecstatic about the call to Redeemer, but also his request for three months of clinical pastoral education (CPE) training. It would not be necessary for us to move again after vicarage as we had expected. Arrangements were made to end his vicarage year with three months of CPE training at Fort Logan Mental Health Center in southwest Denver.

With spirits soaring over our good fortune, we prepared to leave Springfield. Responding to Art's inquiry about housing, a letter had arrived from Pastor Reetz, outlining the housing situation in Denver. With the unoccupancy rate there listed as 2 percent (considered critical by housing authorities), furnished rentals at a price we could afford were scarce. His appeal in the church newsletter had resulted in three possibilities. Near the end of his letter was a short paragraph that deflated our soaring spirits causing immediate turmoil.

> I am a little concerned about Moses. In all three instances,
> the rule reads "No Pets." Having talked with a couple
> of people today (11–13) who are renting apartments,
> it seems this is quite a general rule concerning rentals.

"What are we supposed to do with him?" I snapped angrily. "Leave him behind? Doesn't he understand that Moses is an important member of our family? With whom could we leave him? Who would love him like we do?"

Art was silent for a while, absorbing the thunder of my anger. "I'm sure something will work out, Wife," he reassured. "We won't leave him unless we can find him a good home."

Eventually I, too, concluded it was time to forego sentiments and be practical. If taking him with us would complicate matters, we would leave him behind. We turned to family and friends in desperation. After several calls to Michigan explaining our predicament, my sister Barbara agreed to take him. With the cloud overshadowing our move lifted, we proceeded to pack with joyful hearts.

After taking Moses home to Michigan at Thanksgiving we returned to Springfield and loaded the U Haul trailer.

Our thoughts were preoccupied with questions; "What will it be like?

Will the people like us and we them? How will I fit into the 'vicarage' picture?"

Chapter 8

VICARAGE

"A time for tearing"
Ecclesiastes 3:7 (JB)

"e're about a hundred miles from Denver," Art noted, looking down at the odometer. "They say the mountains are visible from a distance of a hundred miles on a clear day."

"Really, you can see them that far away?" I looked at him skeptically.

"That's what I've heard. We should be able to see them pretty soon now."

I leaned closer to the windshield, squinting, searching the horizon. "The only thing I see are low clouds far off in the distance."

We drove on in silence our eyes still glued to the low-hanging clouds.

Art interrupted the silence a while later, "Over there," he said excitedly, pointing ahead. "Do you see them?"

By now I, too, had caught sight of the faint outline of mountains now distinguishable amidst the clouds. "Wow, kind of takes your breath away, doesn't it?"

Art continued to gaze at the mountains. "Yeah, aren't they something?"

"Imagine what the early settlers must have thought when they first came upon them after months of traveling on the plains," I said dreamily, suddenly feeling a kinship with the weary travelers of long ago. "Just think of the wonder and amazement they must have experienced when they saw that huge wall of mountains towering before them."

We continued to marvel at the scenery as we drew closer to Denver. What a magnificent sight! We were viewing for the first time the immense city spreading on the east with the Rocky Mountains standing majestically on the western border as far as the eye could see.

My stomach fluttered nervously as we approached the city limits, my eyes focusing on the map in my hands. We passed the airport and turned south on the Valley Highway; then we passed the Denver Bronco Stadium to an older neighborhood on the city's southwest side.

"A block off Alameda on Irving. . . . That must be Redeemer over there," Art said, drawing my attention to the modest brick structure on the left. He slowed the car in front of the church for a better view. "It's a lot newer building than I thought it would be."

"Yes, somehow I had envisioned a large stone building, something like Christ Lutheran back home. That must be the church office behind it," I said, pointing to the small frame house south of the church.

Art parked in the parking lot near the church office, and slowly we walked up the sidewalk. "The sign says to walk in," Art said, reaching for the door. We walked through the kitchen to a larger room piled with furniture and other office materials. Behind a desk in one corner of the crowded room sat the church secretary.

"We're the Newhouses," Art announced, trying to ignore the disarray.

"Oh—we didn't expect you until tomorrow," she said in embarrassment. "I . . . I apologize for this mess. As you can see we're in the process of painting your office. We hoped to have everything put back before you arrived."

Art flashed an understanding grin, glancing sideways to peek into the office.

"I'll tell Pastor Reetz you're here," she said, excusing herself. Within a few minutes she returned followed by a tanned, handsome man in his late thirties dressed in a business suit.

"So you're the Newhouses," he said extending a welcoming hand. "I'm Duane Reetz." He gazed at Art curiously. "I must say you look better than the picture you sent."

Art and I exchanged glances. "If he only knew what we went through to get that picture," I thought, recalling the day his letter had arrived, requesting a current picture of Art for publicity purposes. Pressed for time, Art had scurried around trying to borrow a Polaroid camera. Inexperienced as a photographer, I had used the entire roll of film before finding one suitable to send.

"We've arranged for you to stay at the home of the chairman of the congregation until you find a place to live," Duane offered, anticipating our next question. "They have an extra bedroom and plenty of space in their garage to store your belongings. Both Floyd and Helen work, so you'll be free to come and go as you wish during the day."

Grateful for the provision of our needs, I breathed a sigh of relief.

"It's almost noon," Pastor Reetz said noting the time, "I'll call Mary and tell her you're here and that we'll pick her up for lunch."

After a brief phone call to his wife, he again returned to the outer office. "I have some free time this afternoon. If you would like me to, I can drive you around after lunch to look for apartments. It'll help familiarize you with the area."

"Do you want to walk down to the corner with me to pick up a newspaper?" he said, turning to Art. "We'll check out the ads in today's paper before we start out."

Art nodded and left me standing alone in the office with the secretary. "I hope this incident is merely an oversight and not an indication of what is to come," I thought.

That afternoon, and for the next several days, we searched. Before the week's end, we had found a lovely furnished apartment five miles west of the church. Similar to the one in Spartan Village, it was an end unit on the second level of a new brick complex. Unlike the previous others, we could enjoy a beautiful view of the mountains from our bedroom window.

Our first weekend in Denver was a busy one. Anxious to settle in, we spent all day Saturday moving and organizing. On Sunday, Art was installed as Vicar during the first service. I sensed a genuinely warm reception of us as church members greeted us with the proceeds of a surprise food shower—enough groceries to fill two car trunks!

"Mondays will be our day off." Art announced later that afternoon, "Duane asked if we'd like to go skiing tomorrow?"

"Skiing?" I raised my eyebrows. "But we've never been on skis before."

"I told him that. But we'd learn."

I thought a minute, picturing myself atop a high mountain. "Oh no, I'd be afraid. Aren't you afraid?"

"Oh, a little, I guess."

I looked at him curiously, surprised at his interest. "Do you want to go?"

"It might be fun to try."

I pondered the invitation. There was no way I was going to tackle the mountains and skiing; not yet, anyway. "Actually, I'd rather drive up and watch this time."

"Well, what'd he say?" I asked when Art returned after the evening service.

"He just laughed. He said if he drives all the way up there, he's going to ski."

I stared in disbelief. "He said that?"

"That's what he said."

Both anger and pain rose slowly within me. "What are you going to do?"

"Oh, I thought I would try it. I guess some other pastors will be meeting us there."

I felt backed into an uncomfortable corner. The thought of skiing terrified me. Being left behind was even worse. "I guess I might as well try, too." I said half-heartedly. My stomach fluttered nervously just like in high school after the teacher had assigned a speech.

The fluttering continued on Monday as we journeyed the sixty miles to Loveland Ski Area. We met the other pastors and agreed to meet for lunch before Art and I parted company to sign up for ski school. Fitted with ski boots and three-foot skis, we assembled with the other students to wait for our class to begin. A handsome young man with dark hair and a bronze tan joined our group, introducing himself as our ski instructor.

"It looks simple enough," I thought as I watched him demon-strate. The graceful coordination of his body movements with his skis seemed effortless. I tried to follow his directions, "Bend your knees, and put your weight on the downhill ski." My legs were so stiff from the weight of the heavy boots I could scarcely bend my knees. Not synchronizing with my body, my skis acted independently, clumsily carving out their own paths in the snow. The concept of putting my weight on the downhill ski simply did not compute.

I glanced over to see Art busily working on perfecting his tech-nique. "Like this," he instructed patiently, seeing my plight. I con-tinued to watch as he maneuvered his skis, trying to duplicate his movements. It was obvious I had no control over my skis; each time I tried, I fell down.

Sensing Art's impatience at my inability to catch on, I turned to observe the other students. While everyone was struggling and falling from time to time, no one seemed as uncoordinated as I did. I felt intimidated and alone. A rush of heat came over me as my chest tightened with panic. I dared not speak with tears rising. I stood in silence, watching the instructor work with the other students. "He's so arrogant and self-assured," I thought, "He doesn't even notice I'm having trouble."

"Okay, class, now we're going to take the chair lift and get off halfway up," the instructor announced after an hour on the "bunny hill."

I lifted my eyes in the direction he was pointing and turned to Art in disbelief. "Halfway up the mountain? He's got to be kidding."

"I don't think he is."

Real fear crept in to replace the butterflies, "But I don't even know how to get on the chair lift, let alone ski once I get there," I moaned.

Shrugging his shoulders, Art took his place in line. I followed behind still grumbling. When he boarded the chairlift, I managed to pull myself on to the chair beside him. "Now all I have to do is worry about how to get off in one piece," I pouted.

All the way up to the top, I prayed silently. "Oh Lord, help me. You know I have no business coming up here. I don't know how to ski. I can barely stand up on these things."

Nearing the halfway point, I watched as the others stood up and skied away from the lift. When our chair came to the unloading ramp, surprisingly I was able to get off and out of the way without falling. "Thank you, Lord," I whispered gratefully, moving to the side of the hill to take my place in line.

Renewed fear gripped me, however, as I glanced down the mountainside. Art watched as each time my turn came, I panicked and would quickly lose control of my skis, ending up in a tangled heap. "Why is it that every time one of the pastors is riding on the lift overhead, I have to be sprawled out on the ground like this," I mumbled, struggling to pick myself up. After several more attempts, followed by a serious fall, the instructor skied over to help me up.

"We'd better get you off the hill before you really hurt yourself," he concluded, after examining my leg. "I'll call the ski patrol to escort you down."

Throughout the lunch hour, I ate in silence, choking back the tears to hide my disappointment and embarrassment, all the while wrestling with the decision whether or not to continue. "Oh Lord," I prayed, staring at my bowl of chili. "What'll I do? I'm afraid if I quit now, I'll never have the courage to try again."

"Don't give up," God gently encouraged. "There is still hope for you." Then in a more serious tone, He scolded, "Your persistence in comparing yourself to Art has contributed to your problem. You won't know to what degree that has hindered you until you get away from him."

For the remainder of the lunch hour I pondered God's words thoughtfully. Although His words had a cutting edge, there was no doubt His assessment was accurate. Slowly, the deflated spirit within me rose to meet His challenge. With renewed determination, I sat up in my chair and turned to Art, "I'm going to transfer to another class," I announced boldly. "I think I'll do better away from you with another instructor."

The discovery that others in my new class shared my inexperience and fear immediately put me at ease. Our likable young instructor exhibited a remarkable talent for teaching beginners, patiently encouraging us to master our fears and continue trying. A miracle took place that afternoon when God opened my eyes to the secret of turning my skis. "It makes sense! It makes sense!" I thought excitedly, the instructor's words echoing in my mind; 'Bend your knees and put your weight on the downhill ski.' How thrilling to be able to maneuver quite well down the mountain! The day begun in humiliation and defeat had ended in personal victory. In future years, I would look back on the events of this day as a significant step in God changing me and changing our marriage.

After spending one day at the first place the employment agency sent me in downtown Denver, I realized that job would be too stressful. The person I was to replace was a chain smoker and a nervous wreck. As soon as I returned home, I called the employment agency to tell them I had decided not to accept that offer. I would postpone the hunt until after the busy holidays.

The first week in January the agency had called to say they scheduled me for an interview with Diners Club who recently had moved their corporate office from New York City to Denver. I felt very confident as I sat opposite the personnel supervisor in the plush new office. I knew I was well qualified for this position. I was very familiar and had considerable experience with bank reconciliations. Working in a relaxed atmosphere was exactly what I needed this year. I sensed the attractive woman behind the desk was impressed with my resume. The interview had gone very well.

"One of the requirements for this position," she clarified, peering up from her desk," is that you be available to spend two weeks training in our New York office. Your expenses, of course, will be paid."

My spirit sank. Leave Art and spend two weeks in New York City? "Oh, I don't think my husband would ever agree to that."

The woman looked at me in surprise. "You don't think your husband would let you go?"

"I could ask, but I doubt very much if he'd approve of my going there without him."

For a minute, she eyed me skeptically in disbelief. "Well, why don't you talk it over with him tonight and call me tomorrow?"

"How did your interview go?" Art asked, when he came home that evening.

I hesitated searching for the right combination of words. "Oh, the interview went great. . . . There's just one drawback."

"What's that?"

"If I accept the job, I'll have to spend two weeks in New York."

"What's so bad about that?"

For a moment I was speechless, stunned by his response. "You mean . . . you mean you don't care if I go?" I replied, struggling to hide my hurt feelings.

Art shrugged. "I don't care. Why would I mind?"

I felt sick and could see there was no point in prolonging this conversation. A mixture of emotions began churning in the pit of my stomach. "I thought I knew him better than that—no objections to my leaving him for that length of time? That doesn't sound like the husband I know. He's not the least bit concerned that I'll be in New York for two weeks without him."

Swiftly my defense mechanism came to the rescue. "If that's the way he feels, I'll surely not be stupid enough to let on how I really feel," I thought, slamming the lid on my hurt feelings. "I'll show him I don't need him, either. I'll go to New York and have a good time while I'm there!"

"Great! I'll call her tomorrow and tell her I'll take the job!"

I would work only two days in the Denver office as arrangements had been made for two employees from our department to fly to New York on Sunday. On Friday, I learned a single girl, in her early 20s, newly transferred to our department, would accompany me. An attractive girl with long, blond hair, Jan had recently moved to Denver from Joplin, Missouri. Neither of us had ever been to New York, and we were very excited and nervous about our upcoming adventure—two expense-paid weeks in the big city. Four others from another department would be on the same flight.

Immediately after the first service Sunday morning, Art attired in the traditional clergy shirt and collar, took me to the airport. Jan knew my husband was a minister but I felt conspicuous as I sat with him, waiting for the others to arrive. One by one, our four traveling companions arrived at the airport and introduced themselves: three women and their male supervisor. Two of the four had previously worked in the New York office.

We boarded and took our seats in one row. The two who had spent several weeks working at the New York office briefed us on their experiences, which had included some fun as well as work. They were friendly to Jan and me, but I sensed they would make themselves scarce as soon as the opportunity presented itself. They had no intention of serving as chaperones for a preacher's wife and her pretty, young companion. After arriving at the hotel, they promised to show us to the office the next day and quickly departed.

Any thoughts that our little excursion would be a vacation evaporated when we arrived at the office on Monday morning. Mass confusion awaited us the moment we walked through the door. Glancing across the huge room, I noticed a tall young man walking across the room. Pointing him out to Jan, I commented, "See that guy walking over there? Now, there is a guy who would make a good husband." Jan laughed and eyed me curiously. Neither of us had ever set eyes on him before.

In addition to the New York employees and Denver trainees, external auditors were also working on the year-end audit. The comptroller from Denver explained that our immediate supervisor was ill, and we would have to do the best we could until she returned. He instructed us to begin reconciling the bank accounts, some of which had not been reconciled for several months. Stressing the importance of bringing them up-to-date as quickly as possible as the auditors needed the information for the year-end reports, he encouraged us to work as much overtime as needed. After directing us to some files, he left us to complete the task.

Jan and I exchanged bewildered glances. How in the world could we bring any semblance of order to this chaos? We both had experience in reconciling bank accounts, but there was no comparison between balancing small business accounts and reconciling the multimillion-dollar bank accounts of a national concern. The immediate challenge was locating the needed files and finding the corresponding computer run of outstanding checks and deposits. Once more, I faced a gigantic puzzle and an assignment that seemed overwhelming. The only factor in our favor appeared to be our determination to prove we were capable of the daunting task.

Lending to the obvious confusion was the underlying current of distrust and antagonism we faced as outsiders. With few exceptions, most of the New York employees felt threatened by the Denver staff replacing them and hesitated to offer any more assistance than absolutely necessary. Given those peculiar circumstances, it was not natural for everyone to work together when they thought they were losing their jobs.

After several long, tedious days working without supervision, two of the single accountants from the Denver office invited us to a Broadway play after work. While I welcomed the opportunity to get away from the office and have some fun, their invitation immediately put me in a quandary. I wanted to go but did not want it construed as a date. Nor did I want to place myself in what could be a tempting situation. Additionally, the group planned to see *Hair,* which I knew was a rock musical with some nudity. All day I wrestled with the decision. I knew Jan would not go without me, and I did not want to be the spoilsport and ruin everyone else's plans. After thinking and praying about it all afternoon, I suggested that perhaps another person could go with us. The fellows agreed and invited another of the single accountants from Denver. Jan and I looked at one another in dismay when we met him. Steve was the fellow I had pointed out to her that first day as making a good husband! Despite my guilt feelings, it was exciting to see Broadway and the diverse crowd that attended the performance.

Our supervisor returned to work later in the week, and by the weekend, sufficient progress in our work justified taking Saturday afternoon off to go shopping. Although the weather was extremely cold and windy, Jan and I dressed warmly and walked the two blocks from our hotel to Fifth Avenue. The highlight of our afternoon came when we noticed a sign in a shoe store, advertising a sale. Never had we seen such a pile of shoes in the middle of the floor; many of which had been separated from their mates! We laughed watching as people clawed through the pile looking for the mates! On Sunday, we took a bus tour to China Town, the Empire State Building, the Statue of Liberty, and the United Nations Building.

The night before our scheduled departure for home, Steve joined us for a late dinner. To celebrate, he offered to escort us on the subway to a small nightclub across town. We enjoyed the comedian and had a delightful time. By the time we arrived back at our hotel, it was three o'clock in the morning! We were so exhausted the next day, we rescheduled our flight for Saturday morning and decided to have a quiet dinner delivered to our room. We were both anxious to leave New York and return to the Rocky Mountains and a simpler life.

I stared out the window of the airplane lost in thought. In just a few hours, the plane would land in Denver, ending my fantasy. Art would pick me up at the airport, and life would resume as usual, or would it? How could two weeks have such an impact on one's life? If only my eyes were not opened. There is no going back and no point in denying the truth. The time we had spent apart had given me time to reflect on our marriage. Some startling facts had emerged. I doubt that life could resume as usual.

Most surprising was the knowledge that our marriage had not fared well under the strain of the past two weeks. How quickly it had happened. It had been easy to go our separate ways. I felt a dangerous uneasiness about the direction our marriage was heading. I realized we were slowly drifting apart. Somehow, we would have to address the problem. We would have no choice. The sick feeling about our marriage was much too close to the surface to bury. Times had changed, and so had we. "I wonder what Art will say? I wonder if he has come to the same conclusions while I've been away, but probably not. He has probably been so caught up in his own little world that he hasn't even noticed."

Within hours of my return, I found myself baring my soul to my husband. "It was strange," I cautiously began, "but while I was in New York, I felt so detached from you . . . as if we weren't even married. I was surprised how easy it was to go our separate ways, you doing your thing and me doing mine. It really scared me."

Art studied me thoughtfully, while I continued, "I don't like what's happening to us. We're becoming selfish and thinking only of ourselves and satisfying our own needs." I stopped abruptly. "Becoming selfish" was not part of the speech I had rehearsed.

"I know," Art nodded his head in humble agreement. There was a certain sadness in his eyes; a pained expression on his face. "I don't like it, either."

A ray of hope shone through the gray clouds. "He agrees! He sees it, too!" His positive response was more that I had expected.

Alarmed at our mutual discovery, we proceeded to carefully analyze our marriage. Something was missing. Was it lack of money? No, we had more money than we had ever had. We were able to meet our expenses, make regular deposits in our savings account, and purchase nonessentials. We could afford to go skiing, go to a movie, or dine out with friends. No, money was not the problem.

Was it boredom? That was highly unlikely, as we were going all the time. Our calendar was full of social activities: choir practice and women's circle for me; church potlucks, and dinner invitations and clergy get-togethers for us as a couple. No, we did not lack for social activity.

As we continued the assessment, God opened our eyes to see the void in our lives. We needed someone to take our minds off ourselves, someone in common to love. Perhaps we needed a baby. We would wait no longer for a pregnancy—a child that may never come. We had a mutual agreement about adoption. There seemed no need to consult a physician. Simply, we wanted children. Exhilarated at the prospect of our dream becoming a reality, we found no reason for further delay. Tomorrow we would take the first step. We would contact Lutheran Service Society.

Within a month, our application was processed and arrangements made to meet with the social worker assigned to us. At our first meeting, Sharon explained the two options of home study available: individual or group. Rather than choose the individual study entailing several home visits, we chose to participate in a group with other adoptive couples meeting at the agency for twelve hours of intense study one weekend. The agency would make every effort to match the couples to facilitate a congenial group for sharing.

We could feel the momentum of our recent decision as we drove to the agency one Friday afternoon a few weeks later. We sensed both excitement and trepidation as our dream began to unfold. Upon our arrival, we found the designated meeting room and sat down on one side of the large conference table. When all four couples had assembled, Sharon introduced herself and John, the other social worker, after which each couple gave a brief introduction. Completing our group of four couples was an Army doctor and his wife, an engineer and his wife, and an Air Force lawyer and his wife.

The relaxed agenda for the Friday's session put everyone at ease as we shared our common bonds: the desire to adopt a child and the joys we looked forward to in the coming months. Some of us shed tears as we viewed a true-life drama of a birth mother, and the emotions and feelings she experienced as she prepared to relinquish her baby. Rounding out the session was a visit from an adopted teenager who shared her story from the perspective of an adopted child. As the day progressed, we felt ourselves moving from passive listeners to active participants. The complete and accurate picture of the adoption process was coming into focus.

On Saturday, I looked around at the vacant chairs waiting for the session to begin. John had directed Art and the other three husbands to follow him to another room, leaving Sharon behind with the four wives. The large conference table now seemed too large for our small group.

"Now," Sharon began, "I would like each of you to talk a little about your marriage." Noting the puzzled expressions on our faces, she added, "It doesn't matter who begins."

I struggled to retain my outward composure, while inside my heart raced; my stomach fluttered nervously. The magnifying glass was zeroing in on a very sensitive area in my life. I should have known it would not escape scrutiny in this situation. "She can bet I won't be the first to speak up," I thought anxiously. "It'll take all the courage I can muster to be the last." I looked down, hoping to avoid Sharon's observant eyes.

I listened closely as each of the other wives shared a little about her marriage. The more I heard, the more uncomfortable I became. No one mentioned marital difficulties or talked about times of stress. "Compared to them, our marriage is standing on very shaky ground," I concluded. "What am I going to say? For the life of me, I can't think of anything but these past few miserable months. What's going to happen to our chances to adopt if I'm honest?"

Another voice inside argued. "Why say anything? Just gloss over it. Talk about the superficial. They'll never know the difference. Who would ever suspect a minister could have marital problems? Why blow your chances to adopt by bringing it into the open now?"

"I could probably get away with it," I thought slyly. "So far I've been quite successful in putting on a façade; nobody has any idea what's really happening. There is no need for me to take the lid off now. Who am I kidding? I'd never get away with it. My feelings are so close to the surface now, I'd never be able to hide them. I'm going to have to be honest. I'll just have to risk it and face the consequences."

After the last one finished, Sharon turned to me and smiled. "I guess it's your turn next, Bonnie."

Swallowing deeply, I sat erect in my chair. Only one thought ran through my mind at this point, "Okay, Lord, I'll say it if I have to, but please . . . please don't let me cry."

"Well . . . I don't know about the others," I said shyly, glancing around, "but right now, our marriage is going through a very difficult time. Our roles have changed drastically these past few months because Art is no longer a student and now he is the main breadwinner for the first time since our marriage." I paused a moment, "It hasn't been an easy time for me." Once again, I swallowed deeply, hoping no one had noticed my crackling voice. I felt like a traitor, talking so openly about our marriage before these strangers. Quietly I sat back, waiting for the rest of my world to come crashing down.

Sensing the depth of my words, Sharon came to my rescue. "Yes, the changes that have taken place in your lives these past few months can place a great deal of stress on a marriage," she said sympathetically. "I'm sure it's been a big adjustment for both of you." Her eyes were compassionate; her voice conveying love and understanding.

I felt like a tiny fragile kitten being rescued from a watery grave. My heart wanted to hug her gratefully, yet I could say nothing. I dared not speak lest my emotions completely give way. I embraced the new set of thoughts and emotions rising to the surface. "She's supportive! She believes and respects what I had to say! She doesn't think I'm crazy or imagining things! She didn't give me a lecture! She didn't react negatively, or use her authority as a weapon! She didn't tell me a Christian shouldn't feel this way!"

Sharon's support gave validity to my feelings. Her positive response gave me the courage to believe in me giving my morale a badly needed boost. The few words she had spoken gave me permission to face the upheaval in my life straightforward: no more denying it, no more pretending and no more games.

Chapter 9

PANDORA'S BOX IS OPENED

"A time to refrain from embracing"
Ecclesiastes 3:5 (JB)

At the close of Saturday's session, we returned home where I retreated to our bedroom, threw myself on the bed, and sobbed. I felt as if a part of my innermost feelings had been laid bare, leaving me naked before the world. Emotionally drained, I wanted to be alone with my thoughts and cry. Coupled with the pain was a measure of relief. At last, what lay hidden in darkness was in the light. No more would I have to live in fear that one day it might be exposed. I knew I had opened up my Pandora's Box and must face the suppressed emotions and pain found there. I was keenly aware, too, that I had verbalized only a tiny portion of what lay buried.

Why am I so unhappy? What has precipitated this crisis? Other than the fact our roles have changed, what lies beneath the surface? Mentally, I made an inventory. One by one, God brought to my consciousness each item. Many were negative feelings about our long-awaited vicarage. It was impossible to face the truth without honestly acknowledging the feelings that surfaced—feelings that frightened, and embarrassed me: anger, resentment, and jealousy. They are getting a part of my husband that I am being denied, and it's not fair!"

"Rather than be uplifting, Sunday had become the most depressing day of the week for me. I hated to sit without my husband in church every week. Though there are many friendly people in the congregation, I felt alone in a world of strangers. I had no close friends; friends just for me. Certainly, there was no one I trusted to confide in. Even my husband is like a stranger to me on Sundays and lost in his own world. Early in the year, I learned not to expect any attention or companionship from him that day. Learning not to expect any has somehow lessened the pain. What a contrast to Sundays for Art."

"Sundays are the highlight of his week. Why wouldn't they be? He and Duane standing there, basking in the limelight, people attentive to their every word, and milling about during the social hour waiting to speak to the pastors. They are willing to wait their turn for his undivided attention. Undivided attention is something I rarely get from my husband these days. How much vicarage has changed him. Obviously, he enjoys his newfound attention and sense of belonging as a vicar. He's become so wrapped up in the role—so self-centered and arrogant, so aloof from me."

"I never expected him to act like this. I get the feeling I don't fit in his life anymore. It is as if he's outgrown me. I fear our marriage will go the way of so many other marriages after the husband has finished school . . . no longer needing the wife who stood by his side during those struggling years while he worked toward his goals and then being cast aside.

"And then there's Art's relationship with Duane. He has become a wedge between us. He is more influential with Art than I am. Art looks to him rather than me for emotional support and approval, needs I previously filled. They share all the confidences and personal problems of the parishioners, all things Art cannot discuss with me. Maybe it would be easier if I felt his influence was always positive."

"Counseling— that's a subject I don't like thinking about. I know many of the people he counsels are women, sharing their problems and pouring out their hearts. I am sure he listens patiently, empathizing and understanding. What a hypocrite. How can he be so attentive to everyone else's needs and so indifferent to mine? He doesn't listen to me. He acts as though he doesn't understand what I'm trying to say, as if I am imagining the problems.

When can we talk? Even at home in the evening, he is preoccupied with the happenings of his day and the problems at church. What part of my husband's time is for me? Like the day he was watching television. There was a time he would have been more sensitive and noticed something was troubling me. I had to turn the TV off and shout at him before he responded. It's as though he watches television to avoid talking with me. He just tunes me out and slams the door shut to any further discussion. I am foolish for allowing him to intimidate me. Why have I let him convince me my feelings are invalid?"

"Sharon, though, she did listen and understand. She acknowledged that many changes have taken place in our lives to account for some of this turmoil. She listened to me with respect. It didn't seem to matter that I didn't finish college or don't hold a degree in some humanitarian field. She valued what I had to say."

"Value is the key word. My self-esteem has plummeted since vicarage had begun. I no longer feel needed by my husband. He is earning a salary and is not dependent on my income. The monetary contribution is not causing the deepest pain. Worse is the feeling he no longer needs me as his helpmate and support. Duane fills this gap and shares his vicarage.

"I don't feel needed at work, either. I thought having no responsibility would be the perfect job for this year. I could just put in an honest day's work and go home, working in a large corporation with three in our department doing the same work where being away for a day was of little consequence to the workload. I never realized the importance of feeling needed in the workplace."

When the tape of the present had played through and my thoughts about vicarage exhausted, it began to rewind backward to my identity crisis at Michigan State. Reluctantly, I found myself taking from the shelf all the stored, painful memories, and unresolved issues. Knowing the pain it had caused me, I had very carefully avoided that shelf for the past three years. Only once since then had I ever approached the shelf; when personality inventory tests had been administered to the students and their wives at the seminary. I feared its contents might be exposed. To my amazement and relief, the tests revealed no major problems in our marriage.

God had chosen a better time. Everything lined up perfectly according to His plan. Circumstances in my life had caused me to be ripe for action, ripe for change. Not only had He forced the issue through the adoption process, He had graciously provided Sharon to listen and to understand. God had moved me into position to take action by allowing me to reach the valley. He knew that pain, depression, and anger would serve to propel me from the valley to a place where I would be willing to stretch farther to climb out of the depths.

"How ironic," I thought to myself disgustedly. "Here I sit, again, in almost the same predicament I was in at Michigan State. Only this time I have no one to turn to, no place to escape. My family is miles away, and I have no close friends. Working overtime isn't an option now, and I certainly won't run to the church to escape. That's Art's world. Besides, there I'm constantly reminded a Christian shouldn't feel this way. 'Be happy,' the choir director always scolds. 'Sing with joy, People!' No doubt her words are true and her intentions the best, but what if I don't feel joyful? She doesn't seem to understand that true joy is like beauty and must come from within. It is not something to be manufactured on the outside or pound into me." The more I thought about it, the more clearly the picture came into focus. My unhappiness, both now and at Michigan State, was the direct result of a change in Art. He had arrived at a place in his life where his needs for a wife had changed."

Gradually, a distinctive pattern came into view. Once again, I had fallen into the trap of taking a defensive role in my life. When things were flowing smoothly, I did not push myself to grow in my spiritual walk. I did not take an offensive role, unless forced by a change in Art. Suddenly, I realized that neither I nor our marriage would survive much longer if I continued to sense no purpose for my life. I dare not allow my happiness or identity to depend on the actions or inactions of another.

Angry and depressed, the road before me looking very bleak, I asked myself, "What happened? What happened to the future that once held such excitement? It's not fair to have come to this fork in the road with only two paths to choose from. I'm either going to have to adapt to the situation and accept this as my lot in life, despite the fact I'm miserable, or somehow reject this unhappiness and actively search for ways to change myself so I can be happy as a pastor's wife." Although I could not see clearly down the second path, I could see the gloom that awaited me down the first. Haunted by the agonizing faces of other wives, who had unknowingly chosen the first path, I knew unless I acted now, my future was certain to be the same.

Determined to find my way back to happiness and fulfillment, I moved toward the second path. I traveled only a short distance when I sensed the unmistakable presence of God walking close beside me, sharing His truths. "I don't will for you to be unhappy," God gently encouraged, "I love you. I care for you." Second, He confirmed the path I had chosen. "Don't wait for Art to change himself and become the same person who once needed you. Do not count on that happening. He won't even be able to help you solve your problem because he is in an entirely different place than you. Only I can help you. You must begin at once, listening and trusting that still, inner voice you have come to recognize as Mine. You must be fully prepared to act whether or not Art understands."

The key to solving my problem came during the following weeks as I studied the Scriptures in my women's circle and Sunday school classes. Through reading God's Word, the Holy Spirit ministered to my needs. "The root of your unhappiness is idolatry," was His startling pronouncement. "You have gradually elevated Art to a pedestal, the same pedestal on which many others place their husbands. He has become the center of your life. Your depression is directly related to your preoccupation with him, his importance, and his activities."

"As a result," He continued, "you now find yourself in the dangerous dilemma Jesus warned about: serving two masters. Your husband has become an idol in your life, and you must take immediate steps to put him back in his proper place of importance. You must take your eyes off your husband and look instead to Jesus. Your dependency on Art must be transferred to Him where it rightly belongs. It is necessary for you to arrive at a place in your spiritual life, where you can say, and mean it, that Jesus is the center of your life. He will totally care for you, filling any needs you might have. You must arrive at a place where you can truthfully say, 'I can get along without Art if that is required of me.'"

Once again, God's assessment cut through my heart with precision accuracy. The familiar First Commandment echoed in my mind: "Thou shalt have no other Gods before me." I never dreamed that God would one day find me guilty of this grievous sin. "Oh yes," my heart cried out. "I had no idea of my sin. Forgive me, Lord." As soon as I uttered the words, I felt God's forgiveness flooding my soul. A sense of peace, relief, and hope came over me. The relief came from knowing I was dealing with a solvable problem. Somehow, all these years I had falsely believed there was no solution short of divorce—that it was somehow too big for God or me to handle. Although unable to see the end of the road, I held hope for the future.

"How God, how do I go about taking my eyes off my husband and putting them on Jesus? He is around me every day. He's so much a part of my life."

"It won't be easy, but it is possible. Remember my teaching to you several years ago, when you were plagued by negative thinking. Do you remember the principles outlined in *The Power of Positive Thinking*? (1) You know these principles work. You have already proven them effective in battling negative thinking. You must follow the same steps in this situation. First, you must carefully monitor your thoughts and train yourself again to be acutely aware of what you are thinking. Second, when you find yourself dwelling on Art or what he is doing, I want you to visualize the face of Jesus. Picture Him as a shepherd caring for you and loving you. Focus your attention on His words in the Bible that have a special meaning to you, and focus on the Psalms of David for comfort and promise. Focus on the positive. Repeat them to yourself until your thinking has been redirected."

"But, Lord, that's such a drastic measure to consciously push my husband out of my mind. It sounds so cold, so cruel. That doesn't sound like something a wife should be doing. What will happen to our relationship? What will happen to our marriage?"

"You will just have to trust Me and have faith in My guidance. Because of the extreme to which you have gone, it is necessary to revert to an extreme to correct your path. When I feel you are safely able to return to a more middle ground, I, myself, will bring it about. You must believe I know what is best for both you and your marriage."

Placing my marriage in God's hands, I proceeded to detach emotionally from my husband. While working, if my thoughts trailed off to Art, I immediately closed my eyes, softly uttering a prayer for help and visualizing the face of Jesus. Other times, I repeatedly said to myself, "*I can do all things through Christ who strengthens me*," (2) until my spirits were lifted and my thoughts clear.

Finding myself vulnerable during the evenings and on the weekends, I made a conscious point of spending some time away from Art, doing things I enjoyed, which did not involve the church. Occasionally going into the bedroom and curling up with an interesting book helped to fill my mind with wholesome thoughts. Sometimes it was necessary to increase the distance by going outside in the sun or going shopping.

Having confronted one major problem area in my life, the adoption process proved the catalyst for yet another issue; one in which I had not yet come to terms. Until now, I never felt the freedom to verbalize my deepest feelings about being a mother; feelings Art did not share as a father. Distancing myself from him, freed me to acknowledge my feelings. Could it be my bondage to him has somehow hindered me from being honest with myself? Deep inside me is an agony and emptiness. Going to the Expectant Parent's Class each week was painful, constantly reminding me I was unlike the other expectant mothers. I envied them as they blossomed with their pregnancy, seeing their maternity clothes and watching their husbands pamper them. Yes, there was agony deep within me.

"What is this pain in my soul?" I asked myself. "Why am I so sad? After all, we too, will soon have a tiny baby in our home—a baby of our own—a precious baby to love and care for. A year has passed, and still I have not become pregnant. Maybe there is something wrong. Maybe I never will be able to bear a child," The barrage of thoughts was frightening, creating a mood of panic. "I may never experience the growth and development of a tiny baby growing within me. Nothing I can do will bring about a pregnancy. Money will not buy it; all the hard work in the world will not earn it. God is totally in charge of this area of my life, and for some reason, He has chosen to withhold this blessing from me."

"Why me?" I lashed out, "Why do I have to be one of those numbers and statistics to be barren? Why are You refusing me this blessing? What have I done to deserve this punishment?"

God did not return my anger but gently heard me out. "You feel my anger has allowed this tragedy in your life, but read about my people in the Bible. Look at Sarah, Rebekah, Rachel, and Elizabeth. They were humiliated by the world for being barren but favored by Me. They were special. I never change, and I have set you aside in this way, too; trust Me."

I meditated on God's answer curiously. "What does He mean, set aside? Does He mean I should look on my circumstances somehow as positive, rather than negative? Does He mean I will bear children later in life like all of them? Does He mean He looks on me with favor? I thought of Sarah. My heart ached for her. How much she must have suffered and how deep must have been the feelings of sorrow she harbored all those years. But to be favored by God? I wonder if she felt it was worth the price she paid. Even though God does not promise me a child, somehow I should have this sense of peace to be favored by Him because of my barrenness?" Then, I too, felt special. I would draw on these words for strength many times in the weeks to come.

"We've completed the study for your adoption," Sharon announced happily one day in late spring. "Your application has been approved, and now it's just a matter of waiting for the right baby to become available."

"When do you think that'll be?" I asked excitedly.

"It could be as early as May or as late as the fall."

Art and I exchanged hopeful glances while Sharon continued, "In the meantime, it would be a good idea to call us once a month just to keep in touch. When a baby becomes available, we'll call you, probably in the evening when we would be most apt to catch you home together."

Preparing for the adoption served to draw us together. Together we prepared the nursery and talked about the event that would no doubt change our lives drastically. This was an event only husband and wife could intimately share together—not pastor, not parishioners, not friends, and not family. Although Art did not identify with my emotions as a woman unable to conceive, we stood together sharing the embarrassment, humiliation, and anger at the invasion of our privacy as news of our adoption became known. "How long have you been trying; is there some kind of trouble?" Equally upsetting was unsolicited advice. "Keep it a secret, there's no need to tell anyone," or "out-of-town people won't ever need to know."

We spent the remainder of the summer riding an emotional roller coaster. On the occasions of the baby showers or when we contacted the agency, we were at an extreme high. Other times we were at a low, as if playing a silly game with ourselves, pretending to be expecting when we were not. "It's as though we're living in a dream world," I told Art one day. "Here we are expecting a baby, but I'm not pregnant and we have no idea when the baby will arrive." Yet each time the phone rang, we were jostled back to reality. "One of these times, the call will come announcing the arrival of our baby."

I quietly tiptoed into the nursery and ran my fingers lovingly along the rail of the beautiful Early American baby bed now piled high with baby gifts. We had such fun when Art's parents took us shopping during their Easter visit and let us select the bed of our choice as their gift for the new grandchild. Were it not for this visible reminder, it would have been easy to forget we were expecting a baby.

Chapter 10

CLINICAL PASTORAL EDUCATION

"A time for embracing"
Ecclesiastes 3:5 (JB)

With Art's vicarage year at Redeemer officially over at the end of August and Clinical Pastoral Education set to begin the middle of September, we scheduled a week's vacation to allow us time to unwind and detach from our vicarage year and spend some time alone together. We would spend Labor Day weekend camping with several families from the congregation and the remainder of the week camping by ourselves in the mountains near Aspen.

Before we left on our camping trip the Friday before Labor Day, we had one more important event: Jan and Steve's wedding ceremony. They had dated steadily since our New York trip, and we had watched as their relationship blossomed into love. We could not have been more thrilled to serve as honored attendants and witness their marriage before a Denver judge and friend of Steve's family. After the service, we joined the newlyweds for a lovely wedding dinner with other family members at the home of his parents.

On Saturday, I accompanied the other women in our camping group to a nearby town to buy food supplies. While they were busy hovering over the meat counter, deciding on the choicest spare ribs, I wandered to other parts of the store. My eyes lit up when I spotted a book display. Making my way down the aisle, I spun the rack around. When the rack stopped, a book by Catherine Marshall caught my attention, *Beyond Ourselves* (1) "An intriguing title," I thought, leafing through the pages. "Just the book I need for this vacation. Not only will it give me something to do by myself," I reasoned, "It'll be spiritual nourishment and help me resist the temptation to fall back into my old way of depending too much on Art."

During the quiet time that week, God used Catherine's book to remind me that:

> Some things are beyond our capacity to conquer, despite our best efforts and intentions. Instead, we must openly acknowledge our weaknesses and admit our helplessness to overcome them on our own. We must stand humbly before Him confessing them and our helplessness to overcome them. Victory will come only when we give them to God to deal with for us. (2)

God had shown me the implications it might have on my life, and I was anxious to put her theory to the test. "For my testing ground, I'll choose one of the most troublesome areas of my life—jealousy, that old problem long a 'thorn in my side' causing me no end of pain. The next time I begin to sense jealous feelings," I resolved firmly, "I'll do exactly as she outlined. I can't wait to see if her theory will really work miracles in my life, too."

The opportunity came not long after, as the black cloud of jealousy enveloped me. Like a lion ready to pounce on its prey, I stood ready to act. "It's those old twinges of jealousy again," I admitted excitedly. "Now is the chance to prove her theory."

"Lord, I need your help. I confess my jealousy," I prayed silently, "I know now that I can't overcome it on my own. I'm giving it to you, Lord, to deal with for me."

To my amazement, the black cloud lifted, and my ugly intruder departed. Yet, there was more to learn. After victoriously coming through the battle several more times, I began to lose sight of the source of my power. "Wow, now I've got that old problem solved," I boasted to myself. Confident in my own ability to conquer this monster, pride crept in. The next time when confronted with jealous feelings, I met complete failure. A blanket of depression loomed over me as I grumbled, "This old problem isn't solved after all!"

"You see," God reprimanded, "The theory does work, but your problem is that you allowed your pride to take over and forgot that the power to overcome your weaknesses comes from Me. You left Me out of the battle and went marching off to war unarmed. Thus, you found yourself no different than before and defeated by your weakness."

I blushed at God's words of admonition. How quickly I had forgotten and foolish of me, "Oh Lord, You're right. Forgive me for being prideful and forgetting it is Your power giving me the victory. I won't forget again." Sure enough, when I encountered the next jealous episode, the lesson God had taught me was foremost in my mind. Immediately I confessed my jealousy, acknowledged my inability to conquer it on my own, and gave my problem to Him. What excitement and joy to find Christ's power giving me victory once more!

"But why, Lord?" I questioned. "Why do I have to have weaknesses? Why is it necessary to go through periods of despondency? Why can't I overcome my weaknesses once and for all?"

God's answer: II Corinthians 12:7–10:

> And lest I should be exalted above measure by the abundance of the revelations, a thorn in the flesh was given to me, a messenger of Satan to buffet me, lest I be exalted above measure. Concerning this thing I pleaded with the Lord three times that it might depart from me. And He said to me, 'My grace is sufficient for you, for My strength is made perfect in weakness.' Therefore most gladly I will rather boast in my infirmities, that the power of Christ may rest upon me. Therefore I take pleasure in infirmities, in reproaches, in needs, in persecutions, in distresses, for Christ's sake. For when I am weak, then I am strong. (NKJV)

It would be a long while before I could stand with Paul and thank God for my weaknesses, but it was a beginning. I needed to remember that my humanness was vital for my spiritual well-being. I was only a vessel, a clay pot in the Master's Hand.

Perhaps it was the knowledge that not only was I human, but the husband God had given me also shared my humanness, that caused me to approach Art's involvement in Clinical Pastoral Education with some skepticism. Mentally, I found myself bracing for another emotional and spiritual battle. No longer the naïve dreamer, experience had taught me to psyche myself up to reality. "I know CPE will have some effect on Art," I surmised, "and I've learned enough about married life to know that what affects him eventually touches my life as well. No doubt, this experience too, will cause another shakeup in our marriage. This time, however, I will go into the situation guarded and expect the worst."

I scrutinized Art's actions closely the first weeks of CPE, watching for subtle signs and changes in his behavior, changes that might signal trouble for me, but signs of arrogance, silence, and aloofness were absent. Surprisingly, the signals I detected were the opposite. Rather than negative characteristics, humility, caring, openness, and respect emerged. Slowly, I realized CPE was to be Art's battleground and not mine. Rather than push my life into chaos once more, it was to have a stabilizing effect on our home. Grateful for the respite, I sat back and looked on sympathetically as Art struggled with God's agenda.

Clinical Pastoral Education involved interacting in group therapy with patients, supervisors, other staff members, and the four other seminarians in the CPE program. The staff met each morning in a large group with the patients, and later in the day in a smaller group to discuss the day's events. Dialogue between group members was open and honest with all participants treated equally. It was imperative the structure of the group be tough and at times unmerciful to effect permanent changes in the lives of the alcoholic patients; themselves experts at playing psychological games. Confrontation was the key. Discussion topics raised were addressed until the truth was exposed. The group's responsibility was to help each member work through their problem areas in a productive, healing manner. Understanding each person's background, combined with a mutual respect for one another in an atmosphere of love, the group setting was most effective.

With the CPE group's participants coming from various backgrounds, experience, and denominations, Art found himself challenged both spiritually and intellectually. He was not allowed to retreat or withdraw into himself when the discussion became threatening as had often been the case during our disagreements. Instead, he was required to deal squarely with the issues. "I was forced to take a look at why I was functioning the way I was," he explained to me one day. "I was confronted with my inconsistencies." The outcome for Art was positive. Just as he had played an active role in supporting and helping other group members work through their difficulties, he found the same help offered to him.

The overflow of the program into our marriage was remarkable. I sensed a new respect for my own opinions in our conversations. The result was a new trust developed between us and respect for each other's feelings. Freedom to speak caused us to become better listeners. We were more honest in communicating our feelings to one another. Now we could discuss our vicarage experience objectively.

I sat quietly listening as Art spoke about vicarage from his point of view. There were no angry words and no tears shed. This time I listened attentively as if no longer a character in the story.

"They didn't teach us at seminary how to handle all the attention," Art confessed, "To be looked up to and given all that respect. I'd never been in a situation where all that attention was showered on me, and I didn't know how to handle it." Arts eyes searched mine. "I didn't mean to hurt you, but it was the first time in my life that I really felt good about myself."

It was true we had been coming from completely different places. My emotions and my own involvement had rendered me incapable of understanding Art's peculiar circumstances. In his efforts to make the transition from seminary life to vicarage, he was incapable of seeing the situation from my point of view. Both of us had stepped off a fast-moving escalator when vicarage ended. CPE became the vehicle to a better understanding and deeper respect for one another and a healing force in our marriage.

I sensed we had climbed some very high mountains this year and had traveled some very rocky terrain. My self-concept had reached a new pinnacle. I could sense my life; our lives, beginning to come together with honesty instead of games, trust instead of suspicion. My preoccupation with the past at last satisfied, the future held renewed interest. "I wonder what else God has in mind for us, and what other pieces to life's puzzle are yet to be revealed." Even as these thoughts were on my mind, God had already begun to make His next move.

We were two weeks into CPE when I returned after my coffee break at work one afternoon to find a note on my desk. "Someone called several times while you were away," the message read. "She left no name but said she would call back."

I stood at my desk for a moment examining the note curiously trying to guess who the caller might be when the telephone rang again. Quickly, I leaned over to pick up the receiver.

"This is Bonnie, speaking."

"Hi Bonnie, This is Sharon. You're a hard one to reach this afternoon. This is my third call."

I looked up at the clock and blushed. "I guess our fifteen-minute break did stretch into more like a half hour," I admitted.

"I was so excited," Sharon continued in her bubbly voice, "I couldn't wait until you got home . . . We've got a baby boy for you!"

"You have our baby?" I was speechless, hardly believing my ears.

"Yes the relinquishment papers have just been signed. You and Art can pick him up tomorrow afternoon."

Through a veil of tears, I hurriedly scribbled the information Sharon relayed about our baby on a small piece of paper on my desk. Seeing my tears, Jan and my other co-workers hovered over my desk reading as I wrote. Someone wheeled a chair under me, and I slowly sat down.

Sharon ended the conversation, realizing her news had rendered me speechless, "I'll give you my phone number. You can call me at home later this evening."

By the time I hung up the telephone, the entire second floor was buzzing with the news of our baby's arrival. Tearfully, I clutched the tiny piece of yellow paper and stared at my scribbled handwriting: a boy . . . ten days old . . . 3:00 tomorrow . . . bring a change of clothes. Were it not for the tiny piece of paper, I would have remembered nothing except our baby was a boy.

In the excitement, I did not call Art at Fort Logan Mental Health Center but began at once clearing out my desk. "Today's my last day of work," I reminded myself. "Tomorrow I won't be coming to work. I will be a mother." Somehow saying the words seemed like a dream. When the comptroller, my boss, walked by a few minutes later and looked in my direction to see what all the commotion was about, I suddenly realized I had not told him the news that our baby had arrived, and today was my final day of work.

"We got our baby. He'll probably look just like you!" I called out across the room.

Still visibly shaken when it came time to go home, Jan suggested she drive me to Fort Logan to pick up Art. Steve would follow behind and take her on home. Grateful for the offer, I bid farewell to everyone, gathered my belongings, and followed her to the parking lot.

One can well imagine the thoughts that raced through Art's mind when our little entourage arrived at Fort Logan a half hour later than usual.

As soon as the car drew up to the curb, I flung the door open and jumped out. "We got our baby," I yelled to Art, still some distance away. The worried expression on his face lifted, his mouth dropping in surprise. "It's a boy," I continued breathlessly. "Sharon called me at work this afternoon; we can pick him up tomorrow at three."

At two-thirty the next afternoon, we were sitting in the reception room of Lutheran Service Society. "Guess we wouldn't have needed to leave quite so early," I whispered to Art, glancing at the clock. "I don't think I've ever been a half hour early for an appointment before."

At three o'clock we were ushered into Sharon's office where we spent what seemed an eternity discussing the final details of the adoption and the legal papers. When we finished the paperwork, Sharon escorted us down the long hallway to the nursery where our little son was crying loudly. For a moment, we stood gazing into the crib as if frozen in place. He was the most beautiful baby I had ever seen, with reddish-brown hair, delicate features, large, alert eyes, and tiny fingers. Seeing neither of us move to pick him up, Sharon looked at me and smiled broadly, "I think he wants to be held."

I leaned over and lifted Benjamin from the crib. "Can it really be true that he's ours?" I thought, staring at the tiny bundle in my arms, "That we can take him home with us?" I held him a few minutes and then looked up at Art standing close beside me. "Do you want to hold him?"

Art beamed, "Sure." Carefully I placed our baby in his outstretched arms. "Somehow the reality of this moment still seems like a dream," I thought as I watched Art lovingly peer down at our tiny infant. Continuing to ogle over our new baby, we took a few snapshots of each of us holding him in the rocking chair, and then changed him into the outfit we had brought for the journey home.

Despite the adjustments of acclimating to the needs of a tiny baby, our hearts filled with joy and thankfulness. We were a family at last, and each person was in his proper place. How thankful I was that Benjamin had arrived after vicarage as now Art's schedule was less demanding, and he could be home in the evenings and have the opportunity to experience being a father. It was easy to see the wisdom in God's timing and the grave importance of working through the problem areas in our marriage before the baby's arrival. His perfect timetable became even more evident in the ensuing weeks.

When I received an invitation to attend a belated wedding shower and luncheon for Jan on Saturday, October 23, I eagerly looked forward to the break in my new routine and an opportunity for an afternoon away to socialize with friends from the office. Steve invited Art to bring the baby and spend the afternoon watching football games.

We had just taken our seats in the living room after the luncheon, waiting for Jan to begin opening her gifts when the telephone rang. I nudged a friend beside me, "Probably Art wondering what to do with the baby," I giggled.

My laughter turned to concern, however, when seconds later the hostess gently tapped me on the shoulder and whispered, "Your husband is on the phone."

My heart raced as I left my seat. "I wonder what the problem is." I thought. "Something must be wrong with the baby." I knew Art would not disturb me at a gathering such as this one, were it not important.

"Hi . . . Is something wrong with the baby?" I blurted out.

"No, everything is okay with him." He hesitated and then continued. "My . . . my Dad's been killed in a car accident!" The familiar voice of my husband was trembling. I sensed he was on the verge of tears.

"What . . . what happened?" I asked in disbelief.

"Guess he was on the way back to work this afternoon . . . there was an accident . . . he was killed instantly."

"How did you find out?"

"When Tom couldn't reach us at home, he called Duane. You must have mentioned to Mary earlier this week where we'd be today."

My heart suddenly ached for my husband. "Oh honey, I'm so sorry. I'll leave right away."

Briefly explaining the nature of the telephone call to the hostess, I quietly excused myself and asked a friend to drive me to Jan and Steve's apartment. Steve had already made our airline reservations to fly home to Michigan the following day by the time I arrived. It seemed incredible that the day I had so eagerly anticipated had quickly turned so sour.

In thirty minutes, we were back at our apartment and in a daze. I sought for words to console my husband but found none. "What can I possibly say to comfort him?" I asked myself. "He lost a brother in one tragedy, and now his father, too, has abruptly been taken from him. It's unfair, just too much to ask of one family." Silently, we proceeded with the immediate tasks before us. I cancelled appointments and arranged for our absence the following week, while Art made a trip to the bank.

I got out the suitcases to pack. A flurry of thoughts passed through my mind as I wandered about the apartment. "It seems impossible that Art's father is dead. I am so thankful we have Benjamin. Maybe his presence will somehow fill the emptiness in Art's heart. Dad never had a chance to see a picture of his newest grandchild, we just got the pictures developed last week. I haven't even mailed them yet, I was so looking forward to our homecoming with our families, so anxious to show off our new little son. Christmas would have been so perfect this year. No, this unexpected trip home in October for Dad's funeral is not the homecoming I've imagined after having been away a year."

When our plane landed in Lansing the next afternoon, we discovered no member of the Newhouse family had yet arrived to chauffeur us to the family home. Instead, we found my parents, sister, and younger brother and his family waiting at the gate to greet us. Briefly thrusting aside the reason for our trip, Art and I beamed proudly as I carefully folded back the blanket and presented our new little son to his grandparents. When Art's uncle and cousin arrived to drive us to St. Johns, we quickly gathered up our belongings, bid farewell to my family, and departed. The bad dream became reality.

As details of the accident slowly unraveled, we cried out to God. "But God, it doesn't make sense; it's not fair! Why should the other driver emerge from the accident with barely a scratch and Dad be killed? He was not at fault! Why did you allow this to happen? Where is your justice?" Our questions remained unanswered, yet God's comforting presence was unmistakable as we felt the warmth of His love envelop us and gave the family strength to draw together to face our sorrow.

Although we experienced some of the same anger and resentment toward God that we felt when Bernard had been killed three and a half years before, it was clear we had grown spiritually. In the midst of our grief, there remained a glimpse of hope, a light for the future. Experience had taught us that beyond the sadness and pain of today looms a brighter tomorrow. We knew our lives would go on. Most important, our relationship with God was more trusting. We were not afraid to be honest with Him in expressing ourselves. We knew He understood our angry feelings and loved us despite the anger. We did not allow our anger to break our lines of communication with Him, nor did we stop praying.

Yes, in the midst of our grief, there was evidence of God's perfect timing. I did not believe it a coincidence that Art was in a group where he had help working through the grief process. He could not suppress his feelings and withdraw but was encouraged, if not prodded, to vent his angry feelings and talk about his loss. Equally important was the fact that circumstances in our life prohibited us from focusing on ourselves and dwelling on our grief. Art's work in CPE was intense while I was engrossed in the new adventure of motherhood. Together we were preparing for our move back to Springfield within a month. We were looking forward to the joys of parenthood, the excitement of our final year of seminary, and our future life in the ministry.

Chapter 11

OUR LAST YEAR

"A time for searching"
Ecclesiastes 3:6 (JB)

od's presence in our lives had been evident these past few months, proving that we could trust Him with our future. Not only had He safely guided us through the turbulent waters of the past year, we had awesomely watched as He provided for our needs our final year of seminary, our baby's arrival at the perfect time, and the unexpected letter from my boss in Springfield offering my old job back. We also heard from Bruce and Ann, our seminary friends, telling us their landlord had an apartment that would be available approximately the same time as our expected return to Springfield.

When several minor complications arose our last week in Denver, we realized our faith was being put to the test. By far, the most unsettling was a letter from our new landlords; the Smiths, explaining that due to a delay in the construction of their new home, the renters were still in our apartment. They had, however, arranged for us to stay temporarily in the home of some of their relatives while they were away on a trip. Anxious to move into our own place, we did not look forward to the inconvenience of staying in someone else's home but did appreciate their concern and the arrangements made for us.

Our previous plan to tow our car behind the rental truck was thwarted when Art went to pick up the tow bar, only to discover the ball on the rental truck did not fit the tow bar. The truck was already packed and changing trucks would mean transferring the entire load to another truck.

"We won't be able to tow the car," Art said disgustedly upon his return. "You'll have to drive it back to Springfield."

"I can't do that," I vehemently protested. "You know I've had little experience driving on an expressway and never with a small baby; I'd be too scared." I could feel my chest tighten in panic. "There must be another way."

Art shook his head. "No, Wife, there's no other way to get there. You're going to have to drive."

"But what'll I do when he cries?" I argued. "How will I change and feed him?"

"We'll just have to stop," Art said firmly.

I began to sense my protests were useless. Like it or not, I was being forced to do what seemed an impossible task. Our little trip back to Springfield would be anything but relaxing.

Resolved to make the best of the situation, I channeled my thoughts to the positive events of the day. Although hectic, moving day had been fun. Several friends from Redeemer had helped us pack and load the truck while others stopped by just to say good-bye. Some of the well-wishers had given us monetary gifts; others brought gifts for Benjamin. A warm meal and bed awaited us at the home of Wayne and Thea, the CPE couple with whom we had developed a close friendship. We did not feel sad as we prepared to leave Denver, nor did we feel we were saying good-bye, never to see these friends again. We were well aware that a number of Redeemer's members favored calling Art back as Assistant Pastor after graduation. In the back of our minds was the hope that we would return.

We set out for Springfield early the next morning, having agreed that I would follow the truck and if Benjamin needed attention, would pass Art as a signal for him to stop. Had it not been for the illegality of stopping on an expressway except in the case of an emergency, our system for traveling would have been flawless.

"Oh, this is an emergency," I boldly told the Nebraska State Policeman who joined our caravan at the side of the expressway later that morning. "The baby was crying!"

Still frowning skeptically, the officer returned to his patrol car and pulled back onto the highway.

We breathed a sigh of relief when at last we saw the Springfield sign, signifying the end of our long journey. Our trip had been uneventful, except for the little mishap that afternoon near Davenport, Iowa. Visualizing the incident brought a chuckle. Pulling into the shiny new gas station and hearing the sound of smashing glass, I had looked back to see overhead lights dangling by their wires with broken glass everywhere and the sheepish look on Art's face after realizing the truck was too high to clear the overhead lights. Now we could see humor in it. Settling the claim would come later.

We met our new landlords, Margaret and Franklin (Smitty) Smith, who led us to the two-bedroom home that would serve as our temporary residence. After they left, we sorted out our belongings: we moved those we would need into the house and the remainder we stored in an unoccupied room above our new apartment. In an effort to eliminate the task of having to replace groceries when we left, I cleared a space in the kitchen for my own food items. In addition to setting up Benjamin's baby bed, which was essential, we moved in several nonessential items to help us feel at home; a small set of my dishes and the new stereo system purchased with money received from our farewell party at Redeemer.

We were thankful Art was able to schedule his classes in the mornings, leaving him free to care for Benjamin while I worked in the afternoons. Yet, when the day came for me to leave our baby, I fought back tears as Art drove me to the office—tears of guilt for leaving him and tears of grief at the separation. "It's not that I don't think you'll take good care of him," I whispered. "It's just that . . . well, I'm his mother. It's my responsibility."

Art looked over at me puzzled by the outburst, yet trying to understand. "But, Wife, I'm his father," he reasoned, "Besides, it's only for half a day for just a few months." Then reaching over he squeezed my hand. "I'm sure he'll do fine."

Once I reached the office and the initial detachment had taken place, I felt better. There was little time to dwell on the painful separation with the year's end a few weeks away and much work to do. In fact, I was quite surprised to find after a few days that it actually seemed good to get back to familiar surroundings and the books that had previously been my responsibility. As the family adjusted to the new routine, it was obvious there were some positive results of this change. I enjoyed getting out each day, and my absence gave Art a chance to develop his own relationship with Benjamin who seemed to be managing quite well.

We had been in our temporary home ten days when we received a telephone call at ten o'clock one night from our friends, Bruce and Ann. "Ann and I have a problem. We wondered if we could come over and talk to you about it."

"Well, sure," Art responded. "You . . . you mean now?"

"If it's all right with you, we'll come right over."

Art stared at the receiver and then looked at me perplexed. "That's strange. That was Bruce, wondering if he and Ann could come over and discuss a problem with us. I don't know what it's all about."

My heart fell. "Gee, I hope they're not having marriage problems. It must be something serious to bring them over here at this hour on a school night."

A few minutes later, they appeared at our front door. "Actually, we're here because Smitty asked us to come over and break the news." Bruce began, "He just got a call from his sister in Arizona. Some problems have come up with them, and they are returning home from their vacation earlier than expected. They'll be arriving here in Springfield by noon tomorrow."

Art and I shot a startled glance at one another while Bruce continued. "You don't have to worry; everything is taken care of. We have already talked it over with Smitty. You can stay at our apartment, and we'll sleep across the street in their guest room."

"But wouldn't it be easier for us to stay there?" I questioned, thinking it sounded like a complicated solution.

"No, Margaret and Smitty feel it would work out better this way since our bedroom is big enough for Benjie's baby bed."

The days that followed were marked with inconvenience, confusion, and sometimes tense moments for everyone, to be sure; yet, we did not overlook the humor in our present living arrangements.

One morning, I was unguarded when the seminary office called and asked for Ann shortly after she returned home ill from her teaching job. I paused only a moment before replying. "No, Ann isn't here," I explained, "She's . . . she's sleeping across the street at the landlord's house."

So began the most chaotic Christmas season experienced thus far. The mix-up at the post office by two change-of-address cards filed within a two-week period did not get resolved until Smitty, a retired post office employee, made a special trip to the post office to explain our situation. Even then, many of our Christmas cards did not arrive until after the holidays. Christmas home in Michigan with our families became the fantasy that sustained us, a welcome respite from the confusion since leaving Denver. Hopeful our apartment would be available by the time we returned, we moved all our belongings into the upstairs room above our apartment before leaving.

Our ten-day stay in Michigan proved no escape. The atmosphere was not joyful, as we had expected, but depressing. Christmas was not the same without Dad. His recent death loomed over the Christmas celebration, leaving a void felt by every member of the family. There had been a quiet strength about Dad, a strength now noticeably absent. The family was like a ship moving about in the water without a captain.

I began to feel myself sinking under the pressure of the past few months. Clearly, the stress was taking its toll. Our lives had been turned upside down with Art's job change, my leaving work, the arrival of a new baby, the sudden death of Art's father, moving back to Springfield, Art returning to school, my going back to work, the lack of privacy, and not being able to settle down in our own apartment. A sense of panic seized me as I realized I could not endure indefinitely this way.

"Let's leave right after Christmas," I suggested to Art. "I think we need to get settled in our own place. I just don't think I can take all this confusion much longer."

"I know what you mean. I'm beginning to feel that way, too. But, what if the renters are still in our apartment? We won't be able to move in anyway."

"We'll just have to pray that our apartment will be vacant," I said shaking my head, "God knows we have reached our limit."

We arrived back in Springfield to find our prayers answered. Not only was the apartment vacant, but our friends had planned a special surprise by moving all of our furniture into the apartment, and placed in the proper rooms!

Our new apartment was located at the end of the block, on the opposite side of the street from Bruce and Ann. Attached on one side to a tavern, the old two-story house had been converted into two apartments. Our two-bedroom apartment was on the ground level while another seminary couple lived upstairs. Of the four apartments owned by the Smiths, ours was the only one Smitty had yet to remodel, a negative factor for most people but a positive one for us. The lower rent was more suitable to our budget, and the large old-fashioned rooms with their long windows and steam radiators created a warm atmosphere. Margaret and Smitty had added a clothes washer in the basement to accommodate the needs of our baby, followed a few months later by an air conditioning unit in the living room.

Once settled in our new home, life resumed with some measure of normalcy. The addition of a part-time job for Art to supplement my income left little idle time for either of us. Now it was necessary to do the greatest portion of his homework during the afternoons while I worked; no easy task when caring for a four-month-old baby. I, too, felt the added pressure of parental responsibility as I spent more of my time at home alone with our son. The same question haunted us both: "How does one balance parental responsibilities with the pressures of school, jobs, and housework?"

"I never feel I'm doing my best at anything," I complained to Art one day. "Regardless of the choices I make each day, something or someone is being neglected." My greatest concern by far, was the negative affect our lifestyle might have on Benjamin. Would he receive enough love and attention during these first crucial months of his life? Would he somehow suffer later as a result? "Oh, Lord," I prayed, "You alone know our circumstances. Watch over our family this year and especially see that our little boy doesn't lack something that will cause him problems later." How I longed for the day when I wouldn't feel guilty about these important roles in my life and my own inadequacies to fill them.

As I thought about my roles, I drew some encouragement in the knowledge that one role in my life had at least been resolved. I felt a sense of peace and confidence about my role as a pastor's wife. Placed back into the same job environment with many of the same people had proven a blessing for I could clearly see the difference the past year had made in me. The valleys of the vicarage year had caused my faith to be deeply rooted in God. I knew I walked on solid ground and was no longer easily shaken by the expectations of others. God had shown me that despite the circumstances around me or the opinions of others, He would guide me to Truth. Even more important, I had learned to trust the leading of that still, small inner voice I had come to recognize as His. The lessons taught me during vicarage had made a profound impression; an extremely important step in my personal growth.

With that lesson behind me, God began dealing with me in another important area—finances. In the past, I had always set up a reasonable budget and knew months in advance where every penny would fit in. Now, I had to give up my previous job of tightly controlling our finances because it simply would no longer work. Not only was our income unpredictable with both of us working part-time jobs, but our expenses, too, varied from month to month. For the first time in our married life, we were paying all of our utilities, and with a small baby, there were additional expenses for periodic visits to the pediatrician for colds and shots and other necessities for Benjamin.

Each month when the bills came, I filed them away, trusting that somehow, some way, the Lord would provide. Twice a month we deposited the checks we received and took from the file the bills that were due. Each time, there was enough money. During the months our expenses increased, God provided additional money. Sometimes it would be a preaching date for Art, other times we would receive monetary gifts from various sources. Our home congregation and district grants covered Art's tuition. By releasing control of our finances to God, He showed us He was capable of caring for us much better than we ever could have imagined.

While my battleground was in the area of finances, Art was absorbed in a battle of his own—making the transition from vicarage back to life as a seminary student. Vicarage had given him a taste of life in the ministry, and he was more enthusiastic than ever before. Ministering to people and preaching God's Word had given him a sense of self-worth, that he was part of an important mission. Now he had to reorient himself, replacing people with books to read and papers to write. Prior to vicarage, Art had gone to school every summer, and now felt his mind was saturated. Applying himself to his studies did not happen until midterm.

More important than the surface battle, however, was the deep, inner, raging conflict—conflict between seminary teaching and actual experience with people. Not everyone he encountered during vicarage had agreed with him. Questions had been raised for which he had no answers, questions not clearly answered in the Bible. Some of those teachings had been challenged, both by Redeemer members who had come from other denominational backgrounds and by those involved in the charismatic renewal. His clinical experience also exposed him to other theological viewpoints.

When challenged, Art's only defense was to respond in the words of someone else. His first reaction was to become defensive and then realized not only were they not his answers, but that he, too, had unanswered questions. As a result, Art began to face some of the issues. What is the practical value of theology? How does it relate to sin, divorce, and marriage? Does God love the homosexual? Is there such a thing as speaking in tongues? Is forgiveness more important in life than being doctrinally correct?

Art had not been encouraged to think independently or to search the Scriptures for the Truth as God revealed it to him. The seminary had not encouraged a questioning attitude regarding theology and faith. The prevailing attitude at the seminary was that the interpretations of the learned scholars were correct theological doctrine. Art realized his first two years of seminary training had been spent merely absorbing, without question, the material presented him by his professors. Having been given new insight, he made the conscious decision no longer to look to man for those answers, but to test what was being taught and to trust God to lead him to Truth.

Yet, as Art began to ask questions, he found very few students willing to discuss them. His professors were even more determined to avoid any controversial areas or issues. Nobody wanted to address the everyday questions of sin, divorce, and marriage—the things that go on in the lives of people, even the lives of church members. Art's question to the professor of his class on the Holy Spirit about the validity of speaking in tongues, was never answered.

On another occasion, Art observed one of his fellow classmates question another professor about the historical critical method of biblical interpretation. The professor was astonished and the following day came to class with an armload of theological books, called the student forward, and proceeded to have him read from the books all the statements discounting that method of biblical interpretation. Before long, Art began to see that to pursue these issues could mean that he might not be certified. He resolved at that time to remain outwardly in agreement until he was in the parish. Then he would be free to make those decisions for himself.

More concerned about our future stability than Art's peace of mind, I encouraged him to suppress his feelings and not "rock the boat." We had spent years in preparation for the ministry, and I was not about to have it aborted abruptly at this late stage by what seemed to me insignificant issues. With my own limited knowledge of the Bible and church doctrine, I found all of this discussion very unsettling. Much like the reaction found at the seminary, I chose to ignore that which I did not understand.

Having made the decision to remain silent and complete his final year, Art directed his energies to his Bachelor of Divinity thesis. Feeling he should make use of his clinical experience, he chose as his topic, *The Pastoral Counseling of the Families of Alcoholics.* Neither choosing to work with alcoholics during CPE nor picking this topic for his paper was a coincidence. The fact that my father was an alcoholic had given him valuable personal experience. Through my husband, I was to receive a special gift from God—release from the bondage of family shame.

Later as I typed Art's paper and read about the families of other alcoholics, inner healing began to take place. I realized our family was not unlike the others, nor were the emotional scars I carried different from children of other alcoholics. Little by little as the paper progressed, I drew from that dark closet in my mind those painful memories of my childhood. Art's paper became a channel of communication between us, and gradually I was able to share more of my experiences with him. The result was a closer relationship with Art and, for the first time in my life, a new freedom to talk about it openly.

This freedom was a new gift from God. Now, coupled with the lesson that God had taught me on vicarage, I set out to prove a theory. Was my vicarage experience unique, or had other wives experienced a similar loss of identity? The monthly newsletter called, *Vicar Views* that we had received while on vicarage seemed to discount my theory. The compilation of letters from seminarians and their wives while away on vicarage seemed to include only the heartwarming stories about joys serving in the ministry.

"I don't believe it!" I had protested to Art. "I just can't believe everyone's life is as rosy as this. Did they really have no problems? There is nothing written about adjustments or disappointments! It sounds so superficial. I don't think they are telling the whole truth!" After a few more months of the same, we both reached a point where we refused to read them at all.

The first clue to support my theory came one night during a conversation with Bruce and Ann, "The vicars where we were formed an informal vicar cluster group," Bruce explained to Art. "It served as a support group for vicars in the Greater Cleveland area. The wives also participated."

My ears perked up. The fact that such a group had been born indicated to me that others, too, had seen the need to support one another. "I'm going to broach the subject with some of the other wives at my first opportunity," I promised myself determinedly.

One evening a few weeks later, the subject of vicarage came up in my Seminary Wives' class. When the door opened, I quickly stepped in. "I don't know about the others," I boldly began, "But I faced an identity crisis on vicarage. I found I couldn't survive as a person riding on the coattails of my husband." When I finished speaking, I relaxed in my seat, waiting for others to come forward with their own confessions. Instead, the room was silent. No one spoke or offered their support. Realizing I had once again bared my soul to my peers only to meet with deafening silence, a warm flush came over me.

Bowing my head in embarrassment, I murmured silently, "Oh Lord, why did I even speak up? Why did I have to make a fool of myself in front of this class? Why did I assume my experience on vicarage was not unique? When will I ever learn I'm not like they are? I never have been and never will be. Why do I always have to be different?" I wanted to run from the room and get away from these strangers.

"Don't give up so easily," the Still, Inner Voice encouraged. "Just because no one spoke up doesn't mean you were alone in your experience. Maybe they don't have the courage to speak up in a group as you did. Pursue the issue. Ask some of them individually—away from the others." My spirits lifted. I simply would have to continue to trust my feelings and move forward. Maybe my theory was valid.

Speaking to several of the girls after class, I found a few willing to be more honest on a one-to-one basis. Reassured by their response, I prodded on in my investigation. I talked openly of my own experience and asked questions of other wives. Gradually the puzzle pieces began fitting together. What had happened to me on vicarage was not unique. The problem was real, not only for me but for others. Other wives had expressed some of the same feelings. The change in roles on vicarage had placed a strain on other marriages as well. Some had also experienced an identity crisis.

Satisfied my theory was indeed valid, I analyzed the situation, "What is the solution?" I questioned. "Surely, there has to be a solution. Hoping I won't have to confront another identity crisis in the future is foolish. I'm convinced this final year of seminary is only a temporary reprieve. In less than a year, Art will receive a call, and once again our lives will change drastically. I've no guarantee the adjustment then will be any less difficult for me." Although the course of action was not visible, I knew the wise thing to do was to begin at once to prepare myself.

God's answer to my question and the missing piece to my identity crisis came through my Seminary Wives' class a few weeks later. "I have a copy of this book for each of you," the instructor said, holding up the narrow blue book. "I'd like all of you to read it before next week's class. The book is called *Eighth Day of Creation*," he continued, as he unpacked and distributed the books. "The author is Elizabeth O'Connor. (1) I think you'll enjoy it."

That weekend as I read the book, my heart leaped with joy at the author's message. It was as though God was speaking directly to me! "You are important to me. You are special and unique. I didn't pass you by with my gifts. You too have received special gifts. The secret to your identity lies in the gifts I have given you. The pain and anguish of spirit you have experienced in the past is a direct consequence of having buried your gifts." I created you for a purpose.

"Created for a purpose? God created me for a purpose?" Electrified by the power in those words, I cried excitedly. "That's it, that's it! The secret to my identity crisis is in my gifts! But what are they? What are those qualities that make me special and unique?" The author's words came to mind. "You are responsible for uncovering and spending your gifts. Pray asking God to reveal your special gifts and talents . . . Don't limit God by putting boundaries on your prayer, but pray with an open mind."

With mixed emotions, I set out to take my petition to God. Trepidation accompanied my excitement over the nugget of Truth God had revealed, for I knew that once God's plan for my life was unveiled, I'd have no peace unless I carried it out. My thoughts flashed back to the first year of our marriage. "That's why Art tried so desperately to suppress the fact that God wanted him to be a minister," I thought, "He knew if he allowed it to surface, he would be obliged to do something about it. He knew he would have to act on God's direction."

With my heart racing excitedly at what might be revealed, I made a conscious effort to release from my mind any limitations to my prayer, "Lord, my heart is open to what You have to say." I began. "What are the special gifts and talents You gave me?" Expectantly, I awaited an answer.

Slowly, I began to sense a rising to my consciousness of certain aspects from my past, things I had never put together before. Mother had often said I should write a book because so many unusual and oftentimes humorous things had happened in my life. I enjoyed writing letters, and people seemed to enjoy reading them. Could these be a clue to one of my gifts? "Lord, can it be the ability to communicate with words is one of my gifts?" I blurted out in surprise. "Could it be that You want me to write a book?" I hesitated for a moment. "If so, Lord, what would I write about?"

God's answer clearly came through the thoughts in my mind. "Yes, writing is one of the gifts I have given you. What should you write? I want you to write about your experience as I have prepared you to be a pastor's wife: share your identity crisis and the important Truths I have taught you. You see others are hurting much the same as you. I can use your experience to help them, too."

"How, God? You know I haven't kept any notes on these past years. I have no record of my experiences, no diary." No more had the questions formed in my mind than the answers given. Suddenly, I realized I possessed the tool needed to carry out God's direction. My memory was a gift; the ability to remember sharp details of my experiences! All these years I've looked on this as a negative quality," I thought remorsefully. "I've misused this gift by remembering every detail when someone had offended me. Clearly, God never intended it for that purpose. Instead, He will use it to bring to my remembrance whatever He wants to be in my story."

When the conversation ended, I felt the closeness of God leave me as though emerging from a dream. Satan immediately moved in to taunt me with self-doubts.

"You must be crazy. You, write a book? Who are you? Who's going to listen to you? The whole idea is outlandish."

Instantly, the author's words came to my defense, "We fail to try for fear of failure."

Uplifted in my battle of the mind, I retorted. "So what if I fail? I won't be any farther behind than I already am. I have nothing to lose in this venture!"

Aware that this minor skirmish was only the beginning of Satan's future ploys to discourage me, God then gave me three special gifts with which to carry out His mission. The first, a burning desire planted deep within my soul to tell my story exactly as I had experienced it.

The second was a vision, a glimpse into the future of the book's cover. The third: the gift of faith to believe God would guide and direct the work He set before me, regardless of the obstacles I might encounter.

Sensing the need to protect the idea germinating within me from the outside world, I divulged my experience to only one person; a close friend sworn to secrecy. "I'm not even going to tell Art about this," I decided, "at least not until I feel more comfortable and secure with the idea. Then if for some reason I find I'm unable to carry through with the plan or should fail in my attempt, I can spare myself the embarrassment of having others know. I'll have no one to answer to but God."

A wonderful peace flooded the depths of my soul and confirmed the validity of my experience. The compelling urge to keep reaching for something was gone. "God has a purpose for my life," I thought proudly. "I'm special, too!" Satisfied my inward self was at last in order, I directed my attention to an unsettled area in my life.

"What I need to do now," I concluded, "is to strive for perfection as a wife and mother." My thoughts trailed off as I envisioned myself home every day in a strange community with a toddler, while Art was away tending to the needs of a congregation. "If I'm smart, I'll begin preparing myself now for next year when I won't be working outside the home." Once more, the wheels in my mind began turning. "Magazines, that's what I need. I'll treat myself to a luxury this year and subscribe to some women's magazines. Not only will they keep me informed on the latest fashions, they'll give me up-to-date advice on how to be the best wife and mother."

Each month I anxiously awaited the arrival of my magazines, eagerly devouring the articles advising how one might become the ideal woman. A few months later however, twinges of guilt dampened my spirits — guilt about my lack of interest in the Bible; a book rarely opened these days. One day, God spoke to me.

"Bonnie, your frantic search for the quality way of life is unnecessary. You already have access to the Truth; answers to any questions you might ever have. Long ago, I provided for the needs of my people. Read your Bible and learn what I have to say about the best way to live. Everything you need to know can be found in its pages."

My heart filled with joyous expectations, I arose early the next morning and opened my Bible to the New Testament. "How strange," I thought as I read. "I've heard and read these same words before, yet for some reason they don't seem so dry; so remote. It's as though they've come alive—as though they're written just for me!" The following morning, and each morning thereafter, found me in quiet retreat nestled in one corner of the living room. When I reached the sixth chapter of Ephesians some weeks later, (2) I knew why God had directed me to His word:

> Put on the whole armor of God, that you may be able to stand against the wiles of the devil. For we do not wrestle against flesh and blood, but against principalities, against powers, against the rulers of the darkness of this age, against spiritual hosts of wickedness in the heavenly places. Therefore, take up the whole armor of God, that you may be able to withstand in the evil day, and having done all, to stand. Stand therefore, having girded your waist with truth, having put on the breastplate of righteousness, and having shod your feet with the preparation of the gospel of peace; above all, taking the shield of faith with which you will be able to quench all the fiery darts of the wicked one. And take the helmet of salvation, and the sword of the Spirit, which is the word of God. (NKJV)

Clearly, God's message to me was urgent. "Satan does exist. You are involved in daily spiritual warfare with him, and he will continually try to divert your attention and draw you away from Me. If you want to live a victorious Christian life, you must reevaluate your priorities. You must not give priority to appearances, whether your home or yourself. Your priority must be to prepare yourself daily for the spiritual warfare certain to await you. Without this preparation, you will not stand. You must be alert and aware of his activities at all times. You must remain spiritually strong. You must pray and read your Bible daily for this is the means My power is transmitted to you. The same Spirit that causes you to stand in battle will empower you to complete the task I have assigned to you."

Chapter 12

GOD PAVES THE WAY

"A time for uprooting what has been planted"
Ecclesiastes 3:2 (JB)

*T*he news that Redeemer had made the decision to call another vicar came as a surprise and disappointment to us. We had been so hopeful Art would be called there as assistant pastor after graduation. "Many of the members feel Redeemer isn't financially in a position to call an assistant," wrote a friend. "The fact that our vicar will be returning to seminary in September while you won't be available for a call until November was also a consideration. That would mean Pastor Reetz would be left with no help to carry out the ministry here for three months." With the door to Redeemer officially closed, we joined our classmates in wonderment about our future.

"I talked with my advisor today," Art said one night a few weeks later, "He suggested I give some thought to starting a new mission."

I searched his eyes looking for a clue or a glimmer of excitement on his face. "He says a new mission would offer both excitement and a challenge. What do you think?"

I gazed off dreamily. "Well I suppose it would be a neat opportunity for you," I responded with halfhearted enthusiasm. "It would give you a chance to tap your resources even more."

There was no doubt in my mind that establishing a congregation from the ground floor would be a challenge for Art, necessitating the use of all his gifts and talents. Yes, a new mission would be exciting: moving to a strange place, living in a different house, making new friends, and the opportunity to do our own thing for the first time in a parish. Yet, despite the excitement the new mission held, our thoughts continued to wander back to Redeemer.

Had we taken Redeemer for granted? We had been so confident we would be going back. "What is it that draws us to that congregation?" we asked ourselves, "Why are we so disappointed to learn we won't be going back? Is it because the door is closed, or something more? Could it be the confusion of our vicarage year has somehow obscured our vision?" Having had ample time to work through and resolve those issues, we could see the uniqueness of God's ministry there.

The Lord's presence was evident there. A feeling of enthusiasm for the Lord's work permeated the air, with many actively involved in the life of the congregation. The ministry was diverse, meeting the needs of young and old. Sunday school, Christian day school, and the youth group served the needs of the young people. Seven circles offered the women of the congregation the opportunity to serve in a variety of areas and grow spiritually through Bible study. Four adult Bible classes, each structured differently and studying various topics, were well attended by men and women. The contemporary folk service once a month was a favorite with members of all ages. Redeemer was a congregation alive in the Lord with tremendous opportunity for growth and service. The more we reflected, the more we realized our heart's desire was to be a part of that ministry. Whether our dream would become realized remained to be seen.

One morning several months later, Art returned home from school his face radiant; his blue eyes dancing. "Wife, I've got some good news," he announced exuberantly.

"What's that?"

"When I registered for spring quarter this morning, I found out that I'll be able to finish up this summer—I'll be able to graduate with my class!"

"You will?" I squealed in surprise. "But I thought you wouldn't have enough credits and that we'd have to wait until the end of fall quarter."

Art grinned proudly, "So did I!"

"Oh, Honey, I'm so excited," I said reaching up to hug him affectionately, "Just think, after all this time you'll finally be able to go through the pomp and circumstance of graduation!"

"Yeah," he added shyly. "The banquets will be starting next month. I guess we'll be able to go to those, too."

The wheels of my mind turning wildly, I drew away. "Maybe there's still a chance we can go back to Denver. Don't you think we should let Redeemer know?"

Art hesitated. "But, they said they'd decided to call another vicar. Besides, even if they wanted to call me, they couldn't afford to pay my salary."

"I know," I prodded. "But I think we should call and let them know our circumstances have changed. Who knows; it still might work out."

"I suppose it won't hurt to call," Art said beginning to show some interest in the idea. "Maybe I'll give Duane a call right now."

Art's conversation with Pastor Reetz revealed yet another interesting piece to the puzzle. One of the male teachers who had served the school a number of years planned to resign at the close of the school year. The difference in his salary and that of a new hire would leave more funds available in the budget to replace the vicar with an assistant pastor.

In light of these new developments, Pastor Reetz called a special meeting of the church council to review the situation. The church council passed a resolution, extending the call to Art to be assistant pastor. Whether the Seminary Call Committee would agree to place him there, would not be revealed until Call Night.

A festive mood of gaiety and excitement swept through the graduating class as we joyfully anticipated the end of our seminary years and the beginning of our pastorates. Banquets honoring the graduates and their wives were a special treat; an evening out together without the children was a rare occurrence these past few years. Family and friends made plans to travel to Springfield for the Call Service.

With the service scheduled for later in the evening, I had taken the day off work to enjoy the company of my mom and dad and Aunt Helen, who had arrived from Michigan for the celebration. After breakfast, Mother and Aunt Helen excused themselves to visit some of the Lincoln tourist sites in town, while Dad and Smitty sat at the kitchen table swapping stories over a cup of coffee. My spirits soared as I bustled around the kitchen preparing food for the open house.

"Things are taking shape very well for this party," I thought to myself confidently. Mary, our upstairs neighbor, had already sent down the dessert she had prepared. Smitty had delivered the floral centerpiece and punch bowl from Margaret. A lovely flower arrangement arrived from Art's family. John and Donna, Art's cousin and wife and their baby would be arriving later in the day from Bloomington to attend the service with us. Margaret had offered to help with the open house and care for Benjie.

Filled to capacity, the auditorium was jubilant with seminary families and guests. The air tingled with excitement. Once again, efforts to concentrate on the sermon seemed futile as we awaited the Distribution of Calls. At the "Amen," a noticeable hush came over the audience. Moments later, representatives of the Call Committee slowly strode to the microphone bearing the white envelopes containing the calls. The room was still with everyone's eyes focused intently on the action in front; ears finely tuned, listening for familiar names.

" . . . Robert Bruckner, Walther Lutheran High School, Melrose Park, Illinois . . . David Buegler, Assistant Pastor, Trinity Lutheran Church, Jackson, Michigan . . . Bruce Frederickson, First Lutheran Church, Mt. Ayr, Iowa . . . Arthur Newhouse, Assistant Pastor, Redeemer Lutheran Church, Denver, Colorado . . . Robert Nichols, Worker-Priest, Shepherd of the Desert Lutheran Church, Page, Arizona . . ."

"We got it!" I whispered in delight, grinning broadly at my parents seated beside me. Straining to see Art's reaction, I watched as he accepted the envelope placed in his hand and returned to his seat. Common sense and tradition prevented me from racing up to squeeze him and share this thrilling moment.

Following a brief welcoming meeting with Dr. Waldemar Meyer, President of the Colorado District, we jubilantly returned home to celebrate our good fortune. "It's hard to believe school is nearly over," I reminisced out loud, breaking the silence of the drive home. "Just think . . . for more than six years we've worked toward this goal."

"Yeah," Art sighed, gazing at the road ahead, "It's been a long haul, seems kind of strange to have finally reached the end—sort of like a dream come true."

Friends came and went from our apartment bringing with them the cherished envelope containing details of their call. Everyone was exhilarated at the evening's revelation. Like grandparents proudly comparing snapshots of their grandchildren, seminarians shared congregational statistics, housing facilities, and salaries. As the evening waned, it was clear all thoughts now focused on the situations that awaited us. Seminary life was past.

Ordination Day was the afternoon of Sunday, August 27, 1972 at our home church in Lansing, Michigan; the day before our seventh wedding anniversary. Wearing a corsage pinned to the canary yellow chiffon dress that I had painstakingly sewn, I carried eleven-month-old Benjamin down the aisle of Christ Lutheran Church. "Please, Lord, help Benjie be quiet today, of all days," I silently pleaded as we took our places in the second row.

Nostalgic memories surrounded me, as I sat quietly waiting for the service to begin. The beautiful stained glass windows of the old stone church had witnessed my confirmation vows, our marriage, and now Art's ordination. Our aging pastor, Reverend Woldt, was officiating today as he had on each special occasion. This was a special day for him, too. Art was only the second young man in the congregation to go on to the ministry under his leadership. Another face familiar to this pulpit had returned for this occasion. Reverend David Tews, Art's brother-in-law and Christ Lutheran's first vicar, would be preaching the ordination sermon. We had introduced David to Art's sister, Barbara, during his vicarage year and had served as honor attendants at their wedding here later the same year.

The upbeat tempo of the organ signaled the beginning of the Processional jogging me back to the present. Everyone's eyes turned to view the participating clergy dressed in ceremonial garb slowly process down the aisle. I beamed with pride when my eyes caught sight of my husband. How handsome he looked in the sparkling white surplice. As the processional neared the front of the church, the visiting clergy members filed into the front pews while Art made his way to the lone chair standing at the head of the aisle.

I listened closely as David read the sermon text from the third chapter of the Gospel of John. Verse 30 (1) caught my attention: "He must increase, but I must decrease" (JB).

Repeatedly the words rang in my mind: *"He must increase, but I must decrease.* How intriguing," I thought. "I don't recall ever hearing that verse before."

"As Christians grow spiritually," David continued, "We fade into the background, and Jesus increases and becomes the stronger power within us. As He becomes the center of our being, the things of this world become less and less important."

Attempts to choke back tears and remain composed were futile. I dabbed at the tears streaming down my face with a tissue. "What a contradiction," I mused. "Flowing robes, magnificent processional, awed guests, honored position, and pride in our accomplishment. What a contrast all this is to God's message for us today. God's way is always opposite the world's way; He requires humility, not pride; decreasing in importance, not increasing in importance. The church has worked on the visible: education, appearances, knowledge, while God's hand mysteriously works on the unseen preparation: changing the heart, molding from the core into a vessel for Him to use. Yes, the message for today is not one congratulating us on the job finished. Rather he is saying:

Although it seems your educational journey has now ended, I say to you your journey has just begun. There is still much to do. I have a long way to take you. I have many things yet to teach, but my pace is slow. The road ahead has many curves. Yet, I will bring to completion that which I began. You are my servants. I will take you where I want you to go.

Chapter 13

HE MUST INCREASE

"A time for throwing stones away"
Ecclesiastes 3:5 (JB)

Two weeks after his ordination, Art was installed as assistant pastor of Redeemer Lutheran Church in Denver, Colorado. Proudly I took my seat in a front row pew of the familiar church and quietly waited for the service to begin. With the experience of his ordination behind me, I had given considerable forethought to this day. First, as I was determined to fully enjoy the beauty of the service without the distractions of our toddler, I had arranged to leave Benjie home with a babysitter. Second, I had resolved to refrain from emotionally involving myself to avoid the embarrassment of having to sit through another service uncontrollably dabbing my tears with a tissue.

My eyes drawn to a beautiful banner hanging in front to the left of the altar, the creation of Mary Reetz, wife of the Senior Pastor, the inscription read:

"ARTHUR, I HAVE CALLED YOU BY NAME AND
YOU ARE MINE"

A chill came over me as the words pierced the depths of my soul. Tears of joy filled my eyes at the thought that God had mysteriously left His throne on high to share intimately this occasion with us and to personally speak words of endearment to my husband. For a few moments, I basked in the presence of God unaware of the others. The magical spell was broken when a stream of tears ran down my cheeks, and I self-consciously reached into my purse for a tissue. Awed by His presence, yet unwilling to relinquish control of my emotions, I abruptly turned away.

The processional ended, and the clergy took their places in the front pews on the opposite side of the aisle. I gazed over at my husband solemnly sitting in the lone chair in front, and once again, my eyes brimmed with tears. Struggling to regain composure, I quickly redirected my attention to the district president standing in the pulpit. When tears continued to flow as I listened to his sermon, there was no alternative than to mentally block out his message and passively stare at the altar until the service ended. My tears resumed at the reception afterward, when the choir director distributed song sheets with songs she had composed about each member of our family. Ushered in by a lesson in humility for me, our ministry at Redeemer had officially begun.

With Duane and Mary scheduled to journey to the Holy Land soon after our arrival, he suggested that both families might benefit if we temporarily stayed with them, take our time looking for housing, and be on hand to care for their three children while they were away. Our search ended a few days later, however, when we found an attractive two-bedroom brick duplex with a lovely fenced-in backyard for Benjamin. Anxious to settle some of our household and allow both families a few days' privacy before their trip commenced, we moved our belongings into our new home before they left.

Like a deflated balloon plunging to earth after a high flight, my life suddenly returned to normalcy during the Reetz's absence. "I should have known this emotional high couldn't be maintained indefinitely," I scolded myself. "Past experience alone should have warned me to prepare myself for the inevitable return to reality." The month of celebrations was over: the end of Art's formal education, my twenty-seventh birthday, Art's ordination and reception in

Lansing, our seventh wedding anniversary, family parties in Michigan and Iowa as we made our way to Colorado for Art's installation, a reception after the installation at Redeemer followed by a clergy gathering at the Reetz's, and cards and gifts. All had now ceased. Our place of honor had abruptly ended.

With another lesson in humility, I was thrust from the center of attention to the role of a domestic servant, caring for four children, preparing meals, maintaining a large home, and coordinating the activities of a busy household, all while Art was immersed in shepherding the congregation left few precious moments to communicate, not only with my husband but also with God.

Quiet moments with God now swallowed up in the busyness of life in the parsonage, my spiritual reserve was dwindling dangerously low. Slowly and subtly, self-doubt and fear began creeping into my thoughts as I lost sight of the vision God had given me. Seeing myself with a purpose in life, with gifts and talents apart from my husband's, became difficult. Panic set in. The spiritual warfare had returned.

So you thought you found a new identity, did you," the voice chided. *"Don't you know that was just a dream; a false high you were on? Oh, it may have sounded good when you were in Springfield, but remember, life is different here. Look at you. You don't really have an identity of your own. You're not a writer. Who are you kidding? You've never written anything. And even if you were, you'll never find time to write in this busy place. Face it. Your real identity was in your job. Now you don't even have that. Without it, you have no identity.*

I mulled over the thoughts crowding my mind. "You're probably right," I agreed halfheartedly. "I guess I was in a fantasy world for a moment. I wanted so to believe it. It's not as if I don't know how difficult it is to maintain an identity separate from my husband's in this profession. Maybe if I could find a part-time bookkeeping job, I could keep my identity and still stay home with Benjie most of the day. I'm sure I could find a babysitter." With a surge of self-confidence, I eagerly paged through the evening newspaper, circling an ad to call the next morning.

The following morning I woke up with the flu. I was so nauseous I could scarcely move from a horizontal position on the living room sofa. I readily accepted the neighbor's offer to take Benjie for the day and help with the older children. Breathing a sigh of relief, I closed the door behind them. "Quiet—peace and quiet. Were it not for the queasy feeling in the pit of my stomach, I might have enjoyed this change of pace," I thought as I curled up on the sofa. Talking on the telephone to anyone about a job or any other subject was the last thing I wanted to do. The solitude of the empty house was conducive to restored communication with God.

"Lord," I pleaded. "I'm so confused. Was I imagining the vision you gave me, and the new direction for my life? Somehow, I can't see it now. I guess I've lost my faith. I'm so afraid of the path before me. I'm not sure I can follow through, and it scares me to think about the time before when I had no identity of my own and felt no seeming purpose for my own life. Do you want me to get a job?"

"Don't be so willing to give up and return to the old familiar way of life," He gently responded. "Don't be afraid to give this new identity a chance. True, life has been hectic since your arrival here, but you will soon be settled in your own home and be able to maintain a schedule more suited to your needs. Yes, what I said in Springfield is true. It wasn't just a fleeting fantasy for you, but it will not happen overnight, either. You must continue to think positively about the new direction I gave you. It is a matter of complete faith now, but slowly you will see it begin to take shape. You must continue trusting Me and be willing to step out in faith. You do not see it now with your human eyes, but it can be seen with eyes of faith."

The warmth of His presence and words spoken with such power and authority inflated my spirit and revived my dwindling faith. Once more the vision was clear. I would find myself drawing on this confirmation repeatedly over the next several months when temptation to seek a part-time job came disguised in yet another cloak.

How will you possibly get along without working? How will you ever get control of your bills and on a workable budget?

Yet each attempt to return to work was thwarted, with God ultimately closing the door to working and guiding our financial decisions.

Events occurred in January, which had a significant effect on both Art's ministry and my personal spiritual growth. Extenuating circumstances prevented Pastor Reetz from flying to Cape Girardeau, Missouri, for training in the Kennedy Evangelism Program, paving the way for Art to go in his place.

Returning, it was obvious Art had changed. Not only was he exhilarated about the call to evangelize, he was moved to action. Enthusiastic about the new way of sharing Christ and anxious to implement the program at Redeemer, he searched for two trainees; a man and a woman for his evangelism team. When the team was complete, the sixteen-week training period began with the group meeting in our home every Thursday evening.

Seeing my husband's enthusiasm sparked my curiosity. "I wonder what happened at the workshop to spark his change of heart," I puzzled. "What's so unique about this program? Art has heard about evangelizing before. He even took a class at the seminary." Intending to conduct an investigation, I planned to take advantage of this opportunity. I would remain uninvolved, and yet close enough to the group to discover the secret.

Quietly, I pulled up a chair. I listened and observed that first evening, peering at the small group: a teacher, a milkman, and Art. Their only credentials appeared to be a willingness to take seriously the call to evangelize and a covenant between them to set aside one night a week for the next four months. In addition, reading assignments and memory work were essential prior to each week's class. The thick red notebooks propped up on their laps gave evidence to the enormous task. After discussing the first week's material, the team prepared to go out. I bowed my head as Art offered a simple prayer, asking the Holy Spirit to go with them on their calls, to give them words to speak, and open hearts to receive the message. The sincerity of his words convinced me he knew the job exceeded the human capabilities of the team. Acknowledging their own limitations, they had agreed only to be vessels used by God.

"That's it! That's it!" I thought excitedly, after they left. "That's the secret! There are actually four members of this evangelism team! The spiritual power comes from the fourth member—the Holy Spirit! Truly, they are placing their trust in Him, not only to give them words that will be effective but also to open the hearts of those they visit. I could see He had already endowed them with enthusiasm in their mission and boldness to speak about Christ.

Having joined with them in prayer before leaving, I too received the Spirit's power. "If the Holy Spirit can guide, direct, and empower them to carry out their mission, He certainly must have the power to do the same for me," I reckoned. Fired with enthusiasm, I hurried into the bedroom to find a notebook and pen. Returning to the dining room table, I began to write my story. I repeated this procedure for the next sixteen weeks.

By September, the first training session ended. Now the three trainers were each prayerfully searching for a man and a woman to begin the next round of training. I knew the teams were incomplete, yet when Stan Tweten telephoned one afternoon to ask if I would be willing to be on his team, I was surprised.

"Oh, I don't think so," I declined. "What . . . what would I do with Benjie?"

"That's all taken care of," he answered cheerfully. "Glen said she'll be happy to come over and babysit Wednesday nights."

"She will?" I could not imagine anyone being willing to make such a commitment after teaching school all day.

"Sure, it won't be a problem. I can just drop her off when I pick you up."

It was clear I was going to have to think of a better reason to avoid getting involved. "Well, I'll have to talk to Art," I stammered in desperation. "I'll let you know tomorrow." I felt Art would agree with me and think my place was home caring for our son.

Stan was not discouraged. "That's fine. I'll pray about it."

All afternoon I wrestled with my decision, seeking a legitimate excuse. "Sixteen weeks is a long time to commit one's self to any project; even for a good reason," I told myself. "Who knows what circumstances might interfere with this Wednesday night obligation?"

Then, I remembered Stan's wife, Glen, and her offer to make a four-month commitment to watch our two-year-old son after teaching elementary children all day. The school year had just begun. With so many unknowns, Glen was willing to make this commitment to me, being willing to shuffle her schedule and to reprioritize her tasks for that evening despite the unknowns. Each time I thought of another feeble excuse, I remembered Glen.

The afternoon wore on and no honest reasons came forth. Repeatedly the same chain of questions haunted me. "Weren't you sincere about your enthusiasm for the program? If it is so worthwhile, why wouldn't you, too, want to become involved? What kind of hypocrite are you?" In my soul searching, the truth emerged.

There was no doubt about the worth of the program. I had seen the result and the power at work behind the scenes. I did not consider myself a hypocrite. Truthfully, I was afraid. All my life, I had carefully avoided classes or other situations where I might be called upon to give a speech. Furthermore, I was no evangelist. How could I present the gospel in a natural and convincing way to others? Would I feel uneasy speaking to them about something as personal as their faith in the presence of Stan and another trainee?

I recalled the conversation with Stan. "It'll be several months before you'll be asked to present the gospel," he had reassured. "Don't worry about that now. It'll come." He was so matter-of-fact and his manner so easy. He seemed so confident I could do it.

"What faith he has! True, his call did send me into all this turmoil, yet at the same time, I feel honored he chose me for his team. In spite of all these negative feelings, there is a twinge of excitement as I face a new challenge." By the end of the afternoon, Stan's faith had ignited my own.

"I'll do my best to prepare by studying the material," I promised Art later that evening, "and I'll just have to trust God for all the rest!"

The measure of peace about my forthcoming adventure dissipated when I learned Pastor Reetz had accepted Stan's invitation to be on our team. My heart sank.

"I don't want to witness in front of *him*!" I groaned to Art. "He's the pastor. He's had all that theology, all that training and experience.

Evangelism is his job. Who's going to listen to me if he's there? They'll wonder why he's keeping quiet."

Without sympathizing, he listened patiently to my grumbling. "Oh, Wife, they will, too. Don't worry about it."

God opened my eyes to show me that my distress was rooted in feeling unevenly yoked as a team member with the pastor. My sin of idolatry was still with me. I had to remind myself that I must not adulate any pastor: not Art, not Pastor Reetz, nor place anyone else on a false pedestal. The problem was mine to overcome if I was to be successful in the program. God's words were clear and direct. "Take your eyes off the pastor and his position. You must concentrate only on Me and the mission before you."

Humbly acknowledging my sin, I obediently plunged into the workbook, memorized Scripture verses, and quietly absorbed Stan's technique and style for sharing Christ. Even with preparation, I found the magnitude of the task overwhelming, continually forcing me to take my fears and insecurities to the Lord in prayer.

"Oh, Lord," I pleaded. "Give me the power and boldness to say what needs to be said. And please take away this fear in my heart that I'm not the one for this job, that I'm not spiritual enough to try to help someone else."

The Lord honored my petitions as each week I felt more at ease with sharing my faith. As before, God dealt gently with my weakness. Pastor Reetz missed several training sessions and was not present the nights I was required to give the presentation. By the time the training period had ended, I had become familiar with the program and had acquired enough self-confidence to view myself as an effective member of the evangelism team. I looked forward with excitement to the time I would be a trainer.

I learned that team members reaped unexpected blessings as a result of their submission to God. The door to God's principle for abundant living had been unlocked. The more we shared our faith, the stronger our faith became. Our lives were enriched as we interceded for one another, gaining a new dimension as we witnessed the power of the Holy Spirit working in the lives of His people. How exciting to see lives changed and to have had a part in their spiritual growth. God's decision to strengthen my faith and draw me into closer communication with Him as an intercessor at this particular time proved no coincidence.

With Advent came news from Michigan that my father's ill health had taken a sudden turn for the worse. Hospitalized and in serious condition, family members were called home. "If you want to see Dad alive," they warned, "you'd better come quickly."

With reservations to fly home the next day, I tucked Benjie into bed for the night and packed our suitcases. I hoped tomorrow would not be too late. I lay awake long after Art had fallen asleep, my father's impending death swirling in my mind. How easy it had been for me to be so involved in my own life; always thinking my parents would be there when I had more time. Everything that had taken priority in my life suddenly seemed unimportant. I thought about all the times I neglected to take a few minutes out of my day to write my parents a letter I knew they would appreciate receiving, all the times I failed to tell them how much I missed them or say "I love you." Somehow, I had lost forever, precious time with my Dad.

"Oh Lord," I pleaded. "If only you would give me some extra time to make up for the precious time I've wasted. While I slept, Jesus appeared to me standing in the clouds with arms outstretched. Although He spoke no words, I could feel the warmth radiated by His presence. When I awakened in the morning, the memory of His appearance remained vivid, the warm glow now manifest by a spiritual exuberance.

"I wonder if I could have actually seen Him?" I thought, mystified by the experience. Quietly, not wanting to awaken Art, I stood on the bed and pulled back the curtains to see if He might still be there. My heart sank in disappointment to see my view obstructed by heavy plastic covering the window.

"If I couldn't have actually seen Him," I pondered, "what exactly did happen? Wonder what Art will have to say?"

I broached the subject with him shortly after he awakened, making a conscious effort to appear calm and nonchalant. "I . . . I had the strangest experience last night. I saw Jesus standing in the clouds. He . . . He didn't say anything. He just stood there looking at me."

Art eyed me curiously as I continued, "At first I thought I actually saw Him, but when I looked out the window this morning, I realized

I couldn't have seen Him that clearly because you had covered the bedroom windows with heavy plastic. I don't understand how I could have seen so clearly last night. I tell you, it was as though He was right here with me. I actually felt His presence. His eyes seemed to look right through me."

Art shrugged his shoulders. "I don't know, Wife. It must have been a dream."

"Maybe so," I responded, feeling foolish for dwelling on the incident. Changing the subject, I added, "Guess I'd better call home and let them know when we'll be arriving."

Compared to the day before, the noticeably cheerful voice of my brother Wayne answered the telephone. "Dad seems to have passed the crisis in the night. In fact, he has improved so much, it doesn't look like you'll even need to come home."

In the following days, Dad's health continued to improve. To everyone's amazement, Dad was released to go home before Christmas. There was no question in my mind that God had miraculously extended his life. Regardless of Art's explanation, I knew in my heart there was a connection between Dad's healing and what I had seen with my "inner eyes" that night.

Buoyed into the New Year on a spiritual high, I should not have been surprised when immediately following, came the temptation to cast it all aside, to come out of the clouds, and to focus my attention on the worldly.

I answered the telephone one day in early January to hear the voice of Norma, wife of Redeemer's school principal. "The company I work for is looking for some part-time help. Would you be interested, or do you know of someone else who might be?"

"Gee, I don't know. What would I be doing?"

"Survey work; most could be done by telephone from your home. You wouldn't even need a babysitter."

"I really appreciate you thinking of me, Norma, but I'd have to give it some thought. I'll talk it over with Art and let you know."

For the next several days, I wrestled with my decision. The thought of doing survey work was not particularly appealing, even if I could do it from home. The prospect of having some extra money was definitely a temptation. It would be nice to have money for going out to dinner, to go skiing more often, and to buy material to sew new clothes. Why, with more money, I could even buy some clothes!

Having reopened the door to the subject of returning to work, my dilemma led to another question. "If working part-time is in the plan, why not work at something you're familiar with, where you've had previous experience?"

"What do you think?" I asked Art that evening. "Rather than do telephone work though, maybe I should call and see if that accounting office is still interested in hiring me. If I'm going to work, I'd much rather do something I am familiar with."

"Whatever you want to do," he said. "I guess it makes sense." His interest in the subject appeared to be lukewarm at best. Obviously returning to work was not something he was pressuring me to do.

The next morning, I reluctantly telephoned the firm only to learn they had a complete staff and no longer were in need of my services. Breathing a sigh of relief, I hung up the receiver. Maybe going to work was not in God's plan after all.

"You know, if you do go to work, even part-time, not only will your commitment to evangelism suffer, the book I have directed you to write will come to a standstill. Are you firmly committed to this project, or are you merely using it as an excuse for not finding part-time work? The time has come for you to decide whether you will take your writing seriously. Choosing to take it seriously will mean you must make sacrifices and exercise self-discipline. Not only will you have to forego the luxury of extra spending money that a part-time job would bring, you must learn to be frugal with your free time. No longer will you have the option of choosing whether to spend it sewing new clothes to wear or writing."

I choked back tears at the stark realization of God's words," Give up sewing, no new clothes? How can I?" Yet, I knew God had spoken the Truth. My love for sewing was an obstacle hindering my progress as a writer. Unless I chose to lay it aside now, I might never see the fulfillment of God's promise to me. Faced with that alternative, my choice was easy because deep within was my heart's desire to see a finished work.

"Yes Lord, I'm willing to renew my commitment and to bind my promise to you, I vow not to sew any new clothes for myself until I have finished the book." Having spoken the words, I laid my love for sewing on the altar, trusting God to provide for my needs.

God's response was immediate and positive. Not only did He give me inner peace but He also added a blessing; a sense of urgency about my writing. With my father's recent close encounter with death had come a new awareness of the importance of living each day to the fullest. "Don't take for granted that you will be given unlimited time to complete all the loose ends in your life," He warned. "You cannot afford to postpone until tomorrow what you should be doing today for you don't know what tomorrow will bring."

God had already set into motion another essential element to motivate me to action and encourage me. To know His truths had worked for me was not enough. I needed proof that others shared my feelings and would be able to identify with my experiences to be able to write about them with boldness and enthusiasm.

"There's a Marriage Counseling Workshop coming up later this month," Art announced one night after dinner. "It's for pastors and their wives in the Colorado District."

"Wives?" My ears perked up. Conferences for pastors were routine, with wives occasionally attending. Seldom, however, did the conference specifically include us.

"Yes. The pastors go for four days in January and then return in February with their wives for four more days."

"Where's it going to be?"

"Down in Colorado Springs at a Catholic Retreat Center. They say it's a beautiful setting at the foot of the mountains. I'd really like you to go with me."

"But, who could we get to take care of Benjie?"

"I'm sure we can find someone," he assured.

"This little excursion is beginning to sound too good to be true," I thought as I began to focus in on the picturesque setting Art had described. "I could use a little vacation away from it all: no cooking, no cleaning, no responsibilities, adult conversation, and quality time with Art."

"It might be kind of fun," I said enthusiastically. "How much will it cost?"

Art brightened at my response. "Nothing, for us anyway. The church pays all the expenses." He hesitated for a moment. "The only requirement is that we take a personality inventory on ourselves and each other before we go."

"What do you mean by a personality inventory?" I asked, eyeing him suspiciously. "Why do we have to do that?"

"It's similar to the questionnaire we had to fill out at the seminary before vicarage. You remember. At some point during the workshop, we'll be called in to go over the results and see how we scored."

Obviously, this little vacation was more involved that I had anticipated. "Go over the results with whom?"

"I suppose with Reverend Fritze. He's from the Board of Parish Education and director of the workshop. After we come back, I'll be able to use the same test when couples come in for marriage counseling."

"Oh, I see. We pretend we're going in for marriage counseling. What else will we be doing there?"

"Well, in addition to the lectures and small groups, everyone will be assigned to an Encounter Group that will meet separately at scheduled times every day."

"Encounter Group?"

"One of those little groups where you sit around and share experiences and feelings, like we were in when we adopted Benjie."

A queasy feeling suddenly came over me in the pit of my stomach as my mind's computer searched for stored data about those little, sharing groups where you find yourself revealing private information.

"Oh, no, not one of those," I groaned. "I don't know if I want to go through that again."

"Oh, Wife," Art gently reassured, "It won't be that bad. After all, you don't have to say anything you don't want to say."

"I'll think about it," I promised, ending the conversation.

For the next several days, I mulled over the decision. Would it be worth risking another emotional upheaval for a few days' vacation? Art's words echoed, "You don't have to say anything you don't want to say." He was right. Whatever input I offered in the group was my choice. I could remain silent.

"One thing is certain," I promised myself. "If I agree to go, I'll be very guarded about what I share. I'll certainly know better than to reveal anything too personal, nothing that might cause me to feel uncomfortable. The lid needs to stay on my Pandora's Box." With an air of confidence that the issue was resolved, I arranged to go.

One variable not within my control, however, was the random placement of couples in the encounter groups. As soon as Reverend Fritze walked into the room and announced his role as our facilitator, I felt the walls of my defense weakening.

I listened as he spelled out the group guidelines. "Feelings are feelings and should not be labeled as good or bad," he emphasized. "We're not able to control the feelings we have. What is important is what we do with those feelings."

"You're kidding." I thought as I glanced around the room. "No one will judge our words or condemn how we feel? His philosophy sounds great, but I can't imagine anyone foolish enough to actually follow through with his directive."

With my curiosity sufficiently aroused, I sat up a little straighter, listening attentively and observing the expressions on each face as the ball of dialogue passed among the members of the group. In doing so, I found my eyes lingering on Reverend Fritze.

"It's his eyes," I concluded. "There is something about his eyes— those droopy eyelids—that's it! He reminds me of Dad, Yes, and his brothers, too. He has those same droopy eyelids characteristic of Dad's side of the family." It was impossible to look at him without seeing my father's eyes. "Strange how those familiar eyes are so disarming," I mused. "It's as though I'm sitting around the room visiting with the family, hardly the atmosphere for holding back feelings."

The constant reminder of my father and uncles served as a catalyst to prime the pump for forcing the river of angry thoughts to the surface, a level too intense to ignore or suppress. Despite my preconceived strategy for remaining uninvolved, I plunged into the conversation, reacting with surprising candor.

I shared the pain as the daughter of an alcoholic, my humble state throughout childhood, and the knowledge that Dad was looked down upon by his family. He was the "black sheep." Oh, it wasn't that I doubted the validity of their reasons for avoiding Dad. I was certain each had legitimate cause and felt justified in doing so. But, what did that have to do with the rest of us? Were we, too, "black sheep?" All those years of growing up, I felt their rejection. True, they lived out of state, but if they really had cared, couldn't they have stayed in a motel knowing we did not have the means to house and feed guests?

The words bursting forth surprised me. I thought I had confronted and worked through the pain of my childhood during our last year of seminary. Hadn't it been thrust upon me when Art chose "Counseling the Families of Alcoholics" as the topic for his Bachelor of Divinity Thesis? Many times, tears had clouded my vision as I labored over my husband's paper. Healing had taken place with each page I typed, realizing my experience was not unique, but God knew there was yet another area for healing.

Perhaps I might not have given it much thought had we not crossed paths with my relatives a number of times since Art entered the ministry. What a coincidence that Art's sister had married a Lutheran minister who served congregations near my father's family. To include a stop to see Barbara and her family when traveling from Michigan to Denver was natural; visiting my aunts and uncles along the way was just as natural.

How hospitable they were whenever we visited. Yet, while I enjoyed reestablishing ties with Dad's family, part of me resented their attention. Was it because now I was grown and we could establish a relationship apart from Dad, or was it because my station in life had changed? I was married to a Lutheran minister and being Lutheran was part of my Dad's heritage. Reverend Fritze and the other group members, including Art, sat in silence as I poured out my story. When I finished, Reverend Fritze spoke up. "For your homework tonight, I want you to write a letter to your uncles and tell them how you feel," he instructed. "Whether or not you mail the letter is up to you. But I think you need to get that anger out."

I curled up on my bed that night with notebook in hand. The process of putting down on paper the thoughts verbalized earlier in the day was not difficult. Having decided not to mail my letter helped me to be even more candid. Somehow, my confession brought peace of mind as well as paved the way for God's forgiveness in my heart.

The subject of my anger came up again when we met with Reverend Fritze to go over the results of our personality inventory tests.

"I'm wondering if there isn't something else that could account for your high level of anger," he said, pointing to my profile. "Any idea what might be causing you to feel this way—something you haven't already expressed?"

I stared in amazement at the paper lying before him, wondering. "How could that maze of graphs be so revealing?" An answer would not require soul searching, for the source of this anger was barely hidden beneath the surface; so intense, so real, so current. I glanced at Art sitting beside me, searching his eyes for a sign to proceed. Now we were getting into "shared territory." Only recently had we discussed our mutual feelings and anger.

"There is something else," I confessed. "We're in the process of adopting our second child. We didn't have to go through all this the first time. With the shortage of babies, we have to provide the agency with medical proof of infertility before being approved."

My eyes met my husband's as I continued. "We've had to undergo a fertility study and take tests. The whole thing has been so humiliating." I paused as I struggled to retain my composure. "It's been hell having to take fertility drugs, take my temperature, and keep a chart. It's all been so degrading to put our intimate relationship on the level of laboratory tests. Our private life has become an open book to be analyzed and scrutinized. It has been such an emotional thing for us, yet everyone else acts so nonchalant about it. Don't they realize we are real human beings and this is not just a textbook case?"

"As a matter of fact, next week I'm scheduled to have a laparoscopy, the final step of the work-up. It's no big deal, only minor surgery, but I resent that I have to go through it."

Art nodded in agreement while I rambled on. "And what's more, since this is our second child, we had to give the agency names of close friends for character references. Now, our friends are sitting on the judgment seat, critiquing our parenting skills. Why should we have to go through all of this when others just have their babies? I resent this intrusion into our private lives. It's so humiliating!"

Reverend Fritze had remained quiet. "In light of all this," he said thoughtfully, "I would recommend you postpone your surgery until you can work through your anger."

I shook my head emphatically. "No, I'm not going to postpone it! I want to get this over. I want to get our baby girl and go on with life. I can handle it. It just doesn't seem fair."

After the session ended, the flurry of thoughts continued swirling about in my mind. What was it about the laparoscopy that made me so angry? What was its significance? Was it because it represented the final step of the emotional roller coaster ride? Up and down, up and down . . . Nothing had worked, yet somehow we had never lost hope that something miraculously might happen. Now we were at the end of the road. If the results prove negative, we will have to face the reality that I might never get pregnant and robbed even of hope.

As the week progressed, God's presence among us became abundantly clear. Group selections had not been coincidental, for each group member there had been another person in the group who could identify with them, regardless of the feelings that emerged. It was heartwarming to witness others join me in removing the mask and stepping forward in honesty. Freedom to talk about all feelings was a new experience for many of us, yet crucial to the healing process. Our decision to risk bearing our souls was not received with condemnation but genuine love and support of the group.

Throughout the week, my interest remained intense as I waited in hopeful expectation for confirmation of the words and direction God had revealed to me in private. If I had correctly interpreted God's message, my own experience would echo in this place. This was the arena for those truths to be tested. Like capturing nuggets of pure gold, I grasped tightly those truths, as presented by various speakers.

One such nugget came during a lecture on marriage and divorce. "Changes will occur in a marriage as a result of the growth of one of the partners," the speaker pointed out. "These changes will necessitate the growth of the other partner if the marriage is to survive."

I choked up with emotion as my memory's tape rewound to vicarage and Michigan State when I faced that crisis. With the pictures came the pain, agony, and fear that had engulfed me during those turbulent times. How frightening to know the person I lived with was not the same person I married but a stranger. What had happened to us? Why did it have to be this way? What was wrong with the way

158

things had been? Why couldn't he love me the way I was? Why did I have to grow and change? It wasn't fair.

The lecture on feelings and communication, provided another gem. "Statistics show lack of communication as the cause for many marriage failures. Neglect of this crucial area is extremely dangerous to a marriage."

"And for the pastor's family," I thought to myself. "The problem is even more critical when so many hours in the day are spent counseling in confidence. How does the shepherd relate to his family at home, when his thoughts are still focused on the crises of his sheep?"

I was most deeply touched in the workshop for wives: *Role of the Pastor's Wife*. I listened attentively as one after another shared her thoughts, feelings, and frustrations in her role as a pastor's wife. Some had already worked through an identity crisis; others were still struggling to be their own person while living in the shadow of their husband and his role.

Compassion filled my heart as my own spirit identified with their agony. Hearing them speak brought back all the emotions I had experienced: Frustration over my futile attempts to please everyone and fit into their mold, and anger to realize someone would always be dissatisfied with my efforts.

What a joy to hear the workshop end with a challenge to the wives: "If you are unhappy in your role as a pastor's wife, you are not bound or helpless. Do something about the situation!" I wanted to stand up and shout "Amen! God doesn't will for you to be unhappy!"

Chapter 14

OUR SECOND YEAR

"A time for speaking"
Ecclesiastes 3:7 (JB)

lthough Reverend Fritze suggested, I consider post-poning the laparoscopy until I was able to work through my hostility, I chose instead to proceed. A few weeks later, I went alone for my final check-up, and the doctor gave me the results of our previous months of testing.

"You have a twenty percent chance of becoming pregnant," she said. "By that, I mean given the problems the tests indicate, only one in five women ever become pregnant."

Tears flooded my eyes as I left the doctor's office. I had not expected the discouraging news or the impact her words would have on me. How I wished Art had been with me to hear her dismal report. The only comforting thought was with the tests now com-pleted, the way was clear for receiving our baby girl. That thought helped cushion me from the grief I felt.

There was little time to dwell on my grief as we prepared for her arrival during the following weeks, spending all of our free time looking for a home to buy. In addition to needing an extra bed-room for the baby, we hoped to find a house with a fourth bedroom for out-of-town guests. When our realtor showed us an attractive, four-bedroom ranch, with a finished basement and family room, there had been no question in our minds. That was the home for us.

We moved in Easter week in 1974, second only to Christmas as being the worst possible time for a pastor to move his family. Art was extremely busy with the extra services during Holy Week, leaving the tedious job of unpacking the endless line of boxes to me. Unlike our previous moves when as renters, the apartments had been thoroughly cleaned, and quite presentable before moving in, there had been no time to clean the house while unoccupied. Now, I faced walls to wash or paint, floors to clean, windows to wash, and numerous other little jobs, while at the same time working around the unpacked boxes. "This is what I've been waiting for all these years?" I complained.

We had waited so long for a house of our own; we should have been thankful and rejoicing. Strangely enough, we did not feel that way. Rather than being content with our new home, acquiring it had triggered new frustrations as we found ourselves caught up in a vicious circle of wanting material things to go in the house. Having already extended our budget to its limit, however, there was no money available with which to buy them. I felt guilty to admit my ungrateful heart and my preoccupation with material things.

I thought back to where my spiritual life had been before and after our move, and felt as though I had climbed up three steps only to slip back two. Not only did it have a negative effect on my work in the evangelism program, I could not concentrate on my writing. I gave myself one month to get over the "new house fever" and all the busy work I had involved myself with it and vowed to let nothing keep me from my original goal. Immediately, I looked for a quiet place of retreat. I set up our card table and a borrowed typewriter in the extra bedroom upstairs and each time I walked by the room, I was reminded my goal was to finish writing the book God directed.

A few weeks later, my temporary office was disrupted when I answered the telephone to hear our social worker's voice.

"Bonnie, this is Sharon. We've got your baby girl!"

"You're kidding!" I could not believe what my ears had heard. Eighteen months of waiting was over. It seemed impossible I could be shocked, again, the second time around!

She assured me she was serious, explaining she had just come from an agency staff meeting. The staff had chosen us as the best possible match for the baby girl just relinquished. She had purposely called during the lunch hour, hoping to find us home.

"Art's not here yet," I told her, glancing at the clock.

She gave me a few details about our baby: date of birth, weight, length, and nationality, which I hurriedly scribbled on a piece of paper. "You can come to the agency between three and three thirty tomorrow afternoon to pick her up," she said excitedly. "Remember to bring an outfit to dress her in."

I hung up the phone and called the church. When I learned from the church secretary that Art was out of the office, I asked her to have him call me when he returned.

"Why did he have to choose this day not to come home for lunch?" I mumbled aloud. Hoping Benjie had not yet fallen asleep for his nap so I could tell him, I peeked into his bedroom. He was sound asleep, so I quietly closed his door and proceeded to pace from room to room around the house crying for joy. "Who could I tell? It had to be someone special, considering I had not yet told Art the good news.

"I know who to call! I can call Wayne and Thea. "We've already asked them to be the baby's godparents. Certainly they have the right to be told first," I rationalized. Fortunately, I found them both at home and overjoyed at the news of our baby's arrival. Before our conversation ended, we decided to have her baptized the coming Sunday as they would be leaving for a three-week European vacation on Monday.

Having released some of my excitement, I was able to focus on the practical things. I was much less prepared this time and would have to go shopping tonight for our new little daughter. As I threw a load of baby clothes into the washer, I made a mental inventory of the needed items: a diaper bag, one dozen cloth diapers, two packages of rubber pants, two kimonos, one package of undershirts and some diaper pins.

A short while later, Emma, our neighbor across the street, came over to show me the sweater set she was knitting for her new granddaughter. As soon as I saw a break in the conversation, I blurted out, "We're getting *our* baby girl tomorrow!" We were still visiting when Art returned my call—almost two hours after Sharon's call.

Quickly I told him the news adding a few scolding remarks for not letting me know where I could reach him today, of all days! He explained Pastor Reetz had invited him to be his guest at the Kiwanis International Convention meeting that week in Denver.

By the time Art arrived home, Benjie was up from his nap and together we set out to go shopping. Halfway there, Art remembered he had an appointment scheduled in less than an hour that had completely slipped his mind. Checking his appointment book and discovering the needed telephone number was at the office, he took Benjie with him and left me at the department store. My spirits soared as I carefully selected the essentials. The events of the day still seemed unbelievable. Tomorrow our routine would change to accommodate a two-week-old baby.

Like a rerun of the night before Benjie's arrival, after calling our families, we passed the time writing announcements identical to the ones we sent before. This time the name read, Danielle Theresa Newhouse; a name chosen over a year before that we had been careful not to divulge to anyone. As I lovingly wrote her name, I wondered what our little Danielle would look like. Benjie was such a cute little fellow with blue eyes and curly reddish hair. Was it too much to expect Danielle to be a cute baby, too?

Having begun months ago preparing him for the arrival of a baby sister, he probably thought she was an invisible being occupying the nursery. Now that the time had finally come, I wondered how he would react to her presence. Would he be jealous? Would her arrival have any effect on his potty training? Since some of his little friends would be having a new baby in the family within the next few months, I decided it might make him feel special being the first! Whatever the adjustments, I hoped the transition period would be smooth and pass quickly.

The next day we walked down the long hallway and into the agency's nursery. There in the same little crib, dressed in a tiny blue dress with white booties was our new, adorable baby daughter. She had blue eyes, brown hair, and a little pink pacifier bobbing in and out of her perfectly shaped little mouth. Benjie took one look at her and quickly left the room. He discovered the toy box, lifted a little pull toy out, and wandered down the hall where a few minutes later we found him in the administrator's office about to experiment with the new electric typewriter. After taking pictures and signing the necessary papers, we left with our two little ones. "It seems strange to refer to 'the kids,'" I commented to Art on the way home.

Blessed with two very special children, we both felt our family was complete now. A tremendous joy filled our hearts, and those around us shared our exuberance. The excitement of Christmas filled our lives in June when gifts, congratulatory cards, and letters began arriving from family and friends. The new neighbors gave me a lovely baby shower the week after Danielle's arrival. The women of the congregation postponed their shower until parishioners returned from their summer vacations. Everyone was thrilled for us and eager to share in this special event in our lives.

During all of the excitement, each of us attempted to reestablish some order in our lives, yet with routines turned upside down, the task seemed impossible. The daytime was delightful with Danielle sleeping most of the day; however, I soon realized being able to get all of my housework done during the day meant we were all paying the price later in the evening. Both children were awake until eleven or twelve o'clock each night, with Benjie feeling very left out if the baby was up and receiving all the attention after he had gone to bed. When we did get one child to sleep, the other one would wake up. One night, the entire family was still up at three o'clock with Art holding Benjie and me, Danielle.

"This is the worst experience I've ever been through!" Art blurted out in frustration.

I could empathize with my exhausted husband, "Why don't you sleep downstairs in the guest room. There is no need for everyone to lose sleep. Besides, I can take a nap during the day."

Adding to the confusion in the house, there was confusion outside as well. The city began tearing up the street outside Danielle's bedroom in response to Art's complaint several months earlier about the break in the drainage pipe running in front of our house. Not only had the water pressure caused cracks in our driveway with the first hard rainstorm, the drainage situation had amounted to a three-foot geyser in our front yard. I did not know whether to be thankful or angry because of the noise and confusion it would bring. At first, I did not see how God might use this situation as a diversion for Benjie.

The big machines were most effective in distracting him from his new baby sister. There was far too much excitement outside to waste valuable time worrying about her! Every morning I let him sit on the front lawn where he could watch the men work. Before long, he became friends with the crew, and they were joining him under the shade of our weeping birch tree and sharing their lunches with him. Now, instead of the familiar peanut butter and jelly sandwich, his diet consisted of salami, cheese, and crackers. He loved his new routine where, for several weeks, his naptime changed to two o'clock when their shift ended.

One morning, glancing out the window to check on him, I saw one of the workers lift him into the backhoe. My first impulse: race out like a protective mother and rescue my son. My second thought was that I had better pray instead that the Lord will watch over him and keep him safe for I knew this was a once-in-a-lifetime chance for a little boy. All morning, Benjie sat in the man's lap, while I paced nervously inside, "Surely I need to have my head examined," I said to myself, as I watched the big wheels lifting off the ground and the huge bucket smashing the cement with only two thin supports to keep the machine balanced.

When Art came home for lunch and saw his little boy sitting there, he called out to him, but he turned his head the other way. He felt important now and enjoyed the attention he was getting as all the other little boys in the neighborhood looked on in envy.

Shortly after lunch, he began to itch and we noticed some red spots on his face. Within a few hours, the spots turned to a mass of giant hives causing him great discomfort. When his lips swelled to twice the normal size later that day, we became more concerned and took him to the doctor, explaining we thought his backhoe ride might have frightened him causing him to break out in hives. "No, I don't think so," the doctor said upon examination. "It looks to me like a food allergy. It isn't as serious as it appears, but it could be if the swelling begins to affect his breathing. Has he eaten anything unusual?"

We watched him closely that night and by the next morning, the hives had begun to diminish. Scheduled to appear in court for Danielle's adoption, I did not want to take Benjie with us looking like that! After one look at him, the judge would surely wonder just how well the little family was adjusting. I had misunderstood Art's conversation with our social worker when she had explained to him what questions the judge might ask. I thought she would inquire about the state of our mental health. I searched for a suitable, but honest answer. What would I tell the judge? I knew I couldn't lie to her. I would have to answer, "It's shaky, but getting better every day!"

We exchanged looks of relief when later that morning, instead of questioning us about our mental health, the judge asked if we were satisfied with the mental health of our baby.

"Oh yes, we're satisfied with her mental health," we said in unison.

The judge approved the placement of Danielle in our home and we signed the preliminary adoption papers and left the courthouse carrying our new little daughter. When the adoption process was legally completed, our responsibility to the agency would end. Yet, in our hearts, we knew the agency had merely been God's instrument. Our children were God's children first, and He had directed their placement in our home. We were accountable to Him for the gifts He had entrusted to our care.

That summer while I was busy and content focusing on our two children, and trying to find time to write, more and more of Art's attention, was preoccupied with theological and political issues raging within the Lutheran Church—Missouri Synod (LCMS).* The momentum had gradually been building since Art's arrival at Concordia Lutheran Seminary in Springfield, Illinois in November 1968. From time to time, he would share another detail of the unfolding theological controversy, but it seemed overwhelming. Theology was his world, not mine. I was not interested, nor did I understand all this talk about doctrine, charges of heresy, and infighting among church leaders. Hoping the issues would resolve themselves, I chose to ignore for the most part the rumblings until the summer of 1974. The controversy had made its way from the seminaries and synodical headquarters to the Colorado District. It was time for me to learn what the major issues of the controversy were and why it might affect us.

Art needed me to remove my blinders and become knowledgeable, so we could communicate about the controversy that had been occupying so much of his time and energy. Now whether I wanted to or not, I had to make an effort to put the puzzle pieces together to try to understand why it was not all dissipating and why Art, Duane, and many of our friends in the ministry felt so strongly that they would not nor could not remain silent. All the major issues hinged on the methods used to interpret the Scriptures, and on who was qualified to interpret them.

The historical critical method used to interpret the Scriptures, raised questions for some about the validity of biblical historical events such as the parting of the Red Sea, Jonah and the whale, or the Virgin Birth of Jesus. Another issue involved the inerrancy of Scriptures: whether they were God-breathed or self-interpreted and whether or not the Holy Spirit continues to lead Christians to Truth in the Scriptures. The issue of ecumenism included questions about the exclusion and/or inclusion of believers partaking in communion and of fellowshipping with members of the Missouri Synod. For Missouri Synod missionaries, both at home and abroad, the questions surrounding ecumenism caused major problems involving their primary mission of soul saving and whether they could work collectively with other denominational missionary groups on social issues, such as ministering to the physical needs of the people.

The controversy surrounding the charismatic renewal in the Lutheran Church and the understanding of the role of the gifts of the Holy Spirit had been an issue for Missouri Synod officials for years. Ultimately, the decision led to Springfield Seminary allowing applicants identified as Neo-Pentecostal, admission as general students in the Master of Divinity program but ineligible for the program leading to certification. In addition, all regular students had to deny the presence and experiencing of any of the gifts of the Holy Spirit as outlined in I Corinthians 12.

Perhaps two of the most divisive issues involved the authority of Synod and its hierarchy. What was the status of doctrinal statements adopted at Synod Conventions? Were they binding and equal to the Lutheran Confessions or of lesser importance because they had the potential of abuse by those in power? Ultimately, the two issues centering on interpretation were the catalyst for what began as an issue of biblical teaching at the nation's Lutheran Church—Missouri Synod colleges and seminaries, eventually moving to the districts and finally to the congregations. By the summer of 1974, it made its way to the Colorado District and eventually to the members of Redeemer Lutheran Church in Denver.

Although the Lutheran Church—Missouri Synod became polarized between two factions and eventually choosing to identify with one side or the other, the issue was much more complicated. The two factions were labeled as conservatives and moderates; however, a more accurate description would be authoritarian conservatives and individual-responsibility conservatives.

> There is in fact no firm line between the approaches. Some who take an individual responsibility approach on most issues may take an authoritarian approach on others. And of course the opposite is also true. This happens, because both approaches share many common values: the importance of tradition, the unchangeable character of God's moral law, the need for self-discipline, and dependence on God to vindicate righteousness and to punish evil. (1)

* (For a more detailed report on this controversial subject, see Appendix E at the end of the work.) With the passage of time I have come to understand or see that this dissension in the Lutheran Church Missouri Synod was not unique to the church. It is a controversy that ravaged all Christian denominations beginning in churches abroad, and making its way to America in the 20th century. The result was the break-up of mega-churches throughout the country and most denominations would experience the fallout.

Chapter 15

GOD HAS A PLAN

"A time for gathering them up"
Ecclesiastes 3:5 (JB)

By summer of 1975, Art had grown weary of the turmoil and disillusioned with the ministry, as he watched the politics in the church confuse people as to the real issues. He knew no pastor with an Evangelical Lutherans in Missions (ELIM) membership who had beliefs considered heresy. He saw many valid ministries hampered, if not crippled, and many good pastors and teachers forced to abide by the synodical hierarchy's edicts or lose their called positions. It became increasingly difficult for him to hold fast to his beliefs and remain in good standing with the Missouri Synod. From the serious tone of the rhetoric since the last convention, it was only a matter of time before he, too might be forced to resign from Redeemer—or ELIM.

While synodical attempts to suppress any opposition were stifling, other factors were also involved in his disillusionment with his ministry at Redeemer. He had also become frustrated in his role as assistant pastor and aware of the limited influence he had on the work of the congregation. With the passage of time, he found himself more and more at odds with the senior pastor. As the gulf of communication widened between them, Art longed to be on his own, so he could be an effective influence and be able to minister to the needs of the congregation.

Searching his soul for other avenues to remain faithful to his call, he began to look at the options: He could place his name on a call list and go to another congregation as its sole pastor; however, the synodical issues would remain. Enlisting in the service as a chaplain was another possibility we had not discussed since his brother's death in Viet Nam. Since Bernard had served in the Navy, Art felt a loyalty toward that branch of the military. The chaplaincy program could be an excellent opportunity to gain valuable counseling training in addition to serving his country. Returning to college to obtain a degree in counseling or psychology was less appealing, as it would be expensive and difficult to support his family.

In June of 1975, he initiated procedures necessary to become a Navy Chaplain. The prospect of becoming a military wife, coupled with the fact that my father's health had begun to deteriorate, a smoldering spark of curiosity rekindled. With Dad in poor health, time could be running out to locate my two half-sisters from Dad's previous marriage. If my father died now, there would never be a reunion.

As a young child, I recalled seeing a picture my father carried in his wallet of his two small daughters. During my childhood years, he occasionally mentioned them, but none of us seemed to be interested in Dad's previous marriage. As the years passed, Dad seldom talked about them, and later when I inquired about the girls, he would not discuss them. On a rare occasion when he did, he seemed to know some generalities about them furnished by their mother: both girls served in the Women's Army Corps, and one had adopted children.

When I realized Art and I would be adopting our family, my curiosity about them intensified. Our lives seemed to be following along a similar path, creating an invisible bond between them and me. Perhaps, I thought, there was something inherited I shared with them? I was the only one of the four children from Dad's second marriage unable to conceive. The desire to find them became an obsession as though a part of me was missing, a piece to my puzzle.

Although he never spoke about it, I was certain Dad felt a piece of his puzzle was missing, too. I could not understand why he was an alcoholic. He had a wonderful wife and four healthy children; he had everything to live for, and yet, I sensed an unhappiness. What was in his life that he could not seem to escape? Thinking the source of his unhappiness might stem from the estrangement from his two daughters, I dreamed of one day arranging a surprise reunion.

When Dad's youngest brother came to Denver in July of 1975 for the International AA Convention, he invited Art and me to attend the banquet. I saw my opportunity to discuss Dad with him.

"Do you know the whereabouts of Dad's first wife and her family?" I asked.

Uncle Rocky shook his head, "I can't help you—why don't you ask your dad?"

I hesitated. "Ask my dad?" I mulled his words over. Of course asking him would seem to be logical. Why would I think after forty years, he could get me that information? Why could it be possible now? Unaware God was speaking through Uncle Rocky I dismissed the idea and turned my attention to my own situation.

Art's decision to enter the military had an immediate and powerful impact on me, prompting me to take a closer look at my spiritual life. Until now, I had been content with my spiritual growth and felt relatively positive about myself. I was not sure I had the spiritual stamina to cope with long periods of separation from my husband and to raise two children alone as the wife of a Navy Chaplain. Facing an uncertain future, I recognized my need for a stronger faith and more spiritual power in my life.

I had observed Stan Tweten, my Kennedy Evangelism trainer, and his wife Glen who seemed to have a closer walk with the Lord than mine. Their relationship with the Lord had long intrigued me. They had a special countenance about them: a sparkle in their eyes and a joy in their hearts. What was their secret? How did they attain that strong faith and that close relationship with the Lord? I wondered if the same power was available to me. I knew they were involved in the Lutheran Charismatic Renewal; a movement involving the work of Holy Spirit in the church, whose members claimed to have received special gifts as outlined in I Corinthians 12. (1) I knew Glen had the answers I was looking for and could tell me how I, too, could find that closer walk. I mustered the courage to question her when we attended a women's retreat together.

Over the past year, I had spent many hours working in Art's study on my manuscript and like a magnet, my eyes were continually drawn to a small narrow book; *Aglow with the Spirit* by Dr. Robert Frost (2) in one of his bookcases. Art had removed it from the church library, intending to destroy it three years before. The basis for his judgment had been the doctrinal stance of the Lutheran Church—Missouri Synod, seminary teachings, and the abuses he had observed among a small group within our congregation whose actions had deemed divisive rather than foster unity.

Knowing my husband and our synod had taken a public stand against this deeper experience, I was both fearful and curious about the book. Dare I read it and risk getting involved in this heated controversy? Could it be the magnet drawing me to it was the Holy Spirit, wanting me to investigate this dimension of Christian living because of my need? I struggled with these questions, fully aware of the possible unpleasant consequences of my actions before concluding I must not fear but trust God, step out in faith, and let Him lead me to the Truth.

When I finished reading the book, I went to my Bible to see what God had to say and found my answer in Acts 1:4–5. (3)

> And being assembled together with them, He commanded them not to depart from Jerusalem, but to wait for the Promise of the Father. "which," He said, "you have heard from Me;
> "For John truly baptized with water, but you shall be baptized with the Holy Spirit not many days from now. "

Why hadn't my eyes been opened to the importance of Jesus' directive before? The time had come when I, too, needed that same power Jesus had commanded the disciples to wait for. Convinced my request was in agreement with scriptures, I prayed, "Lord, I need more of Your power in my life. I don't want to go through life any longer with only part of what You have to give. I need to be filled with Your Spirit. If that means I give myself totally to You, then I want to do it now."

It was that simple. I was not ready or willing to go forward publicly, but in December 1975, while alone with God, by faith I received the anointing of His Holy Spirit.

A change came over me. I had a yearning to pray and read my Bible with greater zeal than ever before and an insatiable appetite for more learning. Among the books Glen and Stan shared with me from their library were Merlin Carothers' books: *Prison to Praise* (4) and *Power in Praise* (5), which influenced me to take an inventory in my own life. Two things came to mind as being the most painful: my inability to bear children and my father's alcoholism. For many years, I had murmured against God for the injustice done to me and at the same time prayed for something positive to happen. Now, I knew I must praise God for both. Mouthing these words of praise was one of the most difficult things I have ever had to do.

That same month, Art included a news update in Redeemer's Newsletter:

> Last month, I received a reply from the Armed Services Commission that I had been accepted—but for reserve status only—as there are no immediate openings for active-duty chaplains for the Lutheran Church—Missouri Synod. From the time I applied until the time I was accepted, a great deal of thought and prayer went into my decision. It is my feeling that, the situation in the LC–MS being what it is, I can be more effective in working toward reconciliation and helping to solve the many and varied problems, which face our church from the parish. Thus, I have decided to turn down the Navy's offer.
>
> I must say that the whole experience has been a growing one. It has caused me to do some serious thinking and praying about my role as a servant of our Lord Jesus Christ. Through this process, He has caused me and my family to grow—if not wiser, certainly closer to Him. And after all isn't that what it's all about, anyway? Thank you for your prayers and concerns, and please continue to keep us in your prayers daily. (6)

In early January, we traveled to Iowa to visit Art's sister and her family. While there, Art had a telephone conversation with his brother Bob, a psychiatrist in Traverse City, Michigan. He did not share the "meat" of the conversation until we were on the highway headed back to Colorado.

"Bob wants me to consider going back to school to get my degree in psychology and then join his psychiatric clinic as a psychologist."

"What did you say?"

"I told him I'd talk to you. If I can work something out with the church, he will help pay my tuition. It'd be one way to get my degree."

"I can't believe you're even thinking about it!" I fumed, "You just told the congregation that you were going to stay—to try to help solve the problems!"

For the next one hundred miles, I stared at the open road before us and did not say a word. It was apparent our future was very unsettled. The only door closed was Art becoming a chaplain. Recognizing the futility of focusing on circumstances I had little or no control over, I turned my thoughts to matters within my control.

While in Iowa, we visited some of my father's relatives. Seeing Uncle Rocky again reminded me that I had not followed through with his suggestion to ask Dad about my sisters. After our return home, I constantly thought of Dad. On the morning of January 23, 1976 while praying for him during my private devotions, God spoke to me. It was not audible, but the directions were clear. "Go downstairs and call your father and ask him for his daughters' addresses."

When Art awakened, I told him of my experience and the directions given me. "If you feel God wants you to do that, you should go call," he encouraged. "That's been bothering you for a long time."

With his confirmation, I raced downstairs to the telephone with my heart beating wildly. In the back of my mind was the thought that mother had already left for work and by following through with the directions and calling Dad then, I was doing something without her knowledge. "I'll have to trust God to take care of that, too," I thought.

"Dad, it's Bonnie, I have a request." I paused briefly, and then blurted out, "Could you get Connie and Marion's addresses for me? I'd like to write to them."

There was a long hesitation before he finally said, "I'll get them for you."

I did not prolong the conversation but hung up the receiver mystified by the morning's events. I could not explain his positive reaction to my strange request.

The following week, Denver hosted the Mountain States Lutheran "Teaching Conference on the Holy Spirit." When Stan and Glen invited us to attend with some others in our prayer group, we accepted. I knew God was giving me this opportunity to make a public commitment and go forward for the "laying on of hands." I sensed a testing for obedience. Although I knew I had already received the anointing of His Spirit, God knew my pride was keeping me from making my commitment public. When the teaching session ended the first evening and the invitation to come forward announced, I hesitated, until I looked up and saw the familiar red hair of my close friend, Monika, who minutes before had been sitting in the audience with us, now standing in front. Quickly, I left my seat and went forward. It was not until I opened my eyes after the prayer that I looked around to see Art standing beside me.

Several weeks had passed since my telephone call to my father, and I had not received a call or letter from him with the requested addresses. The excitement of that day faded, and I began to doubt.

"But God, this was my last chance," I pleaded, "I thought I was doing what you told me. I didn't think I had imagined Your closeness and the directions You gave me. If this fails, then I guess finding my sisters was not meant to happen, and I will never know them."

Later, I realized the sequence of events had not been coincidental. It was with each step in faith and obedience, God brought me a step closer to realizing my dream. He was using this delay to test me. Would I still trust Him regardless of the circumstances, or would I become impatient while waiting on Him? The turning point was finally releasing the situation to God and accepting the results.

Our church council retreat was scheduled for March 12 and 13, and I planned to attend with Art, having arranged for a sitter to come and stay with Ben and Danielle. The day we were to leave, however, Ben awakened with a fever and I felt I needed to stay home with him. I was very disappointed to have to cancel my plans and could not understand why circumstances had prevented me from going, but putting into practice the principle recently learned, I reluctantly praised God for the situation.

On Saturday, March 13, my father called from Michigan, overcome with joy and thankfulness! Connie, his younger daughter who was then forty-four, had just called him! I was so elated I could have burst from excitement! My eyes brimming with tears and my hand shaking, I wrote her name and address on a piece of paper and beneath it in large, bold letters wrote PRAISE THE LORD!

After hanging up, I picked up the piece of paper, hardly believing my eyes. Something visible at last; it hadn't been a dream. I had her name and address to prove it, a miracle!

Next, I questioned God, "Now that I have her address, what am I supposed to say to a sister I've never met?" God responded with a word of knowledge, I had no way of knowing except by His revelation to me. Immediately, I knew it to be true. I was to tell Connie my father loved them both very much and had been grieving over the loss of them for forty years.

Before my letter reached her and almost two weeks after her telephone call to Dad, he called me again.

"Guess who's sitting across the room from me?"

Before I could even guess, he told me it was Connie! My heart tingled with excitement as he handed her his phone. Her voice sounded like mine as she talked rapidly in a high-pitched voice, just the way I talk when I am excited. With her bubbly personality and friendly manner, our conversation flowed freely, more like two close friends than two estranged sisters. During our conversation, she told me she planned to visit her sister Marion at Easter time and although reluctant to discuss Dad because of her sister's close relationship with their mother, she said she would approach her.

Connie's letter arrived the first week in April with some pictures. Her resemblance to my father was striking: the same eyes and the same nose. It was particularly uncanny because none of us looked like Dad. I put her picture in a prominent spot on the bulletin board in the kitchen where I could frequently gaze upon it each day.

A week later, a rare letter arrived from Dad:

Sure have been thinking of you all since Connie was
here. After so many years that I prayed for that day, God
answered my prayers . . . I know right now you and
Art will love her. She is just like you, Bonnie. They are
coming through here tomorrow morning on their way to
Ohio to see your older sister Marion. Am sure waiting
to see her on her way home.

On Maundy Thursday, Connie told her sister of the newly found
family. Marion was surprised to hear we existed, as neither of the girls
knew about us. Rather than be opposed to the reconciliation, she immediately suggested Connie call Dad so she could talk to him. Dad was
so thrilled to hear from them that, after calling Mother at work, he
called me.

"I'm so happy," he kept saying amidst the tears. The forty-year
estrangement had ended. What a mountain-top experience to see the
beauty in God's plan as He remarkably prepared each heart, not only to
forgive the past but to risk something for the future. Mother accepted
Dad's two daughters with genuine love as did my siblings and their
families. Dad's three brothers and their wives made plans to travel to
Michigan for a reconciliation party to meet the girls.

When a picture of Marion fell from my parent's letter one day, I was
amazed. She looked like me! The picture, taken several years before,
looked very much like my senior picture and even more like my older
brother and his son. Marion was now forty-six. Another telephone call
from my parents some time later revealed yet another interesting bit
of information. In addition to her career in the Women's Army Corps,
Marion was a published writer. At that time, my mother and my younger
sister were the only members of my family to share my well-kept secret.
"Oh God," I mumbled beneath the tears, "This whole experience is getting to be almost more than I can absorb at one time."

A letter arrived from Mom on April 22, 1976:

Dad is still basking in the delight of his two daughters.
I spoke with Marion last night just after he had gone
to the store for me. They are anxious to know how *our*

family feels about this, and I keep assuring them that we are delighted with the results, which are showing on Dad. He has *hope* and is so much brighter in spirit! He may not be any better physically, but his outlook is so much better.

While the rest of the nation was celebrating the Bicentennial in July 1976, we were having our first family reunion in Michigan. I realized why I had always felt a part of me was missing. In many ways, I was a combination of both girls. It was eerie walking through the door of Connie's home the following summer; like walking into my own home! Our decorating tastes were almost identical: Early American furniture in the living room, Priscilla curtains at the windows, and plants everywhere, many the same as ours. The husbands we had chosen had similarities as well. Both were interested in music; Connie's husband had a radio program of hymns, and Art wrote Christian music and played the guitar.

While Art shared my joy at the reunion, the deteriorating situation in the LC—MS was dominating his life and ministry. A ruling came down at the August meeting of the Commission on Constitutional Matters (CCM) in St. Louis, Missouri that would force the issue to a vote in many congregations in the Lutheran Church—Missouri Synod. Congregations, pastors, and teachers could not hold dual memberships or be affiliated with the AELC (Association of Evangelical Lutheran Churches), and/or its related bodies, without forfeiting membership in the Missouri Synod. Any pastors or teachers holding membership in a congregation voting to join the AELC, would forfeit their position on the Synod's clergy or teacher rosters. The commission also ruled that such congregations, pastors, and teachers, were ineligible to participate in delegate elections for a synodical or district convention and that district presidents and other officers cannot retain their offices while "functioning in any way in any movement creating or encouraging the creation of ecclesiastical organizations in opposition to the Synod." (7)

Throughout the summer, Art investigated different programs at nearby colleges where he might complete his degree in counseling on a part-time basis, and continue as Redeemer's assistant pastor. He learned of a new program in the area of counseling and psychology, to begin in the fall at the University of Northern Colorado in Greeley. Geared specifically to accommodate employed students, the program offered classes every other weekend for a year. The fact the program would be compatible with his work and the church council approved his schedule, indicated to Art that this, indeed, was God's will for our lives and the direction He wished him to take.

By November, the ramifications of the Synod's Commission on Constitutional Matters had reached the Colorado District and Redeemer Congregation. District President, Dr. Waldemar E. Meyer offered his resignation to the Board of Directors of the Colorado District effective November 1, 1976. The same day of President Meyer's Celebration and Thanksgiving service, a special meeting was held at Redeemer, called by the Congregation President and fifteen other conservative members:

"PURPOSE: Prevail on you to attend this meeting and vote. The issues are:

1. Should Redeemer Lutheran Church congregation retain its membership in the Lutheran Church—Missouri Synod?

    (WE ASK YOU TO SUPPORT THIS ISSUE)

2. Should Redeemer Lutheran Church congregation withdraw its membership and possibly join some other organization?

    REASON TO VOTE: Pastor Reetz and Pastor Newhouse have both announced that they are members of AELC and ELIM. They have been, and are now, very active in these groups and have proposed to the congregation members (Their letter 10/24/76) that the Redeemer Church join the AELC. They do not claim that Missouri Synod has violated any doctrine but that there has been political violations by the President of the Synod. We do not agree that there is justification for leaving Missouri Synod as there are certainly doctrinal issues involved." (8)

The Denver Post reported the results of Redeemer's Special Congregational Meeting the following week:

"Another Lutheran Church—Missouri Synod (LC-MS) minister has resigned from his church after a vote by his congregation to remain affiliated with the embattled LCMS. Resigning with him were the assistant pastor, Reverend Art Newhouse and three teachers from the church-operated grade school. Reetz and Newhouse will leave Redeemer November 30. The resignations came after the congregation voted 168–100, to stay with the Missouri Synod. About 275 members of the 750 member congregation attended the meeting." (9)

Art detailed his reasons for resigning in a letter to the congregation:

> The purpose of this letter is to share with and inform you on one of the most difficult decisions I have ever had to make. After much prayer and thought, I have come to the conclusion that I must resign as assistant pastor of the Redeemer congregation effective November 30, 1976. There are many reasons for this decision, none of which I have taken lightly. The most direct reason has to do with the conditions within the Lutheran Church—Missouri Synod. I do not feel that the LC—MS is a viable place for ministry for me any longer.
>
> I am deeply distressed by the present leadership's refusal to listen to the concerns of people who are truly concerned about ministry. I am deeply concerned over the administration's double-talk about what the real issues are and what I consider a lack of honesty and openness in dealing with them. I am deeply distressed over the present administration's "so what" attitude when seminary professors, teachers, pastors, missionaries, and synodical mission staff members are forced to alternate ways of serving their Lord because they can no longer in conscience serve the Gospel ministry through the organization of the LC—MS. I am deeply concerned as I see the LC—MS continually withdrawing the hand of fellowship and association from other Christians under the guise of "maintaining pure doctrine."

It seems clear to me that the LC—MS has developed into an organization for the sake of the organization and has lost sight of what it means to be Church. When anything, be it family, friends, job or church organization, begins to demand more of a commitment to it than to the Gospel and person of Jesus Christ, it is time to reevaluate where one stands. I feel the LC—MS is telling me to be subservient to it. This I cannot do. I am a servant of Christ first and foremost.

I feel I must also say something of the situation at Redeemer. As it stands, I feel that my ministry is no longer effective. By the recent actions and behavior of many within Redeemer congregation, it is evident to me that you, also, no longer consider my ministry viable. For me to continue serving Redeemer would only cause more dissension and discord among you, and I do not want that.

I wish with all my heart that we could have worked things out in a less traumatic way. Unfortunately, feelings were strong—pride got in the way—too many people were hurt and there was not enough mutual respect, trust, and Christian love.

I must confess my own failures in dealing with the controversy among us. I am not perfect and made mistakes, and I ask your forgiveness.

The reality of the situation, however, calls for us to go our separate ways. I pray that your Loving God will be with you, and I will continue to pray for all of you, as I hope you will pray for me. May God continue to bless us all in Jesus Christ and continue to have mercy on us. (10)

Approximately 100 members of Redeemer Congregation followed the pastors' exodus from the Missouri Synod that day. Within the first week an organizational meeting was held to begin a new AELC congregation. The new church, called Peace with Joy Lutheran Church, held its first service the following Sunday in a Community

Center in nearby Lakewood, Colorado. As there were not enough members to support two full-time pastors, the new Church Council voted to have Art as a full-time pastor to enable him to complete his master's program in psychology while Duane agreed to serve as a part-time pastor.

Art was nearly finished with his schooling when a letter arrived from the Department of the Navy, inquiring as to his status and explaining the reason he had not heard from them about openings for active duty Protestant chaplains. There had been a change in command in Washington, DC, and Art's file had only recently been found. Additionally, the results of Art's interview with the Commander at Lowery Air Force Base had never been received, delaying the processing of his application. His file was still open.

Recognizing God's intervention, Art informed them of our present circumstances and withdrew his name. God had closed that door for our family once His purpose had been served.

Chapter 16

BLOOM WHERE YOU ARE PLANTED

"A time for planting"
Ecclesiastes 3:2 (JB)

efore we left Denver, I protested my case before the Lord. One night, during my quiet time, I listed my grievances to God for plucking me from my place of honor and placing me in another city away from my support system. I was growing spiritually and being nurtured in our weekly prayer and Bible study. I had people I could talk to and trusted, friends who valued me as a person with a separate identity apart from Art's. Where would I ever find friends to walk so close beside me? How could I ever replace the small prayer group I would leave behind? I did not know how I would survive spiritually.

Again, I was facing an identity crisis. I was no longer a pastor's wife. I was humbled. No longer could I write "Rev. and Mrs. The wife of a psychologist? In my mind, Art had taken another fork in the road—a worldly fork, one serving another god. I did not know how God would fit into his life and did not support this change. All that education, all those years we spent preparing for the ministry, and now he was not vested; any retirement he had accumulated was gone. We were starting over in every way. In fact, if I could have imagined a least desirable plan for my life, this was it. "God, you are really pushing me this time," I thought.

First, rather than do counseling part of the day as he had in the parish, now he would spend the entire day talking with people, hearing their problems—all of which were confidential. Second, although we would be leaving Pastor Reetz, Art would be working closely with his brother, another strong personality in his psychiatric office. What affect would this have on Art and our marriage?

Third, is the fact that Art's mother also lived in Traverse City. We had never been close, and it had been clear from the beginning that I was not her first choice for a daughter-in-law. Adding fuel to that smoldering fire had been Art's decision to leave the Episcopal Church and become a Lutheran—not only a Lutheran, but a pastor as well. No doubt living nearby would mean having to deal with her criticism more frequently.

Fourth, while Art would be establishing himself in a private practice, even with the referrals his brother sent his way, I would need to return to a full-time job so we could have one steady income to pay the bills. Although Ben would be starting kindergarten, I would have to leave three-year-old Danielle with a babysitter. How would our marriage survive all these drastic changes? God would have to show me quickly that He was still with me.

We left Denver the middle of August and stayed in Minneapolis with Wayne and Thea the second night, August 15. Together, we watched the nightly news reports of Elvis Presley's death. Although he had been a part of all of our teen years, it seemed peculiar to feel so emotionally attached to someone we had never met. For me, the news left an especially sad feeling. Was it because I had been saying goodbye to everyone I cared about so recently—and one more part of our past was gone?

Upon arriving in Traverse City, we unloaded our rental truck, put our belongings in Bob and Jan's garage, and stayed with them the first night. The next morning, there was a strange stillness over the household. Everyone in the house overslept! Bob did not awaken at 4:00 a.m. to go fishing, as was his custom before going to work. In fact, for the first time since he had begun his private practice, he missed his first appointment. Even their dog overslept. While no one else seemed to give it much thought, the confusion that morning had great significance for me. I did not view it as a coincidence. I saw it as an important sign from God assuring me that despite my fears, He was with me in Traverse City just as in Denver. He knew I needed the encouragement.

After breakfast, we left the children with Jan and contacted a realtor. He drove us around Traverse City and showed us three homes that first morning. By noon, we had made our final decision. We loved the beautiful blue ranch-style home with the charcoal-colored brick trim. The new three-bedroom, two-bath home near completion was located in a circle subdivision seven miles southeast of Traverse City. Optimistic about its future for us, we envisioned a finished basement to accommodate future growing family's needs, when money would not be so scarce.

In my mind's eye, I could see the beautiful bay window in the dining area in the front of the house adorned in crisp white Priscilla lace curtains. A second dining area, on the opposite side of the kitchen, also had a chandelier and sliding door overlooking the backyard. With his love for gardening, no doubt Art pictured the now-barren property beautifully landscaped. The fireplace in the living room brought back warm memories of the crackling fire in the fireplace at the old farmhouse in St. Johns. Yes, this quiet neighborhood would be a wonderful environment for raising our children. The small galley-style kitchen may have been undesirable to some, but it appealed to me. I did not want to spend all my time there doing domestic chores; my heart was in my writing. I eagerly looked forward to the time when I could resume work on my manuscript.

We returned to Bob and Jan's house after only a few hours and joyfully announced, "We found a house! It'll be ready to move into in a month!" Art's family was shocked.

The next challenge was to find the ten-thousand dollar down-payment check—proceeds from the sale of our home in Denver that had somehow become misplaced in the boxes on moving day. We made that shocking discovery during our long drive back to Michigan. Art was driving the moving truck and towing his Jeep while I was following in the family station wagon with the children.

"You do have the down-payment check?" Art asked, calling me on the C.B. Walkie Talkie.

"No, I thought you had it!"

We put a stop payment on the check, and proceeded to go through all the boxes in their garage. Eventually we found it, but not before its replacement had arrived, just in time for the closing.

We split the month between Bob and Jan's and Grandma Newhouse's and registered Ben to begin school in our new neighborhood. Having sent letters and resumes to a number of accounting firms prior to our move, I contacted each one personally. Some were already staffed, and others scheduled interviews with me. The firms interested in hiring me were unwilling to pay the wage I expected. Finally, the personnel director at Chef Pierre looked on my resume with favor and agreed to pay an acceptable wage. As a sales secretary, I would join the small staff of young women to take orders from the nationwide network of food brokers.

As I walked through the doors the first day, I mumbled to God beneath my breath. "I want You to know that You are making a big mistake, a pie factory is *no* place for a preacher's wife!"

His response to me came during morning devotions on September 13, 1977. I noted the words in my Bible from Isaiah 61:1 and 66:2:

> Yahweh has given me directions. I must follow through with them. For mourning robe, the oil of gladness, for despondency, PRAISE. I am planted here by Yahweh to GLORIFY HIM! (JB) (1) But my eyes are drawn to the man of humbled and contrite spirit who trembles at My word. (JB) (2)

I got the message, and indeed, it was humbling. My new role seemed very unimportant. Used to playing an important role in supporting my husband in dealing with life's problems on the front line of a congregation, it was not easy for me to make the transition from concern for the salvation of souls to a load of pumpkin pies late on arrival! While my physical body was in place, my heart was not. I felt like a baby, suddenly ejected from a safe, cuddly womb and thrust into an unknown world. My new world was a myriad of sumptuous desserts. I had great difficulty taking any of it seriously.

Seeing my need for an attitude adjustment, God spoke to me through scripture on November 10 in Jeremiah 27:12:

> Be humble and submit to authority. Work for the good of
> the country to which I have exiled you. Pray to Yahweh
> on its behalf since on its welfare yours depends! (JB) (3)

Taking to heart God's stern reprimand, I came to understand it was God's authority I was submitting to. He was my superior, and I was His representative in this workplace. If this was where He chose to place me, then I must do my best work for Him.

The next words God impressed clearly on me were not stern but gentle. When I came to Jeremiah 29:11, a few weeks later in my private devotions, I once again felt His favor and was encouraged:

> I know the plans I have in mind for you. It is Yahweh who
> speaks. Plans for peace not disaster, reserving a future full
> of hope for you. (JB) (4)

God's message to me was that even though I did not understand the detour in His plan for my life, He did. Not long after it became quite clear that His choice of a pie factory for my wilderness journey served several purposes. On the surface was the obvious lesson of learning self-discipline for the sake of my physical well-being when faced with the daily temptation of my favorite dessert. Far more dangerous to my spiritual well-being was another temptation that lurked in the background. That temptation caught me by surprise. God had chosen this workplace to test my faithfulness as a wife.

I had witnessed others fall to the sin of adultery in the past but smugly thought I was incapable of succumbing to this grievous sin. However, when I came face to face myself with the powerful demonic forces of lust and adultery, I realized I did not have the strength to fight and win the battle in my own power. It came as a shock and humiliation to examine my own thoughts for I realized how vulnerable I, too, could be. In fact, it proved the fiercest spiritual warfare I had ever encountered, not just a one-day confrontation to experience and win, but an intense battle that raged every day for months.

Although the battle raged only in my mind, with my thoughts, I knew I stood guilty for entertaining adulterous thoughts. Close enough to the edge to fall in myself, I knew, but for the grace of God go I.

In the thick of the battle, there was a constant barrage of words: God's words and Satan's. The enemy chided, *"You're not a pastor's wife anymore. You don't have to be concerned about adultery. Look at the world. Everyone else is doing it. Now days, it really doesn't matter, look around you."*

I knew otherwise. I knew what God had to say about adultery in the Ten Commandments. Not only had we studied them from Luther's Small Catechism in Confirmation Class, we had to memorize all the supporting scriptures. That knowledge was stored in my memory bank to draw upon at such a time as this. The Holy Spirit also revealed to me the pain and suffering that would come to the families. Trust would be shattered, but even more damaging would be the damage to my character. How could God use me to write anything if I failed Him in this way? It would mean sacrificing all of the preparation for God's plans for my future. I could not cast aside hope for the future for any momentary pleasure.

In the midst of my time of trial, I was too embarrassed to confess the temptation to my husband. "How sad and ironic that the psychologist is so busy offering everyone else helpful advice that he isn't even aware of threats against his own marriage," I thought on more than one occasion.

However, when an opportunity presented itself, I found myself confessing my sin to a female Christian friend. Perhaps knowledge of my battle would be safe with her for she had experience on that battleground. She would not judge. Moreover, having lost the battle and suffered the consequences, perhaps, she could offer some wisdom. Her advice was simple, "Don't go there! It's not worth it!"

I sensed her intercessory prayers for me had reached God's throne, for soon after, He directed me to go to the Christian bookstore for additional help.

The first book my eyes were drawn to, *The Purpose of Temptation*, by Bob Mumford. (5) I recognized the author's name and was familiar with his humorous style of writing. Our small prayer group in Denver had been captivated as we listened to his teaching tapes. "How fitting a title for me just now," I mused as I lifted it from the shelf and browsed through its pages. "You mean to tell me God has a 'purpose' behind this ordeal?" Immediately, the tension in my spirit calmed as I recalled his marvelous gift for teaching God's Truth with boldness yet with a touch of light humor. After reading the summary on the back cover, I was certain his book contained God's message for me:

> Here is a clear, penetrating discussion which views temptation not as something to be avoided, but as an integral part of God's plan. Bob Mumford bases his explanation of temptation on the "Law of the Four P's" which states that God gives us a promise that is linked to a principle (or condition), followed by a problem (temptation), leading to a provision. Temptation, there-fore, is the point at which man decides whether or not to obey God's Word and receive the consequent provision.

My interest piqued; I purchased the book. Every evening for the next several weeks during my quiet time, I read a chapter and thoughtfully reflected. Bob Mumford was speaking God's Truth because I could readily relate to his words.

> The purpose of the wilderness is always to make us recognize our own insufficiency, and God's all suf-ficiency. Once we realize this, willingness and obe-dience follows. When I recognize that I cannot do something on my own, I should be willing to give up trying to do it in my own strength and be obedient to the command of God who *can* get it done. (6) (p. 43)
> Temptation isn't real unless it involves the actual possibility of failure—a moment where you face the issue squarely and it is almost a toss-up which way you will take. When you have faced that kind of decision, you have moved from lip service to God to wholehearted willingness to obey Him regardless of what it may cost you. (7)

He further explains in the wilderness:

> In reality, temptation hangs in a delicate balance
> between three participants: God, man and the devil. .
> . . But powerful as Satan may be, he is not the prime
> mover in temptation. God is. (8)

Scripture quotations throughout the book became valuable weapons
in my arsenal against the foe: Paul's words in 1Corinthians 10:13 (9)

> The man who thinks he is safe must be careful that he does
> not fall. The trials that you have to bear are no more than
> people normally have. You can trust God not to let you be
> tried beyond your strength, and with any trial He will give
> you a way out of it and the strength to bear it.

Clear direction came from God through Paul's words to the
Philippians (4:8):

> Finally brothers, fill your minds with everything that is
> true, everything that is noble, everything that is good and
> pure, everything that we love and honor, and everything
> that can be thought virtuous or worthy of praise. (10)

During my private devotions, God spoke to my heart through
Jeremiah 30:3: "Write all the words I have spoken to you in a book."
(JB) (11) These words greatly encouraged me, bolstering my spirit
and gently reminding me of my new identity, "It's true that you are
no longer a pastor's wife, but I have other plans for you. I have given
you these experiences and the gift of writing to serve as an encouragement to others in their time of trial."

My eyes were opened to appreciate and be even more thankful for
the gift of writing as I realized doing so served more than one purpose. The burning desire to write, that God had placed deep within
me, had caused me to continue writing even after returning to work
full time. Taking my notebook and retreating to my car during most

lunch hours to work on my manuscript was a welcome escape and served to remind me of God's plan for my life.

Although I had continued the practice of getting up early to have devotions, I knew if I was to continue growing spiritually, I needed to find a new spiritual support system—new friends to replace those left behind. When I learned there was a Sunday Evening Praise and Worship service at the Lutheran Church we were attending, I asked Art if he wanted to go with me. Although the group was much larger and more organized than our Denver group, many of the worship songs were familiar. The fact the group's leader was one of the church's pastors was an encouragement. Most of all, I felt the presence of God's Spirit and was uplifted each time.

It was during one of these gatherings a man shared a prophesy God had given him about a Christian radio station to be built in Traverse City in the future. Everyone rejoiced upon hearing the wonderful news of God's plan for us. We knew that ministry would nurture our own faith along with countless others. There, I also met some wonderful new friends, who later became part of a smaller Bible study group that met in our homes. Louise and her husband Dick were both medical doctors whose spiritual walk closely mirrored ours. Later, Louise introduced me to her friend Charlene, who also became a close friend of mine.

For the first few months at work, I made a conscious effort to leave my "spiritual identity" at home and sought to blend into my new surroundings as inconspicuously as possible. I certainly would not think of tacking up Bible verses on the walls of my cubicle for daily reminders as I did in my kitchen at home. When personality clashes and other problems began to surface, however, I realized I could not survive spiritually, even for a day, without some visible reminders of the source of my strength. One lunch hour, I drove to the Christian bookstore and bought some stickers to place on my calendar and around my work area. They became a conversation piece and encouraged several others to follow suit.

At various intervals, I gathered my courage and submitted my manuscript to publishers. When a rejection letter accompanied the manuscript, I would be discouraged. Sometimes the rejection letter would be brief and to the point. Other times the letter would include suggestions to make it more marketable. One particular response was especially troubling to me. That individual discouraged me from the book manuscript but encouraged me to submit several of the chapters individually to magazines. He also advised me to continue developing my skills by writing for local newspapers as opportunities arose.

"But Lord, I don't want to write for the newspaper," I protested, "You told me to write a book!" When my initial disappointment subsided and the period of despondency passed, God confirmed that He, indeed, had spoken through the editor. With no effort or searching on my part, God began to open doors for me to write locally. I knew God was directing me to respond when I read something in the newspaper and felt an unquenchable burning well up inside. Once He had my attention, and I obediently sat down to write, the words flowed easily. The process was exhilarating, and my spirit soared, regardless of the topic. God was teaching me to be an obedient soldier, to use my gifts not to give me honor, but God. Having already prepared us for His assignments, there are many things He needs His soldiers to do.

Prior to the newspaper endeavor and the move from Denver, I had seen the need to continue to develop my writing skills. I had enrolled in a Professional Creative Writing class sponsored by the Rocky Mountain Writer's Guild and had subscribed to a writer's magazine. There I saw an advertisement for membership in the Christian Writer's Guild, which I joined for support. When I opened my membership packet, a press card with my name on it was enclosed. The welcoming letter explained the press card could be useful to gain entrance to events where I might gather information. Although I had not thought of such an idea, I tucked it safely away in my purse in case a need arose.

Chapter 17

MIRACLES

"A time for dying"
Ecclesiastes 3:2 (JB)

*I*n the fall of 1979 during my devotions, I read about Mary and Elizabeth in the first chapter of Luke. I was captivated with their parallel stories—each expecting a miracle; drawn together like a magnet. I began to have new understanding why Mary, upon hearing the angel's words, had hurried to Elizabeth's side. They found strength in each other to continue believing the angel's prophesy. I found myself drawn into the subject I had carefully avoided for years with the news my friend Charlene was expecting a miracle baby in February. Charlene's pregnancy kindled my own hope. Could it be God was using her baby to prepare us and our children for a miracle?

"You could be next!" our friend Louise said excitedly one day.

Outwardly, I laughed at her while inwardly a twinge of hope rekindled. "Maybe, just maybe, I will become pregnant at Marriage Encounter in December," I fantasized, "That would be just like Mary and Elizabeth . . . three months before Charlene delivers her baby."

December came and went, followed by Marriage Encounter, Christmas, and New Year's. Still, I had no pregnancy. Inwardly, I continued to hope, while outwardly I tried to focus on my friend's joy. In January, I attended her baby shower at Louise's home. While all the other guests' eyes were fixed on the expectant mother as she lovingly unwrapped her gifts, Louise's attention was drawn instead to me. She seemed to sense my melancholy spirit as I watched Charlene, beaming with the joy of motherhood, hold up the tiny baby clothes for all to see.

Several days later, Louise telephoned. "You looked so sad," she began, recalling the shower. "Don't you wish you could have a natural child?"

Stunned for a moment and shocked by her intruding question, my private space invaded, I quickly retorted, "No! I'm satisfied with the two children we already have!"

Sensing my abrupt slamming of the door to that line of questioning, she began to reminisce about other details of the recent baby shower. For her, however, that was not entirely the end of her questioning. If I would not talk about it to her, she would talk to God about the matter.

"Lord, I don't want you to force a natural child on Bonnie if she really doesn't want one, but You know her heart. If she really does want a baby, I pray that You would give her the choice."

Later, she shared with me her prayer regarding a baby, based on John 16:24, "Ask and you will receive and so your joy will be complete." (JB) (1)

Yet, it was not until my father lay on his deathbed in February of 1980 that the Lord clearly spoke to me during my nightly prayers. "Bonnie, do you want a natural child?"

I thought about the reality I was about to lose my father. It occurred to me if I had a natural child, a part of my physical body, it would also be a part of my father. In that sense, he would be living on in a "remnant" of me, and the detachment would not be so final. I could hang on to a part of Dad, "Yes," I blurted out. A natural child was my heart's genuine desire.

Uttering the words, I felt guilty as if confessing a sin. Was I ungrateful for wanting more? Was my desire for a natural child a sign of dissatisfaction with the two adopted children God had already given us? I could not retract the words. The truth had been uncovered, a truth God had known all along and my friend Louise had discerned. How strange that despite the grave condition of my earthly father's health, I felt closer to my Heavenly Father than ever before.

Then, my thoughts wandered back to the events of Sunday, January 27. My morning devotional reading had led me to John 21:15–25, and I Chronicles, chapters 11 and 12. The words from the Lord had come to life. Noting the date in the margin of my Bible, I summarized God's message to me:

> These passages confirmed to me, too, that this is what I must do, that these words also speak to me. "Feed my lambs": Cub Scouts, Sunday school kids, my children; as well as "Feed my sheep" and "Look after my sheep" that include teaching ministry through books and other means. I also shared with Art what the Lord had been teaching me about being a soldier and how I had read about David's champions and supporters and that I felt as if God was requiring that of me, too. I was to be like a soldier doing what I was commanded to do, even if I didn't want to do it—even if it forced me out of my comfort zone. Just as a soldier must go where he is needed and follows his commander, so must I. First, coming to Traverse City; second, working at Chef Pierre; and third, being a den mother for Benjamin's Cub Scout troop. I feel that now I have no choice to do what I think I would like to do; I must obey God. He has other plans for me. The Lord spoke to me for the third time in this passage at the end of John: "There were many other things that Jesus did: if all were written down, the world itself, I suppose, would not hold all the books that would have to be written." It has confirmed to me that He is guiding the book I am writing. He has not forgotten, and He will bring it to fulfillment.

It was against this backdrop and faith buildup that I began February 1980. My relationship with the Lord was as close as it had ever been. God had confirmed again to me that though my life seemed to be taking many detours, I was to be obedient and continue working on the book. There was no question but that I was on a spiritual high. I cherished those quiet times to be alone in the stillness of the morning or in the evening. I longed to open my Bible and pray, to listen to that familiar voice of God and His direction. My spirit was also encouraged by Oral Roberts' pamphlet, "Believe in a Miracle." (1)

On Saturday, February 2, 1980, Art's mother, now living in Lansing, called to tell us she had gone to visit my ailing father, but no one was home. When I told her he had recently been hospitalized, she was surprised we had not thought to tell her. I assured her I would call home and talk to Mother. I had to admit, to anyone outside of my family, our behavior looked uncaring, yet we all understood one another. Over the past several years, Dad had been in the hospital so many times that it had become routine for our family. Since all of us had our own families and other responsibilities, Mother made a conscious effort not to trouble us unless necessary.

After hanging up the telephone, I realized just how remiss I had been. I had not talked to my parents for at least ten days after they received my last letter. In that letter, I had shared our recent experience about traveling to Petoskey to make a surprise visit on Bill, my half-sister Connie's husband, who was recovering from open-heart surgery. Upon entering his hospital room, we were shocked to see Dad's first wife sitting by Bill's bedside with Connie. Although she had never met any of us, we knew she had been so upset about the family's reconciliation with her daughters, they could not speak openly about us.

Connie, flustered by the chance meeting and fumbling for words, had introduced us as "friends from Traverse City." Taking her cue, we adjusted our conversation accordingly, and inwardly hoped to get out of the room before the discovery of our true identity. We had discussed the awkward fiasco on our journey home. Beneath the humor, I realized an important bridge had been crossed, a gap between Dad's two families closed. My heart was thankful for this opportunity. I knew my parents would want to hear about the "experience," too.

Prompted to call home, I detected the discouraged tone of Mother's voice. "Dad's not good," she said, choking back tears. "He's . . . he's so weak. He's not able to walk or talk and requires twenty-four-hour care now."

Mother, always a pillar of strength in the family, clearly was weakening under the stress. The past years, with the family's roller coaster life with Dad's health, was not improving as expected. Accustomed to the routine, and his downturn so gradual, we had not realized the seriousness of the matter. It was evident Mom needed our support. "I'll have to wait until Monday to reach Barbie. I'll see if she can come down to Lansing with me next weekend."

My brother Wayne and his wife Lynette were in Detroit visiting friends that weekend. The ladies had gone shopping, leaving the fellows home with the children, watching a basketball game on television. About six o'clock Saturday evening, Wayne suddenly felt impressed by God to pray. Following the Holy Spirit's prompting, he immediately left the room and went upstairs to the guestroom. There he prayed in his prayer language for twenty or thirty minutes.

At home in Traverse City, Art and I, hosting a birthday party for one of our friends that evening as planned, had just finished saying grace before dinner when eight-year-old Benjamin announced he had a prayer to add.

"Jesus, please take Grandpa, and make Aunt Jan's mother well." Having overheard us discussing their serious health problems earlier in the day, he had asked me if Grandpa was going to die. I had told him I believed Jesus would be taking Grandpa soon and Aunt Jan's mother would get better.

At 6:30 p.m. in Lansing, Mother went into the bedroom to check on Dad and found him in distress. Hurriedly, she checked his pulse and could get none on the wrist but a slight one on the neck. Immediately, she called the rescue squad who upon arrival labored over him for thirty minutes before transporting him to the hospital.

My younger brother Rich and his wife met Mother at the hospital. While in the waiting room at 8:30, he described a strange feeling coming into his head "a feeling like everything had been cleaned out," he described. Moments later, the doctor came out and informed the family that Dad was coming around and on the machines.

Meanwhile, my sister Barb who was living in Charlevoix, which is fifty miles from Traverse City, without a telephone in her home, felt impressed to go to a friend's house to call Mother to see how Dad was doing. When there was no answer, she returned home.

It was not until 8:30 Sunday morning that Mother telephoned us to report the prior evening's events. "I'll get a message to Barbie that Dad is in intensive care," I promised, "We'll leave for Lansing as soon as she gets here."

Upon our arrival in Lansing, we went directly to the hospital to visit Dad. I was prepared to see a very sick man as Mom had warned us he had a tracheotomy and couldn't talk, attached to numerous tubes. She had mentioned Dad was angry with her for authorizing the procedure. I anticipated the worst, but not for the look of sheer fright in my father's eyes! His dark eyes, rolling from side to side, darted back and forth. The sight of him reminded me of Art's story the previous day when he killed two rabbits. The fear in Dad's eyes told me of his uncertainty about where he would spend eternity, and about whether God had forgiven him. Dad was afraid to die; afraid of going to hell.

"Oh God," I pleaded, "Give me something to tell Dad to take away his fear. Let him know before he dies so he won't be afraid of dying."

Instantly, the words of Jesus to the repentant sinner on the cross came to mind. *"Today you will be with me in paradise."* (3) Second guessing the significance of the words and thinking perhaps I was imagining these words were God's message for me to deliver to Dad, I said nothing to Dad or anyone else about it.

Barbie and I planned to drive to the hospital separately from Mother on Monday morning and were still getting ready when she left. Barbie was finishing a telephone conversation, while I was in the bedroom cleaning out my purse. I had no intention of reliving the previous night's embarrassing moment when my brother Rich had watched as I fumbled through the clutter in my purse looking for the car keys.

"Why don't you clean that mess out," he had blurted out.

One by one, I took out the various items and placed them on the bed. When I came to my ink-stained pocket New Testament, I hesitated. There, positioned like a bookmark was a garment tag. Knowing I had not intentionally placed it there, I curiously opened up the little Bible to the see what scripture it had been marking. I read Luke 23:17–18, which was not illuminated to me. Still not satisfied it had somehow been placed accidentally, I opened it up once again. This time, my eyes were drawn, to the top of the opposite page—Luke 23:43: *"And Jesus replied, 'Today you will be with me in paradise. This is a solemn promise.'"*

"Praise the Lord!" I squealed in delight.

I intended to keep the Word private until I told Dad but found myself telling my sister who had come into the bedroom when she heard me squeal. She listened intently as I explained the scripture I had found marked and its significance. While she agreed that Dad did have a look of fright in his eyes, the message from God seemed a stretch for her faith.

Arriving at the hospital an hour later, the nurse on duty met us with encouraging news. "Your father seems to be doing better," she said optimistically. Barbie shot a puzzled glance at me, but said nothing. She did not need to, for I knew she was thinking. "Given this hopeful news, will you tell Dad what God said?" The nurse left the room, and my sister soon followed.

I understood Barbie's question because I had the same question. Which "word" would I believe? There was no question they contradicted one another. After a few minutes of mental wrangling between the two voices, I knew I must go with the "familiar voice of God." How thankful I was for the visible answer to my prayer; thankful I had asked for another confirmation.

Alone now with Dad, I pulled from my purse the small oval, pewter necklace with the cross on it having packed it before leaving home. I had carefully selected the necklace given me for Mother's Day last year from among the variety of crosses in my jewelry box. There was something special about this cross—I had never seen one quite like it. The engraved lines extending outward from the center of the cross, seemed to give it life as if rays of energy were being emitted.

Dangling the cross in front of Dad, I leaned over his head and read the scripture God had given me. The frightened look disappeared from his eyes at once, and he soon closed his eyes and fell asleep. Exhilarated from the experience, I fully expected him to die any minute.

The next morning when we visited Dad, the frightened look in Dad's eyes had not returned, and he was still very much alive. While

I was very thankful that Dad's eyes now had a look of peace, quite truthfully, I was very upset with God. "Didn't You tell me, 'Today you will be with me in paradise'?" I felt like a fool for stepping out in faith. What would my sister think? This was no small matter between God and me.

In the evening on Wednesday, February 6, I was visiting Dad with my brother Rich. We were standing beside his bed when Dad, still attached to the tubes, raised his arms up high above his head and was pointing upward.

"Look, Rich, he's trying to tell us something!" I said excitedly.

Nodding in agreement, Rich began pointing to objects on the hospital ceiling, to see which of them might be the subject of Dad's focus. Each time he pointed to an object, however, Dad shook his head, "No."

Feeling frustrated because Dad was not able to express his thoughts, I turned to my brother. "I know what we can do. I'll get a piece of paper out and write the letters of the alphabet on it. Then, I'll give Dad a pen and have him point to the letters to spell the words!"

Rich nodded his approval. I searched in my purse, found a small envelope and hurriedly wrote the letters in large block form. Holding the envelope in front of Dad, I handed him a pen.

Dad seemed to understand what we wanted him to do, but his shaking hand was unable to grip the pen tightly enough to follow through.

Rich and I stood silently at Dad's bedside, realizing he was unable to communicate to us what he was seeing. A few moments later, Mother returned. But, before we could say anything to her, she commented how "animated" Dad was.

Overhearing our conversation with Mother, the nurse replied, "People often hallucinate when they are in your father's condition."

Rich and I looked at each other in disbelief. That may be her interpretation, but we knew far more had been going on. We believed God had allowed Dad to see Jesus and his loved ones in Heaven and had been attempting to point them out to us to no avail. Further, I believed it was God's way of telling us and confirming to me that he was not going to hell. This was the sign I had asked for. This was His confirmation to me.

The next morning, I was home alone in my parent's apartment when the telephone rang. The caller identified himself as the male nurse Mother had hired to look after Dad when he came home from the hospital. "How is your father doing?"

"Well, they say he is doing better," I replied. After an awkward silence, he explained that another job "sort of came his way—a more permanent and year-round job." He confessed to me, he was in a bit of a quandary because he had made a commitment to Mother to take care of my father.

I hesitated for a moment, cautiously thinking how I might verbalize my deep feelings to him. "Well, I can't speak for Mom, but I don't think Dad will be coming home from the hospital."

"You know, I feel the same way," he said, breathing a sigh of relief. "All the while I was talking to your mother last Saturday, I was thinking to myself, 'I'll never be taking care of this man.'"

Sensing God had communicated to this stranger a similar message, I dared to share even more. I told him what Rich and I had experienced the night before, and how we felt certain Dad was already seeing Heaven.

"What church do you go to?" he asked in closing.

When I hung up the receiver, I sat quietly for a moment. "What would Mother say?" In a way, I had just "released" the person she had hired to take care of Dad. I felt as though the Lord was really pushing my faith to its limits. I had enough for a while. I was weary.

With Dad still in intensive care, on Sunday Barbie and I returned home to our families, leaving our brothers to help Mom with Dad. I was glad to escape. I needed to return home to our familiar routines of caring for husband and children. I was thankful to go back to the living.

Just as quickly, my thoughts returned to the present—February 22. During my secluded devotion time, talking to God with no distractions, I heard His voice. God's voice was unmistakable, yet not audible. His message transmitted in the thoughts of my mind. He was speaking to me about my desire to have a natural child.

"You will get pregnant and will give birth to a son, just as you desire."

Impulsively, I blurted out. "Can I have a daughter, too?" As soon as the words passed my lips, I recognized my ungrateful attitude. But there was no retracting my words. They had already left my lips.

God was silent.

Receiving no answer, I opened my Bible to see if God would reveal additional information to me through the Scriptures. Again, the pages opened to the story of Elizabeth and Mary. Again, I felt the strong impression that there was a parallel between Elizabeth and Mary, and Charlene and me. I felt strongly this was God's confirmation, that this event would indeed, take place.

In the meantime, God required some action on my part, some moving forward in faith and obedience. He instructed me to begin eliminating caffeinated coffee from my diet. Several days later, news reports issued warnings to pregnant women on the harmful effects of caffeine to the unborn baby.

"The Lord has told me that we are going to have a baby—a son," I announced joyfully to Art the next morning.

Staring at me in disbelief, he cocked his head skeptically. "He did?"

"Yes," I repeated excitedly, "While I was having my devotions, He told me that we would have a son."

The look on his face spoke volumes. He had tremendous difficulty believing that God would speak to me. Why would He tell me, and not Art, that I would get pregnant after all these years of infertility? Was it that he did not want to go along with this. . . . this so-called prophesy, in case it was false? Perhaps, he did not want to see me get my hopes up and be disappointed. I realized then I would have to rely on the support from my friends—friends who had the faith to believe.

The next day at church, a friend handed me a book she was supposed to give me sometime earlier but had forgotten to bring. In it were personal experiences of great women in the Bible. As I read I understood this was God's plan for me to read it this week. Sarah, Rebekah, Rachel, and Elizabeth were all barren, and God had blessed them with the gifts of babies—all boys. I remembered God's message to me nine years earlier:

You feel my anger has allowed this tragedy in your life, but read about my people in the Bible. Look at Sarah, Rebekah, Rachel, and Elizabeth. They were humiliated in the world for being barren, but favored by me. They were special. I never change, and I have set you aside in this way, too. Trust me.

On March 3, Dad passed from this world to his eternal home with Jesus. Amidst the sadness of goodbyes was peace. I thanked God for giving Dad five more years to live. During the extension, Dad had been reconciled with his daughters from his first marriage. Mother had gained two more daughters, and each of us children had gained two more sisters. I was thankful God had reconciled Dad to Himself and thankful that He had allowed me to know this wonderful news. Now, I looked forward to the future event of giving birth to a son as God had promised.

On March 11, during my evening devotions, I sensed God's voice speaking to me for the second time that day, the word *twins*. Was God telling me there would be two? The thought came to mind—a baby girl, too?

"Yes, I will also give you a daughter."

Turning to Scripture with great excitement, I read from Revelation 11 (4), the chapter was subtitled "The Two Witnesses." Each time I read the number two, it seemed illuminated to me. Believing God's message to me was, "You will become the parents of twins without further delay," I began praising God for His love for me and my family. The fact that we had twins on both sides of the family made it even more probable. Not only were Art's brother and sister twins, but twins had been born in my mother's family for the past three generations.

The next morning when I shared with Art that God had told me we would also have a daughter, he realized this "prophesy business" was not only not going away but, instead, it was even more complicated—more unbelievable. I sensed his faith did not allow him to believe any of it.

Were it not for God's periodic confirmations, Art's disbelief might have caused my own faith to falter. Yet, God was merciful and continued to give me reassurance for on Friday, March 14 during devotions, I turned again to scripture to hear from God about exciting events soon to take place. For the third time, I opened my Bible to Luke 1 and read about Elizabeth and Mary, and the babies that were to be born to them.

"Thank you, Jesus, for again confirming these events." I prayed, "Sometimes, I feel it is a dream, but by faith alone I *believe*. Praise God."

A few weeks later when in the drugstore to pick up a prescription, I began searching for "twin" birth announcements but found none. "Maybe we should have them printed," I thought as I ate breakfast with Ben the next morning. "Yes, that's what we'll do." On a piece of paper, I began to write a rough draft.

"With praise and thanksgiving to God, we rejoice at the birth of twins!"

In the following weeks, two different messages seemed to confirm God's answer. First, Mother mailed me two gifts purchased by her friend on a trip to the Philippines. The two bookends of the Virgin Mary holding baby Jesus resembled two embryos if you looked at them from a distance. The second gift I received from Charlene at a birthday party for another friend on March 29. I was surprised when she handed me two small gifts.

Thanking her for the unexpected gifts, I unwrapped them to find two small picture frames. In place of pictures, on one she had inscribed, "Bonnie, You are His . . . He is Love" The second, "Praise the Lord in Everything," one with a tiny fern, the other with a tiny bow. Immediately I recognized these as messages from the Lord confirming the prophesy He had given me. The tiny pictures would be a reminder of God's promise until it happened. Inside my heart was bursting with excitement, but I did not let on to my friends at the party. It was much too early to talk about, not yet, not to everyone. Now I knew that I must tell Charlene soon.

Early the next week I telephoned her. "Do you know why you gave me the little pictures?" I quizzed, "Or, why you gave me two and not one?"

For a moment, there was stillness. Finally she answered. "I don't know. I just felt inclined to give them to you. Why?"

Realizing she was not aware of their significance, I proceeded to explain the Prophesy. "I know there will be two—a boy and a girl!" I told her excitedly. "The fact that you gave me not one, but two pictures was significant and the fact that they were not the same—that one had a bow and the other one a fern—was God's confirmation to me. I believe they will be twins!"

Elated with the news, she promised to pray for me. I had no doubt that God had given her the faith to believe my story because she had given birth to a miracle baby. After Art's reaction, I needed someone to believe with me.

Next, I shared the revelation with Louise, for it was her intercessory prayer to the Lord on my behalf that started this chain of events. Both believed with me that I would give birth to not one, but two babies—twins! They continued to pray on my behalf, and we all looked forward to the fulfillment of God's promise.

Art remained skeptical and doubted I had really received a prophetic message from the Lord. Besides, he was perfectly content with the two children. There seemed no void in his heart. In fact, he once shared with me that he had always harbored a fear that having a natural child might mean having a child with a birth defect.

Believing I would immediately get pregnant, as each subsequent month passed with no pregnancy, I became increasingly despondent. Yet, each time I questioned the Lord about the matter, He reassured me with the same scriptures as before. By October, my faith began to waver. Having joined me on this faith journey, my close friends continued to pray for me.

Charlene called me on Monday, October 6, and told me while praying for me the day before she had asked God what she could do for me in addition to praying. God had instructed her to fast ten hours a week until I became pregnant. Elated to have this special role in the exciting event, she had begun her schedule of fasting. With renewed faith, we all continued to wait expectantly.

The next day during devotions, I opened my Bible to Micah 5:3: (5) "Yahweh is therefore going to abandon them till the time when she who is to give birth, gives birth."

Once again, I felt the strong impression that the day would come for fulfillment of the prophesy. Knowing I needed to rest in Christ and patiently wait, I did my best to redirect my focus. The only successful diversion was to rededicate myself to working on my manuscript. The process of writing seemed to reenergize that gift within me. The more I wrote, the more enthused I became. Although I was careful not to call myself a writer, I was definitely trying on the "writing cloak" to see if it fit me.

During this time, when Charlene was praying and fasting for me, there were times during her own devotion times when the Lord would direct her to send me words of encouragement. One day in October, the message came in the form of two devotions typewritten on a single page:

FROM THE DESK OF:

Charlene Gierkey

To Bonnie:

EXTRA WORK (Oct. 10, 1980)

I am your Helper. At the end of your present
path lie all these blessings. So trust and know that
I am leading you. Step with a firm step of confidence
into Me into each unknown day. Take every duty and
every interruption as of My appointment. You are MY
servant. Serve Me as simply, cheerfully and readily
as you expect others to serve you. Do you blame the
servant who avoids extra work, who complains about
being called from one task to do one less liked? Do
you feel you are ill served by such an one? Then what
of Me? Is not that how you so often serve Me? Think
of this. Lay it to heart and view your day's work
in this light.

SHAME AND DISTRESS (Oct. 11, 1980)

See, My children, that even in distress,
the first step is Praise. Before you cry in your
distress, bless the Lord; even when troubles seem to
overwhelm you. That is My Divine order of approach.
Observe this always. In the greatest distress, search
until you find cause for thankfulness. Then bless and
thank. You have thus established a line of communication between yourself and Me. Along that line let
your cry of distress follow...Thus you will find I do
My part, and deliverance will be sure. Oh! the gladness
of heart. Lightened you will be, the burden rolled
away, as the result of looking to Me. The shame and
distress will be lifted too. That is always the
second step. First right with Me, and then you will
be righted too in the eyes of men.

Charlene's 2 Devotions

The following day, Sunday, October 12, 1980, the second part of the first reading spoke to my heart: Habakkuk 2:2–4 (6)

> Then the Lord answered me and said:
> "Write the vision and make it plain on tablets, that he may run who reads it.
> For the vision is yet for an appointed time; But at the end it will speak, and it will not lie.
> Though it tarries, wait for it; Because it will surely come, it will not tarry.
> Behold, the proud, His soul is not upright in him;
> But the just shall live by his faith." (NKJV)

Another letter came from Charlene with a little handmade certificate:

Charlene's Certificate

Chapter 18

WAITING UPON THE LORD

"A time for giving birth"
Ecclesiastes 3:2 (JB)

*I*n April 1981, the pastor of our church posted a note in the church bulletin seeking two volunteers to serve as lay delegates to our Synod's district convention in Columbus, Ohio in May. While I knew little about a church convention, I did know it would be an opportunity to escape from household chores and enjoy the luxury of someone else preparing my meals for a few days. I could not see any reason why I should not volunteer.

When I received the large three-ring binder with the upcoming convention's business, I realized there would be some work involved, as well. Leafing through the convention workbook, beginning with the agenda, one item caught my attention. Recently released, Iranian hostage, Kathryn Koob, would be addressing the convention. A spark of energy ignited within me!

My thoughts flashed back to the attractive certificate framed on my wall showing my membership in the Christian Writer's Guild and the press card. When I had joined the Writer's Guild months ago, I had no motive other than loosely associating myself with other Christian writers. I remembered well the exhilaration when I first caught sight of my name imprinted on the certificate and the press card. I also remembered smiling proudly as I tucked it away in my wallet.

What prevented me from taking advantage of this opportunity to interview Kathryn and write a news article? After all, didn't the certificate officially recognize me as a writer and have my name on it? Fired up with enthusiasm, I mustered my courage and called the synod office to find out how to reach her. With her address in hand, I went to the typewriter.

> I have read about the faith, which sustained you during your captivity, and as a Christian writer feel your story has been an effective witness to many people. If your schedule permits during your stay in Columbus, I would like very much to interview you about your unique experience.

Within a few days, I received a call inviting me to attend the upcoming press conference in Columbus, as her schedule did not permit a private interview. The caller warned I would have to be on guard. There would be no advance notice, just a brief announcement from the convention podium of the time and place at Capital University.

I hung up, grinning from ear to ear. "Press conference, I am invited to the press conference! This is even better than I could have hoped for," I squealed in delight.

The wheels of my mind turned, rewinding to the stored data. The camera focused on a scene of a frenzied, fast-paced White House press conference I had observed with awe from time to time on television. The camera moved in for a closer shot. I saw a female reporter; a professional woman, dressed in business attire, ready and alert with notebook and pen in hand. No doubt, she had gained access to this prestigious gathering with an individualized press card!

Hoping to revive my high-school shorthand skills, I rummaged through the basement looking for my old shorthand textbook. After several days of practicing, however, I concluded my skills were too rusty after eighteen years to trust with such important information. Instead, I purchased new batteries for our tape recorder and asked Art to give me a few lessons of instruction, so I could tape the press conference as a back-up plan to my notes. With the intention of submitting an article for the newspaper, perhaps including a picture, I learned that

I should use black-and-white film. Not being a camera buff, I decided not to take Art's expensive camera, but felt I would be more at ease handling the little camera I had recently acquired with a cereal box top for $4.95. Last, I read several published articles about Kathryn's hostage experience and prepared a list of fourteen questions.

I sat near the front at the convention, so I would not miss the announcement. As soon I heard it, I gathered up my belongings and raced to the administration building. I felt like Superwoman, making a quick identity change, except for me, the cloak I was shedding was my cloak of timidity, and I was assuming a bold new one as a reporter. Once there, as nonchalantly as possible, I presented my press card to the person standing guard at the door. My sense of relief after successfully gaining entrance quickly evaporated as I gazed into the room. The large conference table was rapidly filling with frenzied reporters from the major television networks and national publications, as well as local media.

I scrambled to find a choice seat around the conference table, all the while watching the other journalists out of the corner of my eye to see what came next. Once their seats were secured, they began setting up tape recorders in front of them and taking out notebooks and pens. Camera crews from major television networks were setting up large cameras, lights, and more elaborate equipment, placing their microphones directly in front of Kathryn's seat at the head of the table.

Although Fear threatened, *"Who are you to think you are any match for these experienced reporters?"* I pushed Fear aside. I pulled my chair to the table and set up my tape recorder in front of me. While the room filled, I looked over my list of prepared questions and prioritized them.

When Kathryn entered, the room instantly quieted. After a few brief remarks, she began taking questions. Abruptly, the sophisticated atmosphere was transformed into chaotic free-for-all. No mother taught manners here; there were no politely raising hands. The procedure appeared to be to shout out a question, and hope yours could draw Kathryn's attention. At first I was speechless, but quickly realized if I hoped to have any of my questions answered, I would have to be very bold and assertive.

"Lord, You're going to have to help me. Give me the courage to do what must be done." Immediately, my spirit was inspired with new energy, and I heard my own voice shout out my first question in two parts.

"What did you do at first, when you recognized you were discouraged?"

"How did you keep from going into depression?"

Kathryn detailed her strategy at length while everyone listened intently.

> I found that it was usually a case of self-pity. To combat my thinking pattern, I would deliberately set out to remind myself that there were a lot of people in the world a lot worse off than I am. More important, I knew that back in the United States and elsewhere around the world, there was a network of family, friends, and a much wider circle of Christians, who were praying and supporting me. It was as if there was a safety net, with each of you being at the knot in that net stretching out to reach each other in support as we lift each other up in prayer. When I really got discouraged, I could bounce down off that net and rest there, being carried and supported in prayer. (1)

When the frenzy ended, I finished my notes and gathered my belongings. I had been able to ask, and have answered, only two of my questions.

"Don't be discouraged," the Lord reminded. "You will have one more chance to submit questions when she addresses the full convention later this afternoon."

After returning home, I wrote my article, focusing on her response to my first two questions, questions she had answered in detail. The *Traverse City Record Eagle* accepted it and published it on June 12, 1981. I could not deny that seeing my name on the byline was nearly as awesome as getting the story out.

Just as my writing career was igniting, I began to sense an urging to return to work part-time. Logically, the timing seemed wrong.

School was out, and Ben and Danielle were home. I had no desire to go back, even though I had continuously struggled with the tight family budget since I left Chef Pierre two years before. Money had been so scarce we could not afford family health insurance. If I returned to work there, we would have family coverage. But, I had to be sure. I could not take this step unless I knew the detour was God's plan and not the Enemy. I knew there would be considerably less time to work on my manuscript if I returned to work.

"Lord," I prayed, "If You want me to go back to work, You will have to have them call me and ask me to return. Then I'll know for certain that this is Your will for me at this time."

The call came on June 18, when I recognized the personnel supervisor's voice. "Would you be interested in coming back part-time? We're in need of someone to work about twenty hours. You can choose your schedule."

During my devotions that day, the Lord confirmed that regardless of timing, this was what He had planned. "I am doing exactly what the Father told me" (John 14:31). (2)

Two days later, our couple's prayer group met. The scripture given me in my devotions that morning was John 16:32. (3) In the verse, Jesus was talking to His disciples, but God's message to me was the same. "Listen; the time will come, in fact it has come already, when you will be scattered, each going his own way . . ."

The message to our group was confirmed when Charlene gave each of us a piece of a tiny cord and explained that trials would be coming for each of us. By the end of August, amidst the celebrations of our sixteenth wedding anniversary and my thirty-sixth birthday, the doctor confirmed I was, indeed, pregnant! As word of my pregnancy became known, family and friends shared our joy. Having been in on God's plan from the beginning, Charlene and Louise were doubly elated! For those in our close circle, the news came as no surprise as they had been watching and waiting for more than a year.

For me, getting pregnant was only one part of God's promise. He had said there would be two—a boy and a girl. Believing God required me to tell others before it happened as a witness to my faith; I was compelled to tell people outside our close circle.

213

On my first visit to the obstetrician, I told the nurse taking my history and doing the lab work, it was supposed to be twins. Looking up from her paperwork, she smiled, and resumed taking notes. When I met with the doctor, I told him, too. He seemed to take me a little more seriously and noted my comments in his record. Throughout my pregnancy, the doctor searched for two heartbeats but heard only one, and I grew despondent. When I returned home, I would reread the scriptures God had given me and look at the two bookends and the two picture frames, and my faith would be encouraged.

When I returned home from my five-month check-up and the doctor still heard only one heartbeat, I opened my Bible to Hebrews 11:1: (4) "Only faith can guarantee the blessings that we hope for or prove the existence of the realities that at present remain unseen." I made a notation:

> 10/30/81, 5 mos. pregnant, and waiting for the Dr. to confirm twins. I really needed to hear this today as I was disappointed yesterday when the Dr. couldn't hear 2 heartbeats.

Each time I returned from a doctor's appointment, I reported to my close friends that the doctor heard only one heartbeat. Yet, they continued to believe with me. As my due date neared, Charlene had a baby shower for me and gave me matching red and green plaid pants with white shirts; one for a boy, and one for a girl. I remained steadfast in my belief until only one baby was born—a son, Matthew Thomas.

With only one baby, my spirit sank and my faith shaken. Outwardly, I tried to conceal the feelings deep in my heart. I felt so guilty! Instead of being thankful for a healthy baby boy, my unfulfilled expectation overshadowed the blessed event.

After Art left the hospital, I was alone in my room and lost no time in calling out to God in the stillness of the night. "Where is the baby girl You also promised?" I questioned, through a veil of salty tears. "All along I've based my faith walk on Your still, small voice. Now, I can't be sure the voice I'm hearing is really Yours!"

The next morning as I stared at the precious baby in my arms, I still could not believe I could have misunderstood God for all those months. "I am a complete fool; my credibility as a Christian shattered. What in the world happened? Where did the breakdown occur? There's much more at stake than the number of babies," I thought, "The bottom line is my breakdown in communication with God."

As the questions arose in the consciousness of my mind, God's voice, though not audible, reached me. "Bonnie, I know you do not understand, and your faith is being tested. But I want you to recall everything you know to be true about Me, everything you have learned about Me. As you do, I want you to write them down as visible evidence."

Finding a piece of paper, I sat in my hospital bed and made a list of all that God had taught me.

God is love.
God never fails.
Delays are not denials.
With God, nothing is impossible.
God is not a liar.
God is Truth.
God is present everywhere.
God is All-Knowing.
God loves me.

When I left the hospital, I added the list to my faith-building arsenal along, with the tiny picture frames from Charlene and the two bookends from Mother. The visible reminders were crucial for the spiritual warfare I faced inside myself and outside. Although I did not understand, I knew with God, there was hope for the future. He was not finished with me yet.

More than twenty years later, while reading from Oswald Chambers, *My Utmost for His Highest*, I read his devotion titled, "Discernment of Faith" (10/31) as follows:

Faith by its very nature must be tried, and the real trial of faith is not that we find it difficult to trust

God, but that God's character has to be cleared in our own minds. Faith in its actual working out has to go through spells of unsyllabled isolation. (5)

There was only one friend, to whom I confided my thoughts. I poured my heart out to Charlene in a telephone conversation one day in early April. Mostly, she listened quietly while I confessed my disappointment. A few days later, a letter arrived:

> Not to appear as one of Job's friends, that's exactly where I find myself when I try to reach out and help you cope with the moments. In other words, I've found that not one of your friends, all with good intentions (so we think), will be able to heal the hurt you are now experiencing. We are human, and you are beyond the reach of human hand. How can any of us know what it is when we have not experienced what you have—how short of love we all do fall! You need a bridge from abandonment to vindication of hope—*Color of the Night* (6) a real visit from God Himself! It is this book Art gave us I'm reading that suddenly turned on a light. We are seeing into a great mystery—the mystery of walking with God. And my prayer for you and all of us who share with you is that nothing of all this may be lost upon us—that we will all walk deeper with the only One who knows *the* Person who can lead us on to final victory. Perhaps the thing that strikes me most is the way the Lord offered Job's friends the opportunity to change and grow with Job—to go deeper into the ways and mysteries of God to not give up and to say "I still am with God!" I'm still on His side. God gave Job's friends this opportunity to enlarge their perspective—to larger risks of faith—but they drew back. In drawing back, they not only rejected Job but also harassed and attacked him.

And so Charlene, along with my other close friends prayed to God to sustain me, as my faith was tested. Knowing my situation was a topic of discussion, yet not wanting to engage in conversation, I withdrew from the world around me as much as was possible and focused my attention on my family. Resolving not to let my disappointment with God affect my feelings toward our son, I consciously made an effort to give Matthew extra attention. Whenever I would begin to feel depressed, I would hold my baby tightly. Only God knew my heart.

One day, when the weather was warm, I ventured outside to take Matthew for a stroll around our circle subdivision. On the far side of the circle, a neighbor I scarcely knew opened her door and shouted, "I see the Lord only gave you one!"

Her words stung my ears. Could she really have said that? Close to tears, I pushed the stroller back home and went inside. Although I was angry with her, I knew she had only verbalized what others were thinking. How thankful I was that I had quit my job one month before Matthew was born. I did not have to face all my coworkers each day. However, there were still people to face at church every Sunday.

I was very vocal to Art about wanting to leave the church and go elsewhere. For different reasons, he was at the same point. So, when I continued to pressure him, it wasn't too long before he agreed that our family would be better off elsewhere. We transferred our family membership to another mission congregation across town that summer.

Returning to work on my book manuscript became a welcome diversion. In June, I submitted an introduction and three sample chapters. A month later I received an encouraging letter from the publisher, outlining some positive suggestions before sending it back. I retreated to my writing closet during the baby's naptime, quite content to be alone in my world, caring for my family, writing, and avoiding the outside world.

God did not allow me to continue in this pattern indefinitely. One afternoon, I was impressed to call the new Christian radio station; WLJN, and volunteer my services for several hours a week. That would be fun, I thought dreamily. Yes, working at the station would be exciting. Perhaps I could assist in the office with clerical work, filing, and so on. Tingling with excitement, I hurried to the telephone.

I was surprised to hear the voice of the station manager, who I knew from the small praise group that used to meet at Bethlehem Lutheran Church. It was in that small group that Bob had been given the prophesy about the Christian radio station.

"I'd like to do some volunteer work at the station. I was thinking a few hours a week, maybe work in the office?"

"Well, it depends on what we need to have done."

I took a few seconds to gather my thoughts, taken aback at his response.

"Okay. What do you need?"

"Well," he said slowly and deliberately, "We need someone to come in every other Sunday from 2–6 in the afternoon to work the controls, spin records, and so forth . . . Would you be interested?"

"You're kidding," I laughed.

"No," Bob's tone was serious. "We have a real need for someone to relieve the volunteer that works the shift before. It's hard to get volunteers for Sunday afternoon."

Realizing he was not joking, my heart sank and a sick feeling welled up in the pit of my stomach. Me, work the controls at a radio station and spin records? I could not believe what God was asking of me. The job description just did not fit; not me, anyway. I was the last person for a job like this. I was not mechanical! It was five years before I discovered my sewing machine sewed in reverse!

But, if this need was the reason God directed me to call, how could I say no? Despite these negative feelings, I knew I could not ignore the Lord's voice.

"Well . . . I guess if that's what you need. I've never done anything like this before. I'm not very mechanical."

Bob reassured me I could do the job and explained I would not be on my own at the station until after a period of training.

A few weeks later, armed with a notebook for taking detailed notes and a stomach full of butterflies, I pointed my car up the steep road toward the small radio station at the top of radio hill. "Okay, Lord, I'm believing You will help me do this job for which I am unequipped. If You can do this, I *know* You can help me do anything else You want me to do!"

Every other Sunday for the next eighteen months, I drove up the steep hill to the station, praying my car would not slide off the road. When winter came, I would drive past the road to the station to a point farther down the highway and turn around. Each time I would pray no oncoming traffic would be in the path as I accelerated speed and angled off to the left across the opposite lane and up the hill. I knew if I slowed down at all, I would not make the hill.

When my shift began, I exchanged greetings with the volunteer before me and was on my own. The first two hours I played records, alternating between two turntables. Unlike the more modern radio stations with a schedule of what to play, I could choose from a large assortment and manually queue up one record while another record was playing. At various intervals, I played some short commercial spots, an advertisement for a radio show or a public service announcement. On the hour, I had to flip a switch to go to network news from Moody Broadcasting in Chicago. Later in the afternoon, I could relax and listen to Billy Graham's Hour of Decision.

On the days I worked at the station, my butterflies began Sunday morning and continued until my shift ended. I was fearful because I knew I was alone and totally dependent on the Lord. If anything went wrong, I did not have the technical knowledge to fix it. I was so intense about doing my job correctly; if the telephone rang during my shift, it always startled me. If I wanted to leave the room to go to the bathroom or get a drink, I had to make certain I was back before the record ended. If not, the audience would hear silence. Silence was not good. The Lord was faithful and showed me with Him all things are possible. Only once did I have to call someone in to help with a minor mechanical problem.

God used the quiet time at the radio station to bolster my sagging faith. The whole Sunday afternoon was a constant feeding of my spirit—a solid block of time when I pulled away from the outside world, with no interruptions and drew nigh to the Lord. The Christian music and network programs, especially Billy Graham's Hour of Decision uplifted me.

As I strove to move on with my life, my closest friendships changed. The prophesy Charlene had delivered telling us our prayer group would scatter was fulfilled. Charlene, Louise, and I soon drifted apart for a variety of reasons. Charlene was expecting a baby, occupied with motherhood and their family business. Louise was busy with her medical practice and her own family. I knew I was not the only one affected by recent events. After all, they believed with me, and their faith tested, as well as mine. I knew they had once respected my walk with the Lord, and now felt my credibility was damaged.

As far as any thoughts of having another baby—another pregnancy—no one wanted to hear about it or talk about what God might have been speaking to me. Yet, in my heart, that was the avenue to vindication—to a resolution. There was more hinging on this than a baby. My whole relationship with the Lord was at stake; my whole walk of faith.

One day as we walked together, I found myself sharing my deepest feelings with a new friend, Amy, a neighbor who lived on the other side of our circle. I talked about my experience: the prophesy and the circumstances surrounding the birth of our son. I explained my belief that the only way it made any sense was if God were to give me another pregnancy and a daughter would be born. Otherwise, it was irreconcilable, and I would remain unredeemed. God had said two children would be born. I had not heard the Lord incorrectly. Although I had second-guessed those clear confirmations, my faith was nudging me again to believe that I had heard correctly. God would keep his Word—we would have a daughter. Art was even more skeptical this time. Perhaps he did not want to see me so despondent, to believe only to have my hopes dashed.

Amy was given the same faith by God to stand with me. After a year or more went by and no pregnancy had occurred, it was Amy whom God called upon to fast one day a week for me until the prophesy would be fulfilled. It was August 1985, the month of my fortieth birthday and our twentieth wedding anniversary, when I learned I was pregnant for the second time. It had been over three years since Matthew's birth, and I was thrilled! I felt God's favor upon me once again and glowed with the joy from within me. The picture on my new driver's license, taken the week of my birthday captured that glow. Learning of the pregnancy, family and friends rejoiced with us. My sister hosted a surprise birthday party for me, with my entire family helping us celebrate.

After over three years of feeling humiliation, because the prophesy had not been as I understood, I was filled with joy at the prospect of God's promise being fulfilled. I understand more deeply the vow of Hannah in I Samuel 1:10–11:

> And she was in bitterness of soul, and prayed to the Lord and wept in anguish. Then she made a vow and said, "O Lord of hosts, if You will indeed look on the affliction of Your maidservant and remember me, and not forget Your maidservant , but will give Your maidservant a male child, then I will give him to the Lord all the days of his life, and no razor shall come upon his head." (NKJV) (7)

While I had not made such a promise to God, I too, was so thankful, I was exploding inside with gratitude and praise. My spirits soaring and my faith restored, I knew I had to respond to His gentle nudging for over a year. In May of the previous year, I had attended Concerned Women for America's (CWA) Michigan Conference, and felt God wanted me to respond to their appeal for Prayer/Action chapter leaders in Michigan. I did not view myself as a leader, but I believed God would enable me to do whatever was in His plan for our area.

The first week in September, I wrote a letter to Mildred (Mickey) Kallman, Michigan Representative for CWA:

> It has been nearly a year since I received your August-September newsletter. Although you have not heard from me, I have continued to be active in CWA on a national level. I have spent considerable time this past year praying about God's direction for me in regard to my involvement in CWA, both in beginning a prayer chapter here in Traverse City and volunteering as a Home District Liaison in the 535 Program. I do feel that God is urging me to pursue these issues now and have been in contact with the Washington office regarding the 535 Program.

The prayer chapter I have in mind at this time would begin with a cross section from a number of denominations, not necessarily one from the Lutheran church of which I am a member . . . One factor, which will no doubt curtail some of my activities, especially travel, is the fact that we are expecting in March. Since this is only my second pregnancy in twenty years of marriage, I am quite cautious.

Mickey Kallman wrote me a return letter dated September 9, 1985:

Your note is such an encouragement to us. We've been praying for a person to coordinate Grand Traverse County's ladies and encourage them to establish CWA contacts in their churches as well. We'll pray that the pregnancy will go smoothly and that God will raise up other women to do the things you can't pursue.

After receiving a list of women in our county on the national CWA mailing list, I began making contacts. I sent out press releases, notifying the media of our first meeting on November 21 at All Faith's Chapel on the State Hospital grounds. The Christian radio station, WLJN, where I worked as a volunteer, interviewed me on an afternoon radio program. *The Traverse City Record-Eagle* requested an interview, resulting in a lengthy and informative article titled, "Concerned Women Chapter Forming," (8) detailing the history of CWA and ending with the original five and a half lines of my press release. The publicity was beyond anything I could have imagined.

As a 535 Home District Congressional Liaison for CWA, I was flooded with information on the national, state, and local levels. In this position (named for the 435 Representatives and 100 Senators in the Capitol) I would be involved in coordinating prayer chapters in our area to pray, call, and write on specific issues coming before our legislators, both on the state and national levels. My position gave me the opportunity to participate in a local coalition with leaders of other Christian groups: Right to Life, Michigan Alliance of Families, and the National Federation of Decency. From the beginning, educational issues were always in the forefront.

With all the information coming my way, and experience writing letters to the editor of the newspaper, I was quick to respond to one reporter's challenge to the National Federation of Decency in his weekly column:

> Let's see what effect pornography really has on the rate of rape and child sexual abuse. Let's see the links between pornography and abuse of women. Let's see what you can do to overturn the conventional wisdom that pornography is a "victimless crime." (9)

As far as I was concerned, his challenge fell directly on me. In fact, I had only recently received a mailing that answered all of his questions. I gathered the information together and sent off my first forum piece titled, "The Link between Pornography and Crime" on December 9, 1985. (10)

By the end of December, it was becoming cumbersome to get close enough to the turntable at the radio station and all the controls. Additionally, I needed to spend more time home, preparing for the birth of our baby. Although I believed it would be a girl, every time the doctor listened to the baby's heartbeat, he would tell me it sounded like a boy. Hearing this at each appointment left me downcast for a few days until I could have time to spend with the Lord and be reminded once again of the prophesy. Hadn't God said this would be a baby girl?

It was Easter week when I went to the doctor for my final appointment. The baby was a week overdue, and because I was so large, the doctor sent me to have an ultrasound to rule out the possibility of twins. He didn't want to get into the delivery room with a forty-year-old mother considered to be high risk anyway and be surprised.

When I went for the ultrasound, the technician looked at the pictures and then sent me to the bathroom. She wanted to see if the baby would "void" as well. I did so and then returned to the table for more pictures.

"What do the pictures show?" I inquired after she had resumed her ultrasound and was gazing into the computer screen, which was in a position not visible to me.

"This one will be good at the bar," she joked. "Your doctor will call you with the results later this evening."

"Yeah," I nodded and returned to the dressing room. Her off-hand remark about my baby being good at the bar did not serve to humor me as she had intended. I was thankful Mom had arrived a few days early to help with the other children. At this moment in my life, I felt like a child myself and was glad to return to the loving arms of my mother. She would be there to reassure me that everything would be all right just as she had always done. Her strong faith would sustain me and encourage me as I tried not to let negative thoughts creep into my mind as we awaited the doctor's call.

Later that evening, the doctor called me. The ultrasound had revealed our baby had an enlarged kidney. Worse yet, there could be more problems only evident once the baby was born. On Good Friday, the doctor opened his office to meet with us for a final examination to determine whether they would take the baby by Caesarean section or allow me to deliver naturally. The final decision was to allow a normal delivery.

We were both devastated, waiting for the impending birth. The doctors already knew the baby was in trouble, and it was possible there were other problems. My heart was so heavy; I cried off and on for the next several days and was on the verge of tears the rest of the time. There was no way I could go to church on Easter Sunday. Art took the other children while I stayed home with Mother. Anxiously, I awaited signs of labor. How could Art have known that natural children would pose this risk? My father had also mentioned it some years ago—long before Matthew was born. Did they somehow have a premonition years ago that this day would come?

On Monday morning, my doctor called to see how I was feeling.

"Any signs of labor yet?" he asked. "Do you feel like you might be going into labor soon?"

"No, I feel fine," I assured him.

He seemed relieved. "In that case, I think I'll go home and get some rest. I've been up all weekend delivering babies. I'm really tired."

When I did go into labor later that night, another doctor in the practice was on call. We went in just before midnight, and by four o'clock I was in the delivery room and ready to deliver. The doctor had just arrived.

Between contractions, I began to sense the environment seemed much too matter-of-fact for the potential problems the baby might have. Should not some precautions be necessary? Was it safe to assume that these two doctors had communicated the serious nature of our baby's health? Finally, lifting my head I blurted out, "You *do* know that this baby has problems?"

The doctor stared at me in shock, "No, I don't know anything about the baby's problems!" Immediately, he exited the room to call my doctor. When he returned to the delivery room, several other medical personnel were with him. At this point, I felt we were as ready as we could be, and the only thing I could do to help my baby was to proceed with labor.

I tried to block out all other thoughts than my immediate assignment—bringing this baby into the world. Everything else was out of my hands. Just after four o'clock in the morning our baby girl, Traci Louise, was born weighing nearly ten pounds. I breathed a sigh of relief when they examined her and assured us that there were no other visible defects. I looked at the tiny baby placed in my arms. No one would ever have guessed that this little one with a full head of dark hair could have anything wrong with her. She appeared normal in every respect.

A few hours later, Traci was taken from the nursery to have tests run to find out the extent of her kidney problems. Later that morning, the urologist came in to give me a report.

"The pictures show Traci has a duplicated collecting system," he explained as he scribbled a drawing on a piece of paper. "She has two ureters on the left side. One is blocked and the other doesn't have a valve. That's why the kidney is enlarged. The urine doesn't completely empty into the bladder but swishes back into the kidney." He stopped, looking to see my reaction.

I continued staring at the drawing, choking back tears and wishing Art was here to hear the diagnosis. "What can be done for her; what comes next?"

"I'll make an appointment for her with a pediatric urology specialist at the University of Michigan Hospital, in Ann Arbor. As soon as he can see her, he can run further tests to see what can be done. Dr. Bloom is an excellent doctor and was one of my instructors at the University of Michigan Hospital. Do you have any questions?"

"No, but I'll call my husband. I'm sure he'll have some." As soon as the doctor left, I called home to break the news to Art.

When he arrived at the hospital, I showed Art the diagram Dr. Gillette had drawn, and explained our daughter's situation. "Dr. Gillette seems to think it is a fixable problem," I said as optimistically as I could.

Dr. Gillette scheduled Traci's appointment with Dr. Bloom soon after we had come home from the hospital and did his best to prepare us for the experience before us. As we approached the large hospital complex adjacent to the University of Michigan housing Mott's Children's Hospital, we understood why he had described it as a Mecca. It was an intimidating scene. Seeing children of all ages with so many different problems was depressing for both of us. Releasing our tiny new baby to the doctors and nurses for the tests was also difficult.

Finally, several hours later, the test results completed, we met with Dr. Bloom. "She will need surgery," he said putting the pictures up on a screen so we could view the results. "But. . . . we'll have to wait until she is a little older. In the meantime, we'll put her on an antibiotic that she'll need to take daily to prevent an infection. We'll do the surgery in two phases, the first at six months of age when we'll take out the blocked ureter. Then when she's around two or three, we'll need to rebuild the valve system. She'll need to be on medication to prevent infection until after the second surgery.

Leaving the hospital, we were somewhat relieved. Although we knew we faced two major surgeries ahead, we were hopeful our daughter would be able to live a normal life. The doctor told us had we not discovered her kidney problems on the ultrasound before she was born; the ultrasound to rule out twins, we would not have known there was any problem until she became very sick with an infection. Then it would be a problem clearing up the infection before they could operate, and it would be much more complicated and risky for her.

When I notified the CWA prayer chapter that the September 25, "Call to Pray" meeting was postponed until October as Traci's first surgery was September 23 at the U of M Hospital, I asked them to remember her in their prayers. There was never a time I felt as helpless as the moment I had to let go of our baby, lying in the hospital bed with her stuffed animals by her side, as the double doors closed behind her and she was wheeled into surgery. I sat silently beside Art in the waiting room, reading my Bible and praying—praying that God would direct the doctors in their work and that the surgery would be successful. We all praised God when the surgery was over and was not nearly as extensive as the doctor had expected.

In the months and years that followed, we and our family and friends continued to pray that God would watch over Traci and safely bring her through the surgery to repair her body. It was a test for our faith as we watched her grow, but God was faithful in walking with us on the journey. Her second surgery was completed on schedule before she began preschool and was also successful. By the time she reached her teens, follow-up tests revealed the rebuilt valve system had healed remarkably.

Chapter 19

DEPLOYING MY SPIRITUAL GIFTS

"A time for building"
Ecclesiastes 3:3 (JB)

*T*hankful God had answered our prayers and was continuing
to heal Traci, I returned to my activities with renewed faith
and wrote several more forum articles. In September 1987, our newspaper came out with the front-page news on the firing of the Traverse
City State Hospital Chief, Martin Nolan. Martin's wife was my close
friend Amy. In fact, as Amy and I walked each day, I had been privy
to considerable information about the events leading up to the firing.
As her spirits were dragged down by the negative publicity and I
saw the other side of the story was not being told, I felt God nudging
me to write another forum piece, telling the story from Martin's
perspective. This time it was necessary to spend considerable time
researching the facts and reading hearing transcripts.

When the newspaper received my first draft of the piece, Mike
Ready, the managing editor called me to schedule a meeting. Before
he would publish it, he wanted to see my supporting documentation.

I gathered all my files into my briefcase and walked into the
newspaper office.

"Oh Lord," I prayed. "You'll have to give me the words. I've
never done anything like this before."

Mike ushered me into a small conference room with a round table.

228

Looking me straight in the eyes, he asked. "Is Mr. Nolan paying you to write this?"

"Oh, no. . . . It's nothing like that." I said shaking my head, trying to remain calm even though shocked at his first question.

As he began to relax, I began again.

"Well, actually," I said slowly and feeling a bit uneasy at the direction of this conversation. "I've already been paid." Mr. Ready suddenly sat straight up in his chair, preparing to hear my confession.

"You see, his wife is my best friend. She prayed and fasted one day a week until I became pregnant with my youngest child, Traci. When I saw her pain, I knew this was something I could do for her because she has been talking about this case and the events leading up to the firing for months."

For a moment he was speechless, shocked by my response. When he resumed his questioning, there were no more questions about my motivation, but he proceeded to question me about the case. The editor changed only one word in the entire piece—"reportedly." I learned an important word in the publishing business. At the bottom of the forum article, published October 5, 1987 (1), I noticed two asterisks and a note. The newspaper had contacted Martin's attorney, his brother, to ask him to verify some of the facts in my story. He did.

Martin sent a copy of the published article to his brother, and after reading it, he called Martin with a message to relay to me.

"Tell Bonnie Newhouse to 'cease and desist.'" I learned another important phrase. But I did not let his comment trouble me. Martin was happy to have his side of the story printed and Amy's despondency had been lifted. I was at peace.

In addition to CWA, I had gradually become more involved on parent committees in the public school system. It was not something I set out to do, but it simply fell into place. In the fall of 1986, a newsletter had come home with Ben and Danielle from the junior high school. What caught my attention was a notice to parents about the upcoming open house with an invitation to join the junior high citizen's advisory committee. I could not imagine why I felt a tugging to join that committee—nor did I have any interest in doing so. I was perfectly contented tucked away in my writing closet, working diligently on my book manuscript. Yet, when the tugging continued, I had to be sure the sensing was, indeed, from the Lord.

"All right, God," I acknowledged. "I'll do it, but only if I can be certain it is You speaking to me and not the enemy trying to distract me. I'll 'throw out a fleece.' I'll go to the open house; however, if You also want me to go to the advisory meeting, You'll have to cause the chairperson, a mother with whom I was acquainted but not particularly close, to personally extend the invitation to attend the advisory meeting. If that happens, I'll know without a doubt for whatever Your reason, this is something You want me to do."

Satisfied with my proposal, I went to the junior high open house. When I spotted the refreshment table, I breathed a sigh of relief. A cup of coffee and a sweet treat would give me a lift and put me at ease in these unfamiliar surroundings. I reached for a cookie and looked up to see the woman referenced in the fleece.

"Hi, Bonnie," she said smiling, "We're looking for parents to join the citizen's advisory committee . . . Our next meeting is . . ."

I felt out of place in the group of policymakers. Most were stylishly dressed, professional people, who seemed well acquainted with one another. For the life of me, I could not understand why God would have me waste my time like this. Month after month, I listened but contributed little.

Only a few parents attended the May meeting, when representatives to the district advisory council, (DAC) were elected. I might have stayed away myself except I had to drive across town to take Danielle to a choir rehearsal. I learned the DAC was comprised of one parent representative from each of the district's elementary schools, as well as one parent from each grade in junior and senior high schools. The only requirement for membership was the parent had to have a child in the grade represented.

"It's not difficult," encouraged the chairperson, looking for volunteers. "It just means you have to attend one more meeting a month and represent the junior high."

When no one else volunteered to be the eighth grade representative, I raised my hand. "Danielle will be in the eighth grade next year. I can do it."

By the fall of 1987, I was beginning to feel a little more at ease in the school environment. Attending monthly meetings of the DAC, as well as the Jr. High CAC, a few things were beginning to come into focus.

I listened, as parents and teachers fumed after learning school administration officials were proceeding with plans to change to a middle-school concept to solve the overcrowding in our public schools. Their plan was to move sixth graders from elementary schools to middle schools and ninth graders to high school. Costs to taxpayers to build new buildings, renovate old buildings, and convert some schools to middle schools were enormous: $42 million to $64 million. To the spectator, it was as though a step in the planning process was missing. Somewhere, there had been a breakdown in communication between school administration and teachers. Regardless of all the opposition from staff and parents, no force seemed able to change the course of the fast-moving ball.

Petitions presented to the school board showed 80 percent of junior high staff opposed the proposed building plans, and less than half of the elementary school teachers would support it. The junior high CAC sent a letter to the school board, asking for further review and study of the secondary facilities report. In December another letter, signed by 115 junior-high teachers asked for further study. Finally, school officials set up a task force to determine whether the proposed plan was both "suitable and viable." Everyone hoped there would be some resolution to the concerns.

The president of the school board attended the January 1988 junior-high CAC meeting, hoping to bridge the communication gap. Rather than accomplish her mission, she met stiff resistance.

"Why wasn't the junior-high staff given an opportunity to be involved in the planning?" questioned the staff spokesperson. "We were under the impression that another step would follow the task force report."

"Where was everyone last year when we were holding public meetings about the overcrowding problem?' the board president retorted, "Why have the junior-high teachers just now come forward to voice their opinions about the grade configuration issue?"

At our February CAC meeting, one committee member, who also served on the newly appointed secondary facilities task force, gave an update on the committee's work. He told us that other alternatives were not being evaluated and voiced concern for both the quality of information being made available and the time limits involved to study such complex issues. In his view, important issues raised by both parents and staff were being ignored. The thrust of the planned change in configuration meetings appeared to be numbers driven rather than on the developmental characteristics of early adolescents.

The entire committee was troubled by the time he finished his update. As we continued our discussion, we agreed the public needed to know what was going on behind the scenes and soon. My attention was piqued when someone finally made the statement, "Someone has to write a forum article and let the community know what is happening."

"Who would be willing to write it?" asked the chairperson, looking around the room.

I sat quietly, listening to the discussion and waiting to see which one of the others would volunteer. All the while, I knew God had given me the gifts to do the job. Hadn't I written other forum articles? Some were much more complicated than this. Hadn't God helped me every step of the way? Certainly, He would do the same for this issue. He knew what I needed to say.

Finally, when no one else came forward, I knew God was calling me to action so I spoke up. "I'll write to the newspaper," I volunteered, "I've written some other articles." I had nothing to lose going to the front lines. My job was not at stake, and I did not fear losing friends or clients by bringing the information to light. I was beginning to look forward to the challenge.

"Lord, how do we fight this?" I questioned.

"You fight it with the Truth!" He responded.

Praying for direction, I set about to research the issue and gather information. When teachers and others learned of the project, information came to me from a variety of sources. Much of the information had been put forth before but was ignored. Driven and energized, I pursued each lead with a boldness I had never known. Once I acted on one piece, God presented another to complete the task. The project seemed to have an invisible Director and a life of its own. In the end,

He put it all together like a puzzle. It was amazing how smoothly the project went.

Records showed a split on the task force's final vote on the grade-configuration issue and a similar vote by the DAC. Although reports said the elementary- school teachers' petition presented at a recent board meeting indicated "strong endorsement" of the middle-school concept, a closer look had revealed 80 percent opposed the proposed changes. The bottom line was, in view of those statistics, it seemed ludicrous for the board to pursue a $41.9 million building proposal and continue to ignore the feedback of such a large segment of the population. The newspaper published my forum article on April 27, 1988. (2)

The reaction was mixed; teachers and school staff, whose voices had been squelched in fear of losing their jobs, were relieved to have the Truth made known. They were not convinced, however, that any change of direction was possible. I received a note of appreciation from one teacher:

> I want to say how impressed I was with your *Record-Eagle* forum article. I agreed entirely with your statements and appreciate your energy in this matter. I am afraid we are in a no-win situation here, but it is necessary to keep trying.

I sensed despair in the teacher's words, but her note had the opposite effect on me. "Oh, but you don't know just how powerful is the God we serve. This is not a problem for Him." I thought. "If God wants something different to happen in this school district, He can bring it about." That was a certainty to me.

One woman, furious with my article, fired off her own letter to the editor a week later.

> First, she attacked the board's plan, but nowhere in her article did she state how she would handle the same situation. Since she served on the parent advisory committee, I would like to know what her solution to the problem is.

God had blinded me to the possible negative ramifications my article might bring. Had I known, I may have been reluctant to jump into the public fray. The heat was not fun. Having my name bantered in print was devastating. I went to the next CAC meeting feeling despondent.

Sensing my melancholy mood, one committee member approached me in the parking lot after the meeting as I was getting into my car. "You know, Bonnie there is another way to look at this. She challenged you publicly to come up with a better plan. The door is open now for you to do that. You could put forth a better plan. Didn't you read Niki's [DAC representative to the task force] letter to the Editor last week?"

"No," I said in surprise. "I haven't been reading the editorial section. I guess I didn't want to read any more negative letters about my article."

"Well, you'll have to find it," he said enthusiastically. "It was in about a week ago. Let me know what you think."

When I got home, I rifled through the stack of old newspapers and found Niki's letter. The opening line in her letter referenced the writer who had criticized my article:

> (*Name*) asked how Newhouse would solve the secondary facilities configuration problem. Several times I have heard this disarming tactic used in the community when discontent has been expressed over school policy or decisions. I assume it is used to discredit or negate any opposition because they have failed to design the perfect alternative.
>
> While it would be commendable if Newhouse would come forth with a solution for the school district's overcrowding, that task is above and beyond her duty. It is, however, the school administration's duty to look carefully and thoroughly into various alternatives. This they did not do and did not encourage their Task Forces to do.
>
> In all reality, Newhouse alone probably could not accomplish such a monumental task. Her criticism

emerges from the fact that the task forces assigned by the school district did not explore alternatives or fully explore data relating to the proposed middle-school configuration. It would indeed take a serious task force many months to weigh the pros and cons of alternative configurations. (3)

I thought about Niki's letter, "While it would be commendable if Newhouse would come forth with a solution, in all reality, Newhouse alone probably could not accomplish such a monumental task."

By now, the idea of saving face in the public arena appealed to me. If I was able to present a viable plan, perhaps I could regain my credibility. I was beginning to see what God might be doing. My first forum article served the purpose of raising public awareness. Now, whether I liked it or not, the ball was back in my court. "Yes, it's true," I thought. "I can't, but I have a God who can. Only He can put all the pieces to this gigantic puzzle together; only He could give me the answers in a way the community could understand."

With Art's encouragement and the support of my family and CWA prayer warriors, I accepted the challenge of setting forth an alternate plan. I began to see how God had prepared me for the task. This was not my first experience with investigative journalism. I had grown to love digging for information. My accounting background, which included auditing work, gave me the expertise to assemble accurate reports from a variety of sources.

The connection between my school committee activities and my activities as a prayer chain leader was becoming evident. I had a network of other prayer warriors, who were in place to call upon for intercessory prayer. Following my first forum article, I shared with them what was happening on the school front, as well as a door that was open for us. One of the candidates running for a seat on the school board had asked to speak to our group. In order to meet the requirements we had to invite all candidates running for that position.

I recalled the previous year when some of the questions from coalition members, including my own, had been omitted at the public forum—questions about important issues. "What do you think about having a candidate forum?" I asked, "It would give us a chance to affect the school board election and serve the Christian community. That way we will be in control of the questions asked and not have ours passed over."

Realizing our own limitations to accomplish the task, we committed our plans to God in prayer. We agreed to pray and fast, as God led each of us before our voter's forum. Although all candidates were invited, some declined. The result of the school election on June 13 showed the school board president losing her seat and both candidates opposing the school administration plan receiving the greatest number of votes. Viewing this as a mandate from the community, the board voted not to renew the superintendent's contract.

After the success of our first voter's forum, we began to think about a forum for Grand Traverse County probate judge and county prosecutor positions. This time we enlisted the help of several other coalition organizations: The American Family Association and Concerned Clergy. With a mission to help familiarize voters with the issues and candidates, we sent invitations to all candidates seeking the two positions. Of the nine invited, seven confirmed participation. In our press release to the media, we advertised that attendees could ask direct questions of various candidates, as well as those prepared by the coalition.

"Election forum offers surprises," (4) read the headline on July 20, the day after our forum. One participant told the reporter, he had expected to be cross-examined about his position on the favorite moral issues of the Religious Right after he had been invited. Instead, questions had focused on such issues as juvenile justice, the state mental health code, and the most effective way to deal with pornography.

"I thought the questions were very responsible and well thought out," said another candidate. "I wasn't uncomfortable with this group at all."

The lengthy article included a large picture of the candidates waiting quietly for the forum to begin in the community room at All Faith's Chapel. One could not miss the familiar portrait of Jesus on the wall.

Throughout the summer months, I gathered information for the forum article. I visited county and township offices, interviewed parents, educators, and school and public officials seeking answers. As word of my project spread, others sent me pertinent information that were pieces to the puzzle. Our king-size waterbed became my executive desk and very useful to organize the many stacks of supporting information. Each stack represented a paragraph of the finished article. When I had sufficient data to write the piece, I set aside a portion of my day in prayer and fasting to clear my mind to hear God's directives for organizing the information. Two weeks into the new school year, the article was published on September 29, 1988 (5)

While my summer had been spent researching a forum article to support an alternative to the school administration's middle-school plan, school officials were forging ahead with their plan. The architects were busy drawing up plans to present to the school board at a specially called meeting on September 19, 1988. The election timetable was also discussed at the meeting. Taxpayers would be asked to approve Phase I of a $62 million bond issue.

Our CWA prayer group prayed about the situation when we met on October 25. Although only four ladies attended, we claimed God's promise that *"For where two or three meet in My name, I shall be there with them."* (JB) (6) We prayed for our nation, our state, our community, and others.

At the November school board meeting, I followed up my article with an oral presentation. I wanted to share other pertinent information omitted in the published article due to space limitations. Specifically, I had compiled an in-depth analysis of enrollment statistics for each township in our school district, including population and housing start statistics, which I handed out with a printed copy of my presentation. Second, I displayed all of the information on a large 4 1/2' by 3 1/2' surveyor's map of Grand Traverse County. After finishing my presentation, I sat down. The room was silent. No one commented on my remarks. No one questioned me. There was no visible evidence I had effectively gained their attention.

"It was like talking to a wall," I grumbled to Art when I got home from the meeting.

The following week, I received a note from one of the teachers, "How can we get the board to *change* its mind? I keep praying."

I found myself encouraging her, "When you've done all you can think to do," I said, "You stand and wait for God to move. You praise Him for the victory." Speaking the words to her uplifted my own spirits.

Later that week, I received a letter from the school board president:

"*Thank you* on behalf of the children of the school district as well as board members and staff for attending our Board of Education meeting on Monday this week.

"We acknowledge your concern and want you to know we heard your comments with an open mind. Clearly, you are demonstrating exemplary citizenship by taking the time to attend and express your opinions. The letter you distributed will be discussed in more detail, and hopefully, we will be able to answer it more specifically in the near future."

The newspaper on November 22 (7) reported that Traverse City's school superintendent had resigned, saying he had planned to leave the post for the past two years. He went on to say that he announced his retirement early to allow the school board enough time to search for a new superintendent. Board members had already begun interviewing search consultants. The resignation would take effect June 30.

By the December 5 meeting of the DAC, there was talk about hiring an independent consultant. We learned more about the plans in January when the new school board members gave the school board update at our junior-high CAC meeting. Among the items she discussed were plans by the Chamber of Commerce to hire an outside consultant.

On February 3, the newspaper confirmed the reports (8)

The Traverse City Area Chamber of Commerce has hired a curriculum development consultant, not a building engineer, to study local educational needs for the next thirty years. Chamber officials announced this morning that William DeJong of Planning Advocates, Inc., a Columbus, Ohio firm, will arrive in Traverse City in two weeks to study "how education should be delivered in the Grand Traverse area." DeJong will be assisted by Wayne Gardner, a secondary-school planner on the Ohio State University faculty. DeJong will be paid $40,000 to $50,000 for the work and will deliver a series of recommendations to the Traverse City Area Board of Education by April. Most of the cost of the project will be covered by a grant from Rotary Charities.

The article went on to say that the head of the chamber committee who selected DeJong, said the committee decided that the school system's entire educational program had to be evaluated before any decision about building plans could be made. Two public forums would be held to find out what community members consider the key issues in local education. Forging a community consensus on the kind of school system that would best suit our area would be one of the most important tasks of the consultant.

On March 6, I was among several other members of the DAC, who had asked to make a presentation regarding various aspects of the school's proposed building plan. When I entered the room and saw ten to fifteen guests seated in the added row of chairs, I was mortified. Although I had given my presentation to the school board some time earlier, I had no idea outside guests, including the consultant and a number of community leaders, would be present at this meeting. I read over the prepared speech, recognizing some of my statements were bold. Gazing around the room, *a voice chided, "Given this audience, do you still have the courage to deliver this message?"*

Intimated and bombarded with negative thoughts, I prayed, "Lord, help me to calm down and not put these people on a pedestal. Give me the words and confidence in the work You have directed me to do." When it was my turn, I gathered my courage and my visuals, including the surveyor's map of the district, and stood up.

"Where does one begin? I interviewed parents, educators, and county and township officials. I listened carefully to what they were saying and followed every possible lead that might be a part of this giant puzzle. One thing became very clear from the onset, regardless who I spoke to. Had I not taken the initiative to seek their counsel, I would not have learned what I did. The prevalent atmosphere in the community was one of intimidation. Perhaps that's where I had the advantage. I had little to lose by speaking out publicly: not my job, not my livelihood, not position, not votes, and not social standing. That this should be the case in a country such as ours remains a mystery. No one should have to fear reprisal for openly opposing this issue.

"I approached the challenge as seriously as if I were on the job. The first rule is to take nothing for granted. If auditing the books of a pig farm or grain elevator in Illinois, you wouldn't take for granted the figures on the books. You would send accountants out to the farmyard to count pigs or climb in the grain bin to measure the grain. What does this have to do with this issue? If we are going to take the matter seriously, we will have to approach this problem with the same intensity to the extent we are able. We need to seek the advice of the experts in our community *and we must go to them. They will respond honestly if we show respect for their positions*."

A few weeks later, I learned our presentations had caused much controversy at the following school board meeting. In fact, the board president sent a letter to the DAC chairperson, stating it seemed the communication between the board and the DAC needed some improvement. He planned to address our group at the next meeting and instructed her to report to the board on a monthly basis with an update, both on our activities and our discussion.

While I was not confronted directly, it was necessary to defend my right and, in fact, my obligation to make my presentation to the DAC. These were my peers, and I would be negligent had I not given them the same information I had presented in two forum articles as well as two letters to the board.

In addition to attending our DAC meeting, the consultant met separately with other community groups prior to the community forums. Those groups included elementary-school teachers, junior-high school teachers, high-school teachers, and school-board members.

"School officials have to learn to trust the public if they want the public to trust them," said an Ohio planner, who is studying the future needs of the Traverse City Area Public Schools."

"All the actors in the educational process—teachers, parents, and voters—need to be brought more closely into the decision-making process. I have an undying faith in the good judgment of people; if they're properly armed with the right information, they'll always come up with the right decision for their community, even if it isn't the best decision you'd arrive at just by looking at the demographics." (9)

The first community forum, attended by approximately 400 people, addressed the topic: Desired *Educational Programs and Services*. Divided into three groups, they discussed elementary, middle/junior high, and high school, with each group further subdivided into smaller discussion groups of six to eight people. At the end of the evening, each group shared their responses with the consultant and his staff. According to news accounts, "Most said they like the current grade configuration over one favored by the school board." The consultant expressed surprise by the number of participants supporting a second Traverse City high school.

At the second community forum, held two weeks later, 450 people attended. Focusing this time on *Facility Alternatives and Options,* participants divided into groups and discussed the original alternatives proposed. The consensus seemed to be keeping the current grade configuration, building two new elementary schools, and building a second junior-high school and an additional senior-high school. The consultant promised to make his recommendations at the board's April 17 meeting.

After hearing and reading that the school board was worried that the community forums had been "stacked by reactionaries," who were opposed to any changes in the current system, and that somehow a faction from the junior high was responsible, I made one more trip to the April school board meeting.

"I would like to suggest that no human being or group thereof could be given credit for what we have witnessed at the forums. When you circulate 5,000 informational pamphlets and use every means possible to publicize such an event in a community the size of ours, it is humanly impossible to orchestrate who decides to attend, let alone what they might say.

"Only God himself would have the resources available to mastermind such a plot, and only He has all the answers to this gigantic puzzle. It has been my contention from the onset that if He has the ability to create the universe and everything in it, including each one of us, He certainly would not find this local crisis out of His range of capabilities. He is the only one I know who has the best interests of all of us at heart and who can be purely objective.

The decision is up to the board whether to accept or reject the recommendations of the consultants. Perhaps the underlying factor now is to whose authority are we willing to submit? Is it to one another, as some have suggested? The answer to that is that we all have only One authority, and it is to Him we must ultimately be accountable. He has placed you in an awesome position in this community and as the consultant charged us at the first forum: The decisions we make now will affect a generation of children."

I sat in the back of the room when the consultant gave his final report to the board. No one seemed surprised when the consultant recommended that the board keep the current grade configuration, build two new elementary schools, a junior high, and a new high school. He also recommended that two separate bond elections be held; one for $29.5 million this year for two elementary schools and a new junior high and a $35.5 million bond proposal in 1992 to renovate the present junior and senior highs, build a new senior high, and replace another older elementary school.

After the meeting, Niki sought me out in the crowd, "I want you to know I gave the consultant a copy of your last forum article," she said excitedly.

"I wanted him to know that his plan was almost identical to the one you proposed last September. I told him to read it on the plane going home."

The board did accept the consultant's recommendations and put both the millage increase and the $32 million bond issue on the ballot for the June 12, 1989 election.

> "It is obviously the biggest financial questions we have
> ever put before the voters," said the citizen co-chair
> of the millage campaign steering committee. "There
> was a lot of momentum from people in the community
> who wanted to do something about the situation." He
> called the double win Monday historic for the future

of Traverse City. He credited the hundreds of volunteers who worked on the campaign, along with the
community forums, and the Chamber of Commerce
Facilities Study Committee that hired a consultant
and commissioned a $50,000 study on the district.

"I have watched and been a part of the most
important and significant partnership between a
school district and community," said the outgoing
superintendent. "This shows what can happen when
you do that." (10)

As I write this on August 23, 2016 (twenty-seven years later),
we have seen completion of both phases of the building plan. Traci
attended one of the new elementary schools a short distance from
our home on the east side of the school district. Two other elementary schools were built on the city's west side. Both Matt and Traci
attended the new junior high built three miles from our home and
graduated from newly renovated Traverse City Central High School.
Traci's youth symphony orchestra practiced each Saturday in the
lovely new music wing in the new senior high school—Traverse
City West Senior High.

Chapter 20

SCHOOL STUDIES

"A time for speaking"
Ecclesiastes 3:7 (JB)

I was in position now for God's next assignment: a role in scrutinizing the public-school curriculum. He already had me in strategic places: serving on the District's P.A. 226 (Sex Education Committee), Senior High Parent Advisory Committee (PAC), and as the twelfth-grade parent representative to the district's advisory council (DAC). I also served as board observer for the 1990–91 school year for the DAC, requiring me to attend school board meetings. I was receiving valuable information from each group, as well as from Concerned Women for America (CWA) and other organizations with which I was affiliated. Many pieces—The MEAP, Whole Language, Chapter I Classes, SAT, ASCD—to the education puzzle had come to me, and putting them together provided new insight.

Michigan Educational Assessment Program (MEAP)

The new school assessment test (MEAP), to be administered to all fourth-, seventh- and tenth-grade students, was the first topic of focus. Although the media had joined educators in applauding the new test, growing numbers of parents and educators had serious concerns. Unlike previous reading tests, the new test delved into realms not traditionally or appropriately the subject of reading tests. Some questions requested personal data, while others were value related.

Another key issue was that the test was not based upon phonics but the controversial *whole language* approach, focusing on the overall understanding of written words rather than specific reading skills of students. Thus, technically it was not necessary for a child to be able to read the text, only that he understand the basic idea. Some experts had found that children taught by the whole language method needed remedial help. Jeanne Chall, head of Harvard's remedial reading laboratory, had called the move toward *whole language* "shocking." "There has been little research to document the method's success in this country. . . ." (1)

The new MEAP Test was also discussed at the first DAC Meeting of the 1989–90 school year. A week later, we received a letter from the high-school principal, informing us that the test would be given to sophomores later in the month. "The test this year will include reading and math competency testing," noted the school principal. "We will use the results of the MEAP as the criteria for our minimum competency program. If a student does not achieve minimal test scores in reading or math, that student will be placed in an appropriate math or reading class that will emphasize the teaching of skills in which the student was deficient. We believe that we have a responsibility to the students, to you the parents, and to the community as a whole that upon completion of high school every student can communicate and compute proficiently." (2)

His last sentence caught my attention.

"And I, as a parent, also have a responsibility to my children, other parents and their children, and the community to pursue this issue and find out for myself what this controversy is all about and its effects on our children," I thought. My work on the sex education committee for the past year and a half had served to educate me well. We had the responsibility for reviewing and approving every word of sex education curriculum prior to presenting it to students in grades K–12. Recognizing this letter beckoned me for further investigation, I immediately arranged to preview the test.

Whole Language Method for Teaching Reading

After reviewing the MEAP test, however, I became aware that it was not the value-related and subjective questions that troubled me most, but the connection to the *whole language* method of teaching children to read. Someone else would have to investigate other issues of the MEAP test. I sensed God was leading me in another direction. My file was bulging with information related to this issue—information I needed to share with other parents. By November, I had begun to organize the material for a forum column to submit to the local newspaper.

I recognized my local leadership in CWA drew them into the situation. Not wanting to say anything, which might impact that organization negatively, I sought the advice of CWA's attorney who agreed to review the article prior to submission. I also contacted two authors I planned to quote, seeking permission, and any additional information that might be helpful. Because of the complexity of the project, my first draft was not ready for review until December.

While God had drawn me into the issue through our fifteen-year-old daughter taking the MEAP Test. The issue took on a personal level, through our seven year-old son. Had our children not been spaced as they were and some years since Ben and Danielle were in elementary school, we may not have noticed the changes taking place in the way children were being taught basics in the public schools.

We had quietly been observing the changes even before Matthew started school. Rather than enrolling him in school at the age of five or six, depending on our judgment of his readiness, now the district tested all kindergarten-age children for readiness. Children not meeting the standards set by early childhood educators were recommended for primary kindergarten. We were not alone in anxious days, waiting to hear if our child had passed his "readiness tests." When we received a letter recommending he wait another year to begin kindergarten, we were very disappointed and thought we had been neglectful in properly preparing him.

Trusting the educators and believing the test meaningful, we had enrolled him in primary kindergarten as suggested. For primary kindergarten, kindergarten, and now first grade, we had been observing the new methods for teaching children to read and write. We did not assume the responsibility for teaching him to read when we noticed he was not learning it in school, although we knew some parents had. We patiently watched and waited for the new method of teaching children to come together in a visible way as promised. I had remained silent because I did not feel qualified to challenge the school administration in this area. Who was I to second-guess the educators?

My attitude changed prompting me to act however, in the second semester of Matt's first grade year. One day, he brought a paper home with some questions he had answered. My eyes focused on the last question: things I want to learn. "Read and write" was his answer, although barely legible. It was shocking! Not wanting him to see my true reaction to his paper with the red star on it, I turned away. Tears welled up. His plea to be able to read and write could not be ignored.

By the time Art arrived home from work, my eyes were dry and I was bristling with anger.

"Look at this paper!" I fumed, thrusting it into his hand, "We can't wait any longer. I guess I'm going to have to teach him myself!"

Art stared at the paper in disbelief. "Well, we're going to have to do something. You can barely read this. Where are the vowels?"

I felt sick in the pit of my stomach as guilt swept over me. "I only regret we waited so long," I confessed, "I know other parents have been teaching their children. . . . I guess I just thought we shouldn't have to teach him at home. Isn't that the school's job?"

"It is the school's job," Art said, laying the paper on the table. "We shouldn't have to do it at home. We didn't have to for Ben and Danielle, and we shouldn't have to do it for Matt!"

The next day when I picked up the forum piece I was working on, the project had risen to a higher level of importance. From first-hand experience, I knew other children were suffering and would continue to suffer unless educators made changes. I saw each child as a casualty. The article was finished by the end of February and was published in the *Traverse City Record-Eagle* on March 8. (3)

As I began to work with Matthew, I was astonished that after three years in the public schools, he did not know vowels from consonants and omitted most vowels from his writing. Weekly spelling lessons, part of curriculum since I was a child, were absent. When I asked Matt's teacher, she told me that as long as the child understood the thoughts expressed, spelling the words correctly *was not* important. Furthermore, if a child wanted to know how to spell a certain word in his writing, he was instructed to write it down on a notepad and take it to the teacher for help. I ordered a phonics curriculum and resolved to teach him myself that summer.

I realized my recent forum article had aroused interest when a letter to the editor appeared in our local newspaper, in response to my article. The letter, written by a school consultant, listed the names of seven early childhood educators supporting the revised MEAP test, and challenging both my statements and understanding of the *whole language* philosophy. (4)

Chapter I Classes

Rather than discourage me, my determination to continue with my investigation intensified. I listened attentively to comments parents made about their child's educational experience whenever an opportunity presented itself. I was not surprised to learn a number of students were struggling academically. I had not determined how many students were struggling. That information would come in October, when Matt's second-grade teacher called to discuss putting him in a "Chapter I class" where he could receive remedial help with reading. When I objected to that solution to the curriculum problem, she attempted to console me.

"Matt isn't the only one," she offered, "I have ten out of twenty-five students being pulled out for Chapter I classes. All the teachers are playing catch-up because of this early childhood curriculum" (5)

I was shocked! Forty percent of the students needed remedial help in reading! All the teachers are playing catch-up because of this early childhood curriculum! If teachers were aware of the problem, could it be that those in decision-making positions were unaware?

At the next DAC Meeting, school officials announced the expenditure of $350,000 to $400,000 for new reading books. "The new program is piggy-backed on the early childhood program . . . the most expensive adoption we've ever faced," added the administrator.

That was the last straw! If people could not be motivated for the sake of the children, they might be concerned about the waste of tax dollars. I recognized his statement was a perfect opening for my next forum article informing the school district and parents of the pitfalls of the new reading program. Gathering my data, I prepared and presented a paper at the January DAC Meeting (6), challenging my colleagues to authorize a comprehensive follow-up study of the children in the early childhood program, including a parent survey.

The council did not vote for the study. However, school administrators asked for additional time to prepare a formal response to my statement. In the meantime, perhaps to placate me, two of us were invited to attend an in-service for Chapter I aides in late February to hear a reading specialist from Michigan State University address the subject.

Prior to that meeting, the newspaper printed two extensive articles written by Anne Stanton, the education reporter. The first gave a chart comparing MEAP test results for school districts in the areas of math, reading, and science. (7) The second discussed the low test scores on a reading test. (8) After reading them, I saw the new door the Lord had opened up for me.

When I saw Anne at the next school board meeting, I complimented her on her recent articles.

"I found them very interesting," I continued, "I've been doing some research in that area myself."

Seeing I had some knowledge and interest in the scores and their significance, she lingered a short while to discuss them.

The next morning, still reflecting on our conversation, I called her at work. "You mentioned you saw a further breakdown of MEAP scores for individual schools. Could you send a copy to me? That information would be very useful in preparing a report I am working on for the March 4 DAC meeting.

"I don't have a copy. I usually go in and review them at the Administration office when I know they're available. But, you could get them from the school," she said, rather matter-of-factly.

"I could? But I'm not a reporter."

"Oh, they're public record. Under The Freedom of Information Act, anyone can request a copy," she explained.

"Thank you for the information." I said in closing. "You might want to attend the next DAC meeting. It should be interesting as there'll be a presentation on the new early childhood program."

I could hardly wait to call the school to request a copy of the test scores.

"I'd like some information to prepare myself for next month's DAC meeting," I explained after identifying myself to the receptionist. "I need the MEAP reading scores' breakdown by schools."

"I'm . . . I'm not sure we have that available."

"I understand this information is available to me under The Freedom of Information Act," I said confidently.

After a brief silence, she responded, "You'll have to speak with someone else," before transferring my call to the assistant superintendent.

"There are a number of problems trying to compare schools," he cautioned, "Wrong assumptions are made. Part of the problem is due to mobility of students."

Realizing I was not deterred by any of his arguments, he put forth his final plea, "*The Record-Eagle* was kind enough not to make the information public."

A few days later, I received a copy of the District's MEAP test scores, a handbook for interpretation and short note attached; "It may prove useful as you interpret the results."

I was curious what the reading specialist would have to say at the in-service for Chapter I aides and expected to hear propaganda in support of the district's new program. Armed with a skeptical attitude and notebook for taking notes, I found a seat in the back of the room where I could take notes inconspicuously. I was surprised at Dr. George Sherman's statements:

> "People ought to recognize we're on a hot seat because of changes in reading," he told the audience. "Teachers are asking, 'What does this new direction mean? How can I do what I know works without violating the new direction?' How important is reading to our children? Reading is fundamental. It is critical to their self-esteem. They are losing their independence if they haven't learned how to teach themselves to read words. If you are a reader, you have learned four products. All four are needed:

1. Appropriate sight vocabulary
2. Appropriate applied decoding performance
3. Appropriate fluent texting performance
4. Appropriate text comprehension

"If the reader does a good job on the first three things, I don't care if he has the fourth. Michigan . . . focuses on one process: comprehension; .making the assumption that the child will automatically pick up the first three. As professionals, you know there is more to teaching reading than comprehension." (9)

I sat in the back of the room hurriedly taking notes. I could not believe what my ears had heard. The fact I heard Dr. Sherman was even more astounding. Would they have invited me, had they realized that his message would not support the direction they were taking? I doubted so, but God had known and arranged for me to attend.

Although not customary for nonmembers to attend DAC meetings, I had requested that parents be invited. Although not allowed to question the speakers directly, they could submit questions via their school representative. I was delighted to see a number of other parents in attendance, including my husband, and was thrilled to see the newspaper's education reporter also take a seat in the audience. Was it coincidental that two of the presenters happened to be our son's former teachers?

Parents were assured the new program was in line with "extensive research on how children learn best. Regardless of any program used, there would always be some children who, unfortunately, would 'fall through the cracks.' Chapter I classes were available for children experiencing difficulties learning via these methods." When asked if any statistics were available to determine the curriculum's effectiveness, the speaker replied, "No, however, second graders will soon be taking the Stanford Achievement Test to gauge what they're learning as compared to children nationwide."

A lengthy article appeared in the next day's newspaper, detailing the difference between the traditional childhood curriculum and the new early childhood curriculum. She reported on the concerns of some of the parents as well as other information made available at the meeting. After reading her article, I mailed her my list of fifteen prepared questions that remained unanswered. A week later, I followed up my mailing with a telephone call to the newspaper's editor, stating, "I believe they are valid questions and would like to use them as a guideline for further research. Before I proceed though, I'd like some assurance from you that you'll accept it for publication after its completion."

Agreeing to run it as a letter to the editor, I rewrote my statements to the district's advisory council in a letter, responding to the reporter's piece on the meeting.

> That the district should embark on a program of such
> magnitude without first testing the foundation is incon-
> ceivable. A study should be undertaken of the district's
> "guinea pigs" in the early childhood program to deter-
> mine how well they fared under the curriculum. Parents'
> feedback should be a significant part of this study. (10)

Even before the letter was published, I realized no study would be undertaken by the school officials or anyone else. That assignment was mine. My involvement on the DAC gave me a unique accessibility to parents from all seventeen elementary schools for each school had a representative on the council. After learning one parent sought help from the Grand Traverse Dyslexia Association, which advocated the Orton-Gillingham method of teaching phonics, I made an appointment to speak with the director, Pat Dolanski. She confirmed what Dr. Sherman said and elaborated further:

> The stress factor is bigger than life, and is internalized
> into less self-esteem. Instead of the home being a safe
> harbor, parents are forced into the role of educators.
> Hours are spent working on homework. (11)

Next, I delved into the Chapter I classes. I knew that students having difficulty were pulled out of regular classes and sent to a special room and given additional help. I learned the Chapter I reading program is the largest federal-aid program for the nation's schools, providing specialized reading and math instruction to millions of students across the nation. Funding for Chapter I, is based on the number of students qualifying for free and reduced lunch programs. Once a school qualifies, students with high needs in academic areas are serviced by reading teachers, and assistants.

What is the cost for Chapter I programs? I did not have to look far. That information had been included in a packet of information I received after writing to my Congressman about the MEAP testing. He had sent me a copy of the *U.S. Senate Republican Policy Committee Report on Illiteracy* of September 13, 1989. (12) According to that report, the Chapter I cumulative funding from 1966 to 1989 equaled $61 billion. Locally, the grant application for Chapter I for the 1991–92 fiscal year totaled $580,565—the largest federal grant in place in our school district.

Students are selected, based on teacher recommendation and test scores on national referenced tests, specifically the Stanford Achievement Test (SAT). "We can service most students that score in the thirtieth percentile or below," one administrator told me. Following that lead, I turned my attention to the test scores of each elementary school in our district. My next question: How many of the district's children were "falling through the cracks?" I knew the answer was in the test scores. I had to gain access to them for an analysis.

Stanford Achievement Test (SAT)

I mailed my request to the Director of Instruction/Curriculum, requesting the complete SAT results for Grade 2 for each of the seventeen elementary schools for the last four years—those students I considered the district's "guinea pigs." When no response had arrived within five business days, I mailed a certified letter confirming my original request. When the test information finally came, I spent a few days examining the data and noted some pages missing from the test reports. I sent another certified letter to the administrative office, listing in detail the missing page numbers. By early July, all 166 pages had been received and an invoice for $41.50. I gladly paid the invoice and began the task, praising God for showing me the way.

In order to focus on the reporting of the "bottom third" test scores, it was necessary to report the opposite in my analysis. Thus, when given the percentage of students scoring above the national fiftieth percentile, I subtracted this figure from 100 percent to obtain the percentage of students scoring below that. Making a comparative analysis of the scores of the second-grade class on the SAT test for 1991, I was shocked at my findings in the five categories I analyzed: total reading, word-study skills, reading vocabulary, reading comprehension, and spelling. Of the eighty-five separate percentages listed, only twice did the percentages go below 30 percent. In the category of spelling, I found a minimum of 49 percent of the class below the national fiftieth percentile with the figure ranging to as high as 87 percent in one school.

These were startling figures. For when the district was talking about students "falling through the cracks," I knew they were talking about at least one-third of the students. This was not acceptable to me. I was not alone in my concern. In a September 1989 article, Samuel Blumenfeld expressed deep concern for this "bottom third." (13)

> That is why, to this writer, September is the saddest month of the year. It is the month, in which 4 million, eager, healthy, American children will enter the first grade of the parochial public schools, where they will begin the process of learning to hate life and love death. *At least* one third will become "learning disabled" within a year, losing their healthy sense of self, relegated to a life of needless torment, tragedy, and incompetence.

We removed Matt from the public schools at the end of his second-grade year, and enrolled him in the Lutheran school where we knew he would learn the basics. However, I could not turn my head and ignore the issues. What would happen to the children whose parents had no other alternative? From the research I had already completed, I knew the devastating, far-reaching effects on the child's future success. What happens to the "bottom third" as they move into high school?

Association for Supervision and Curriculum Development (ASCD)

As a member of the senior-high parent advisory committee (PAC),

I began to pay closer attention to issues at the high school. My interest was piqued when I learned Traverse City Senior High School was one of twenty-four high schools in the nation, and the only high school in Michigan, to participate in the Association for Supervision and Curriculum Development (ASCD) High School Futures Planning Consortium. Their mission was to work collaboratively to develop or refine a five-year plan for *redesigning* high-school programs most appropriate to their students' future lives." Our school would host the Consortium's third meeting, in August 1991. I would have a unique opportunity to find out first-hand what the plans were both locally and nationally. Believing parents on the PAC should be allowed to attend, I requested we be invited. We had been assured as the date neared we would be apprised of the schedule, as details were not yet finalized.

When in late July, we had not yet received a consortium schedule, we called the high-school principal (who headed the Traverse City Team) to remind him. Five days before the conference, we received an agenda with a note, "You are welcome to attend any sessions at the conference; however, you must call and make arrangements."

I was discussing the upcoming conference a few days later with a board member when I learned they had received a revised schedule. The speaker for Saturday's afternoon session was different. The name sounded familiar: William Spady, consultant outcome-based education.

At the conference, my friend and I moved freely throughout the workshops, giving no advance notice of our presence. Perhaps that is why I was able to hear firsthand the strategy session: *How to deal with people who sabotage your plan.* "Do little things to include them, give them power, let them be co-chairs." The suggestion to send them little notes cued me in. Already this year, I had received three such notes from the chair of the school improvement team.

I was shocked to hear Bill Spady proudly boast that he was one of three given a grant by the Danforth Foundation to *transform* American high schools. The fact that the Danforth Foundation had funded the plan did not surprise me because two years earlier, I learned the Carnegie Foundation had funded the *transformation* of America's middle schools. Their handbook *Turning Points* (14) was the blueprint. The ASCD played a key role in bridging the gap between the foundations and the local schools.

255

I was also familiar with the name of another speaker, ASCD's Executive Director, Gordon Cawelti. Cecile Caldemeyer had introduced him to me in an article she had written:

> A November, 1985 *Education Week* revealed the weight of the ASCD's considerable influence and reach in education circles had been thrown behind the new *global initiatives* in education. In that article, Gordon Cawelti urged a *"world core curriculum"* to ensure a "peaceful and cooperative existence among the human species on this planet." (15)

An opportunity to share some of the information gleaned at the consortium meeting came the following month, when Michigan's Senate Select Committee to Study the Michigan Model held hearings in Traverse City on September 23. In my testimony, I shared the results of my three-year investigation and listed those who most influence the education of America's youth. In addition to the more familiar NEA, Association for Supervision and Curriculum Development, Mid-Continent Regional Educational Laboratory, and the Coalition of Essential Schools, I also listed five of the nation's largest foundations; Carnegie, Ford, Kellogg, Kettering, and Danforth.

Others before me had shared concerns over the involvement of tax-free foundations. In fact, Congress had established the Reece Committee in 1953 to investigate tax-free foundations. In his book, *The Shadows of Power, The Council on Foreign Relations and the American Decline,* James Perloff detailed their findings:

> In the international field, foundations, and an interlock among some of them and certain intermediary organizations, have exercised a strong effect upon our foreign policy and upon executives and advisers to government and by controlling research in this area through the power of the purse. The net result of these combined efforts has been to promote 'internationalism' a particular sense—a form directed toward

'world government' and a derogation of American nationalism. (17)

"Because the founders knew that unrestricted power leads to tyranny.' Government," declared George Washington, "is not reason, it is not eloquence—it is force. Like fire, it is a dangerous servant and a fearful master." James Madison said, "The accumulation of all power—legislative, executive, and judiciary—in the same hands . . . may justly be pronounced the very definition of tyranny." (18)

Actually, the nations of the world themselves act as a sort of check-and-balance system against each other. . . . if our world pluralism is junked for a world government, we are apt to see atrocities far worse than any the world has known. (19)

I closed with a quote from *The Turning of the Tides,* by John Howland Snow and The Honorable Paul W. Shafer of Michigan-Member of Congress from 1937 until his death in 1954:

Responsible investigation is a right and a duty . . .
Inasmuch as there is a movement to make the schools of America into agencies of 'social change,' into promoters of socialism, collectivism, and/or the welfare state, people have every right to: inform themselves of the fact, to discuss the movement, to oppose it, to brand it as subversive, and then to see that educational authorities and members of the teaching profession are held strictly to account for their part in it.

Snow and Shafer do not leave us without hope, however:

For I am convinced that the great majority of our fathers, mothers, teachers, and students can and will organize to stop it—once they see what it is. (20)

Michigan's Select Senate Committee was also interested in the information I gathered at the third consortium meeting of the High Schools of the Future, where the key to their plan was *manipulation*, so clearly outlined that I was astounded by their boldness:

- *Manipulation of money*—grants, stipends, partnerships with business
- *Manipulation of school boards*—board policies will be changed; they will be asked for waivers.
- *Manipulation of Teachers*
  - Each teacher may be required to serve on an action committee
  - Teachers who are kid's favorites will be used for pilots
  - The 'barrier of the closed door,' will be overcome with the introduction of special education teachers in the classrooms
- *Manipulation of Parents*—Several suggestions were offered which included:
  - Try to do little things to include them
  - Send them little notes to invite their participation
  - Give them power; make them co-chairs
  - Invite them for coffee and dialogue. Let them gripe for 45 minutes. Let them air their grievances to gain their trust to show you made a monumental effort
- *Manipulation of Students*—Student service will be required for graduation

In the following months, I remained actively involved and encouraged the involvement of other parents in educational issues. My research of the district's SAT test scores ultimately resulted in three, separate analyses. Some improvement was noted when doing a comparison between the 1991 SAT scores for second graders and the 1992 SAT scores for third graders, On a comparative graph, the evidence was clear. Reading scores ranged from 11 percent to 53 percent below the national fiftieth percentile, and math scores ranged 3 percent to 57 percent below the national fiftieth percentile. Too many students were still "falling through the cracks."

As I write this in 2016, the recent test scores in Michigan reveal only 29 percent of Michigan's fourth-grade students are proficient in reading, 71 percent are not proficient in reading, and 71 percent of eighth-grade students are not proficient in math. (21)

My final forum article on education challenged parents to get involved in their child's education. (22)

> We are seeing a major shift away from academics toward attitudes and values. The question is: Who will determine which outcomes your child must have to graduate? If all this seems farfetched, one has only to read some of the information presented at the ASCD workshops:
>
> • Learners' behavior must show. . .
> • Learners' attitudes must demonstrate. . .
> • Learners will advocate for collaborative change

I ended my piece with a quote from the progress reports given by some participants in the ASCD High School Futures Planning Consortium III from across the nation:

> • Our nineteen-member team has the right to decide where we're going.
> • We can do unorthodox things as long as our board policy leaves room for it.

Another team pointed to the waiver as a tool to change board policy:

• We're asking for a lot of waivers.
• Try to move the perimeters, press for diversity.
• We don't have political restraints—we can do just about anything we want if we have the money.' (23)

There is no question that our schools are at a dangerous junction. Certainly, our interest must not end with community forums. For, if we drop our guard we may well find ourselves like other communities—unaware that crucial decisions relating to curriculum are quietly being made by a small, carefully selected committee out of the public eye.

Two years later, I would have another opportunity to share information I had gathered, when the Michigan Senate Republican Task Force on Education Reform held its first scheduled hearing at Northwestern Michigan College in Traverse City on August 24, 1993. My previous experience testifying proved beneficial for I was more at ease and knew to take advantage of the exposure to present copies of my six-page oral presentation to each Senator, as well as detailed SAT test comparisons.

In my paper titled, "Sound the Alarm", I included a quote from an April 19, 1993 newspaper article written by Anne Stanton in the *Traverse City Record- Eagle*: "Eighth graders, and anyone younger, sit up and take notice. You won't get a high school diploma if you don't score 50 percent or better on a state proficiency exam by the time you're a senior in 1997." (24)

It was the perfect introduction to my four-year comparison of the SAT Scores of second-grade students in the seventeen elementary schools. (25)

And if we find these statistics shocking, when we look at students now coming through the elementary schools little encouragement is offered. We don't need to wait until these students reach the tenth grade to identify children lacking in the foundation of basic skills, they have already been identified.

After I finished my presentation, Senator Welborn asked if I could compile another study, this time including private and religious schools.

"Yes," I assured him, "I will do that." I was confident I could complete his request, for I knew God would guide the project. I praised Him for opening the door to solicit test scores from private and parochial schools, information I might otherwise have been unable to obtain.

Among those attending the hearing with me, was my friend and fellow researcher, Marjorie Yingling. A few months later she told me *Free World Research Report* was calling for papers on educational topics for their First Annual Symposium in Des Moines, Iowa in February 1994.

"I think you should submit "Sound the Alarm" to them," she encouraged excitedly, "I think they would be very interested in the research you've done."

"You think so?" Her excitement was contagious.

Assuring me the subject matter was exactly what the conference was all about, she asked me to stop by and pick up the publication and conference information.

"Maybe I will," I told her, promising to stop by her house on my next trip to town.

My excitement accelerated, as I read about the upcoming conference. The information I had gathered would fit into the conference theme, "Piecing it Together—The Education Reform Agenda for the '90s."

In November, my copy was returned with a number of suggestions, and a brief handwritten note from the publications editor Sarah Leslie:

> Enclosed is the material you requested (writing guidelines). My recommendation for your research paper for our symposium is to broaden its scope. Most people around the country are not familiar with the MEAP test or how it's being used, for example. Let me know if you have questions.

With the deadline of December 15 looming large and the Christmas holidays quickly following, I would need to enlist the help of another friend to rewrite the paper. Immediately, God brought to my mind the name of a friend and co-worker in CWA. My friend Judith Danford also taught sociology at Northwestern Michigan College. I knew she possessed the necessary gifts and talents to help me with the project. "My thought, Judith, is we could co-author the final draft and if it's accepted, present it together in Des Moines."

Our adventure occupied much of our time that holiday season, working early and late hours around Judith's teaching schedule, sitting side-by-side on her computer, adding documentation, moving paragraphs, and "broadening the scope" as Sarah had suggested. Granted an extension, when the deadline neared and our work not yet complete, we were able to finish it by January 5.

On January 21, we received word that our paper was accepted! We were thrilled at the opportunity before us! Not only would we be presenting the paper orally at the symposium, our paper would be included with all the other speakers in a published journal. Having decided that Judith would do the introduction and background and I would discuss my personal involvement and the test scores, we began to rehearse, working with the visuals we had prepared for the conference.

What an exciting moment when the conference schedule arrived in the mail and we saw our own names listed among other speakers from across the country: Berit Kjos, Charlotte Iserbyt, Dr.William Coulson, and Samuel Blumenfeld. The works of Samuel Blumenfeld and Charlotte Iserbyt had been instrumental as I conducted my own investigation.

At the conference, we learned that Charlotte Iserbyt was in the final stages of a major work on education reform: *The Deliberate Dumbing Down of America* (26); an extensive volume detailing her thirty-year investigation of education in the public schools. An expert in the field, she had served as a senior policy advisor in the Office of Educational Research and Improvement of the US Department of Education during President Ronald Reagan's first term of office. After hearing our presentation, Charlotte asked for permission to include some of my research in her comprehensive book.

Upon returning from the Iowa conference, I completed work on my test analysis for Senator Welborn, which included test scores from religious and private schools and mailed my findings to him with a letter in July. (SAT Scores for Grade 2 1990 and 1992, Grade 3 1992, and Grade 4 1993).

In reviewing these comparisons, I continue to be alarmed at the high percentages of students scoring below the national average or the national fiftieth percentile in spelling. Yet, when we look at the superior showing of Living God Christian School, with 0 percent of their students scoring below average in word study and reading and only 5 percent of their students scoring below average in math and spelling, we can be certain they hold the secret to successfully teaching these basic skills to the students.

God provided friends who diligently prayed, encouraged, and supported my work, many times behind the scenes, for me to accomplish all He set before me. I am indebted to local coalition members and other CWA members: Marjorie Yingling, Betty Wrasse, Judith Danford, and others, as well as state and national researchers whose own work provided valuable missing pieces to the education puzzle. When my research was completed and recorded, God provided a friend who had professional expertise to prepare color graphs of the information gathered. My husband and children were supportive and patient during all the hours I spent away from home, attending school and other meetings to gather information.

Prior to this manuscript's publication in 2017 and three months before my retirement, the following article appeared in my email (6/29/2015) at work from HOMEROOM—the official blog of the US Department of Education: The Critical Voice of Parents in Education by Department of Education Arne Duncan, speaking at the National PTA Convention in Charlotte, North Carolina.

> Parents are critical assets in education. Parents can be a voice for high expectations for children and for supporting educators in creating schools where all children receive what they need to succeed. An excellent education is every child's civil right, and while our nation has made great strides, with a record high school graduation rate and college enrollment at all-time highs, we have much further to go to ensure that every child has equal opportunity to learn.
>
> Parents can play a key role, in demanding the world-class education that their children deserve. But, for many parents and families, it can be an uncertain task determining the best ways to support their children or the right questions to ask to ensure their children are learning and growing. (27)

Chapter 21

IN THE MIDST OF THE YEARS

"A time for tearing"
Ecclesiastes 3:7 (JB)

I felt a tremendous let-down after the Iowa conference. After three months focusing on the paper, and then the excitement of presenting at a national conference, returning to my life in Traverse City seemed mundane. I was frustrated and discontented. Was it a midlife crisis? The more I thought about it, the more frustrated I became. Beneath the frustration, anger was brooding. During my quiet times, I sorted out the reasons for my anger.

Closest to the surface was working in a job that did not challenge me and paid minimum wage—the same as our two older children. Comparing my paycheck to Art's, I was being paid 75 percent less. That fact infuriated me, knowing I was capable of more. Once on that thought process, I became angry at Art because were it not for him, I would not have quit my college education when I did. After all, I was doing well in college when I dropped out.

Determined to seek another job, one in the field of accounting, I updated my resume and answered a newspaper ad for an accounting clerk position in a CPA firm. I was elated when called for an interview! A few days later, I walked into a small accounting firm and looked around. *Fear* swept over me for every desk had a computer, those dreaded monsters that had taken over most offices while I was home raising children.

"I have no experience with computers," I confessed to the office manager.

"That's not a problem," she encouraged, "We'll train you."

"I don't know," I responded thoughtfully. "I. . . . I think it would be easier to take some classes first."

She handed me a business card. "If you change your mind, give me a call."

On the way home, I made up my mind. I knew myself well and knew the hectic pace in an accounting office. I could only imagine trying to learn something as complicated as a computer with the constant pressure to meet deadlines as had been my previous experience as a bookkeeper in a CPA office.

The next day while driving to work, I thought. "I'm going back to school and learn the computer! There is no way I can do on-the-job training with anything so difficult. They'll never keep me, and even if they did, it would be much more difficult." I had no idea where the money would come from. I only knew I was determined to go back to school. Nothing else mattered.

"I've decided to go back to school," I announced to Art later that evening.

"You are?" He stared at me in bewilderment.

"Yes! I'm going back to school and learn the computer. There's no way I can be trained on the job."

If he had any negative thoughts about my plans, he knew better than to verbalize them for the tone of my voice and the fire in my eyes indicated rock-solid determination. After all these years, he knew no words could discourage me.

I began moving toward my goal. Soon, my plan broadened. I called my friend Charlene, who, having received her doctorate in education, held the position of Director of the Bridge Program at Northwestern Michigan College. (NMC) The program assisted adults returning to school. Although I had been out of touch with her for several years, a co-worker had told me about the program and its benefits.

Charlene was excited to hear about my plans and promised to try to find additional funding. In the meantime, she suggested I schedule an interview with a job counselor at JobNet, a state agency partnering employment and training, to assist me in career research and exploration.

In June 1994, I met with a case manager to discuss my plans, previous education, and experience. He concluded that since my accumulated average grade point was above average, rather than enroll in the Bridge Program, I should consider completing my Bachelor of Science (BS) degree in accounting. Drawing up an action plan with a timeline, my first assignment was to schedule an appointment with a guidance counselor at NMC to develop an educational plan.

A week later I met with the NMC guidance counselor, who also suggested I pursue completion of my degree. I could complete whatever classes remained at the community college and apply for admittance to Ferris State University (FSU). The two-hour drive to the main campus in Big Rapids was not necessary as Ferris offered a BS in accounting through their new University Center in Traverse City. Financial aid was available to help with tuition and expenses.

I walked away from the second interview, bursting with excitement! I had not been surprised God would use Charlene to encourage me, but to use two counselors who did not know me? I sensed God's Hand in a mighty way, confirming that this new spark of energy I felt was, indeed, His doing. What had begun as a simple plan to take a few computer classes was snowballing into the reality of an unfulfilled dream. Confident I was on the right path, there was absolutely no stopping me; I was focused. Whatever it took, whatever obstacles to overcome, I was prepared to do it.

I ordered my transcripts from Lansing Community College and Michigan State University, and formally applied to Ferris. Having left Michigan State in the second term of my junior year, I assumed I had little more than a year, attending full time. I had not considered that requirements had changed since I began in 1963. Now it would take three years, going full time, to complete the same degree.

My announcement at age forty-nine that I was quitting my job and going back to college became an interesting point of discussion for everyone in my life.

"We'll have to get her a backpack as a going-away present," chuckled Marianne, my boss.

"Oh, I don't need one—I never needed one before." I grinned, unable to imagine lugging a cumbersome bag around all day.

Two days into the first semester, however, I was between my car and the classroom in a downpour of rain. I glanced down at the expensive books, and darted into the bookstore. While I browsed through the stylish assortment of backpacks, I remembered Marianne's words. For the next three years, my backpack was my most valued and constant companion.

Just as I expected, the most significant change in college and the workplace between 1963 and 1994 was the use of computers. Culture shock hit the first day of class. With four classes, three requiring the use of computers, I was in a new world. I was thankful for the young man about Danielle's age, in my electronic spreadsheet (Lotus) class, who sat beside me and showed me how to turn the computer on. My intermediate accounting class also required Lotus projects, I learned the first day. "There is still time to back out," I thought eyeing the door.

As soon as class was over, I sought out the professor. "I'm taking Lotus now," I said anxiously. "I don't know if I can do this."

"Don't worry," he gently encouraged with a smile. "You'll be working on your Lotus projects in small groups outside of class; I'm sure they'll be able to help you. You'll be fine."

Midway through the first semester, Art and I evaluated the disruption in our home caused by my new routine. If we wanted to preserve family life, we would have to invest in a home computer. By installing Lotus and some basic programs, I could work on my assignments at home and be more accessible to the family. I also would have scheduling options: working in the early morning or late in the evening when the computer lab was not open.

I also realized I needed to swallow my pride and find a tutor if I wanted to get a passing grade in my Lotus class. I needed someone to sit beside me at the computer and show me, someone available to answer the myriad of questions I had. Mustering my courage, I visited the tutoring office and pleaded my case. They assigned a part-time student who met with me in the computer lab twice a week for the remainder of the semester. She was an invaluable help and great encourager.

"You won't believe it," I told my brothers during dinner the following Christmas, "The bottom line of computer technology is nothing more than off and on switches!" They stared at me in disbelief as I continued. "I'm serious. The very bottom line of computer technology is nothing more than a circuit of switches. It's just that simple!"

By the time I reached my third and final year, I was more at ease with the computer. College had been successful in taming the "enemy." It was now my friend and would be a valuable tool with my writing. I remember sitting by Judith's side, watching with envy as she moved and deleted paragraphs in the paper we presented in Iowa. Now, I could do that and also prepare my own graphs and charts.

As graduation neared, I realized college had brought me up to date on the many changes in the business world over the past three decades. When I first enrolled as an accounting student, I was one of three females in the class. Now, over half were females. Advances in technology had transformed the classroom. Adding by hand was obsolete. Going to class without a calculator was unthinkable. In fact, I had to buy and learn to use three different high-tech calculators. Electronics also offered options when communicating with instructors. You had options in turning in assignments or receiving your grades.

"Who faxed their assignment from Florida?" asked the financial management professor one evening. We learned the answer the next time our class met. A student out of town on her honeymoon had faxed the assignment and neglected to include her name.

Perhaps most significant was the array of choices and the options now available to obtain a college degree. Through the University Center and long distance learning, I was able to complete all requirements for my BS in Accounting from FSU without ever having set foot on their campus.

After graduation, I began submitting my resume, hoping to find the perfect job. I did not want to return to the field of public accounting where each day I would work on an entirely different set of books. Instead, I hoped to enter the private sector in an entry-level position. The problem was when businesses received my resume listing my past experience, they were reluctant to hire me. Twice during job interviews, I heard the same concern.

"I'm afraid after six months and you become familiar with the job, you might go elsewhere seeking something more challenging."

Finally, I applied for a position in the corporate accounting department of a large travel agency, preparing airline reports. During my first interview, the finance director offered a new proposition.

"If we hire you, you'll have to choose a new name—an office name to go by." Seeing the perplexed look on my face, she explained, "You see, one of the regional managers is named Bonnie. It's really not so unusual. There are a number of other employees here who have office names."

"Oh, I see," beginning to understand the request. "That sounds like fun. I'll start thinking about what name I'd like to be called." It seemed like a small inconvenience, compared to the attractive travel opportunities that would be available. She scheduled an interview with the owner of the business.

Feeling confident that this job was the right one for me, I mulled over an assortment of names. "It isn't often that one gets to choose a new name in mid-life," I mused, "Deciding on a name is usually a task for expectant parents, not for you!" Names came to mind; names I had always liked, Faith, Dana, Andrea, Joy, and Theresa. I had to admit "Faith" was my favorite and felt I must choose it. Biblically, there were examples I recalled where God changed someone's name and always for a reason; Abram to Abraham, Sarai to Sarah, Jacob to Israel, and Saul to Paul. Maybe God has a reason for changing my name. Maybe it's because I'm going to need faith to see me through the turmoil of starting a new job. I recalled Hebrews 11:1 (1) "Only faith can guarantee the blessings that we hope for, or prove the existence of the realities that at present remain unseen."

When I told the family about the name I had chosen, none supported my decision. But, I was not swayed from my choice. I would be the one called by that name, day after day. With or without their approval, my name would be Faith.

I reported for work in early November 1997. It was not long before I realized my fantasy of having a dream job I could comfortably ease into proved just that: a fantasy. The knowledge I had acquired in my classes seemed to be of little use to me. In fact, the document called "ticket" that I had to process, was as foreign to me as anything I had ever worked with. Furthermore, the desk where I sat was in the most open and conspicuous location in the office, across from the bathroom, next to the copy machine, and at the top of the stairway. All visitors passed by me on their way to the executive offices. For someone as easily distracted and as social as I am, it could not have been a worse place for me.

The first few months I struggled to learn the computer programs, trying to find time to catch up on the tasks put aside after the previous employee left. Sometimes I worked late; some Saturdays I went in for part of the day. Occasionally, I brought work home with me on the weekend where I could work in a nice quiet corner away from all confusion and noise. Even so, my starting pace was not acceptable to my superiors. Twice they called me into meetings, where we discussed my "time management." I longed for the day when it would all run smoothly, a day when I felt confident. There were many days I had serious misgivings about the job. After the closeness I had once felt with God, I could not understand why He seemed so distant now. Peace and happiness had escaped; my self-confidence plummeted. Could I have misread God's direction?

The warning came on January 4 when I read Habakkuk 3:2 (2) God's words seem to speak directly to me:

> O Lord, I have heard Your speech and was afraid.
> O Lord, revive Your work in the midst of the years!
> In the midst of the years make it known;
> In wrath remember mercy.

I wrote "1/4/98 . . . I am 52" in the margin of my devotional.

Later that week, when it was nearly time for my annual appointment to see the gynecologist, I was still so swamped I could not spare the time away from the office. Hoping to change my appointment to a later date, I called the doctor's office and talked to the receptionist.

"If you cancel this one, it will be at least six months before we can get you in," she cautioned.

"In that case, I'd better leave it as it is." I told her reluctantly.

The day before my appointment, once more I contemplated canceling. "I don't know what to do," I confided to Dee (aka Diane), who headed the accounts payable department, and with whom I often worked closely. "I have a doctor's appointment tomorrow afternoon, but we're so busy, I think I should cancel until the pace slows down around here—until summer. But when I called to change my appointment, they said it would take months to reschedule. I'm in a real quandary."

Dee hesitated briefly. "There never will be the right time; just go."

"I'll work through my lunch hour, so I will miss only an hour or so," I promised.

The next day Dr. Abernathy was pressing around on my lower stomach during her examination when she suddenly stopped. "What's that?"

"What are you talking about?"

She took my hand and placed it over the lump she had discovered.

"That shouldn't be there," She said shaking her head. "Can you feel it?"

Unfortunately, I did. Somehow, I never noticed anything unusual there before.

"It may be something, or it may be nothing. I'll have to order an ultrasound to take a look at it." She eyed me curiously, "You never noticed it before?"

"No," I said sheepishly. "I didn't notice anything. I guess with all the talk about middle age bulge, I didn't think too much about excess weight in the midriff."

She noted the location of the lump, commenting it did not appear to be where my ovary was but somewhat higher and to the right of my naval.

Before leaving, I waited for the receptionist to schedule my ultrasound appointment. "Can you make it in the evening, so I don't have to miss work?" I requested.

Realizing my appointment would conflict with a church meeting Art and I had signed up to attend, I told Pastor Jim that neither of us would be able to attend. Art had to accompany Traci to a school activity, and I had an appointment to keep. I did not share any further information. "After all, it's really no big deal," I thought, "Hadn't

Mother had a tumor the size of a grapefruit removed when she was about my age? The doctor removed it, and she had no further complications. I've always been so much like her in addition to looking like her, I guess we'll share this experience, too."

When I went to the hospital for my ultrasound, Traci came with me and waited in the waiting room while I was having it. The technician quietly took the pictures and explained my doctor would notify me of the test results.

On Friday, January 30, I had a routine doctor's appointment with Dr. Ward, our family physician, as he wanted to see me before renewing a prescription. I was about to tell him the gynecologist had found a lump so he could expect to receive a copy of my ultrasound, when he told me he received a copy of my ultrasound the previous night. However, he looked at his schedule for the next day and saw my name, so he decided to discuss the results with me then.

His expression grew troubled as he held my file open, gazing at the report, "The pictures show the lump is a mass in the abdomen, pressing against the ureter on the right side."

"Oh it's probably like my mother's," I reassured him. "She had a grapefruit-size tumor removed twenty-five years ago, and she's doing fine. They even sent her to visit us in Colorado after her surgery to recuperate." I laughed, remembering the time, "We took her up to Pike's Peak!"

Still frowning, the doctor continued to stare at the report. "Well, let's hope your experience is like hers," he said skeptically. He then examined my abdomen to feel the mass and asked the nurse practitioner standing beside to feel it, too.

When I got home at 6:00 that evening and listened to the messages, there was a second message from Dr. Abernathy. Suddenly, I remembered she had called and left a message on the answer machine the previous day, and I had forgotten to call her office. "Too late to call her now," I thought. "Her office is closed on Monday so now I'll have to wait until Tuesday to talk to her." By now, I was most anxious to hear her explanation of the ultrasound pictures.

During the prayers at church on Sunday, Pastor Jim prayed for another parishioner who was having medical tests run. On the way out, I shook his hand and told him my appointment the night of the meeting was for an ultrasound. "I'll let you know how it came out this week," I promised.

Still gripping my hand, he scolded. "You didn't tell me about the test—I could have been praying."

On Monday while working on the airline reports, I thought about the implications of the mass in my abdomen. Over the weekend, I had called Mom to ask her how long she had been off work after her surgery. Her response, "six weeks," had immediately put me in a tailspin. "How will I tell the finance director that I'll be off work for six weeks? Worse yet, I work upstairs! Mother could not climb stairs for some time. What am I going to do now?"

When at work on Tuesday, I found a small piece of paper and wrote down two telephone numbers: Dr. Abernathy's and Art's. I abbreviated so no one else could read it. My immediate concern was how to have a private conversation with them, while sitting at my desk out in the open. There was absolutely no privacy. I decided to wait until the "crew" had arrived, so it would not be so quiet. When Dee came in, she asked if I would mind working in the president's office that morning as she needed to work on my computer. Instantly, I saw God's provision. "Thank you, Lord. That's even better," I whispered beneath my breath as I gathered up my belongings and moved to his private office.

I called Dr. Abernathy's office and left a message and my work number. Periodically, I checked my voice mail to see if she had called back. At about 2:00 in the afternoon I noticed a message, and picked up my message pad and went back into the private office to return her call.

"It's a good thing you told me you had an office name," she laughed, "I might have thought I had the wrong number." Then her voice grew serious. "The ultrasound showed you have a . . . highly treatable cancer."

My heart sank, "Cancer? The "C" word was a word to fear. I could scarcely believe her words. All along, I thought I had a benign tumor like Mom.

"I will need to schedule an appointment for you with an oncologist," she continued. "This is out of my area. Do you have a preference?"

"No, you can go ahead and schedule me as soon as you can get an appointment."

Quickly, I dialed Art's number and left him a voice mail as he was away from his desk. "I talked with Dr. Abernathy. It's . . . it's cancer," I whispered into the receiver, trying to hold back tears. "It's a softball-size mass, 8 x 14 centimeters," I read from my hurriedly scribbled note.

In a few minutes, Dr. Abernathy's scheduler called back to tell me she made an appointment with Dr. Robert Schwert on Friday. I hung up and waited to hear from my husband. I was certain he would be shocked. Although stunned and on the verge of tears, I dared not let anyone know—not yet. "What would all this mean to our future? What about my family, my job?" These questions kept fluttering about in my mind. I could not believe all this was happening. I never dreamed it would be like this.

When Art returned my call, it was clear he was worried. He could not believe his ears. In fact, he had played my message back three times, straining to hear my whispered words. Still whispering, I briefly went over the news from Dr. Abernathy and told him about the appointment. He asked some questions about the procedure and next appointment.

"I can't talk anymore right now," I said. "You can call her, and talk to her yourself. I'll see you at home. We'll go over it all then." I knew I needed to get off the telephone before I burst into tears. Somehow, I had to compose myself and get through the day.

On Friday February 13, Art met me at Dr. Schwert's office to learn what the next step would be in my treatment. He lost no time in getting to the point. The pictures confirmed I had lymphoma, but I would need more tests to ascertain the kind and the stage as this would determine the treatment plan. The pictures showed that my right kidney was not functioning because the tumor wrapped around the ureter on the right side, closing off the stream to the kidney. His first concern was that I had a major organ not functioning. "If the cancer affects your good kidney sometime in the future, you could be left with none," He explained. "Do you want to hold off for a few days on the cancer treatment to try to save the kidney?"

His words pierced my soul, leaving me speechless. I had no idea that I had kidney problems, too. I glanced over at Art to see his reaction to this news, thinking to myself, "Forget the kidney, let's get to the tumor."

Art spoke up resolutely, "I think we need to try to save the kidney."

"I guess we should try to save the kidney first," I repeated to the doctor.

Nodding in agreement, he outlined his plan. He would consult with a urologist to decide how best to deal with the kidney. Perhaps he would be able to place a stent in the right ureter to enable that kidney to resume functioning. We suggested Dr. Gillette, the doctor called in when Traci was born.

"I'd like to admit you into the hospital for three days next week. That will allow time for all the necessary tests. We can get them done much faster if you are in the hospital and available when the various procedures can be done. At this short notice, you will have to be worked into everyone's schedule."

"We'll do a biopsy on Monday, putting a needle directly into the tumor to draw a sample of the tissue to determine the type of architecture, which will show the stage the cancer is in. Another test will be done of the bone marrow to see if it has advanced into the bone." Then he added. "I . . . I may also order another CT scan from the waist up to see if there are any other cancerous sites present."

After the appointment, I left Art to go back to work to finish the project I had been working on and to inform my supervisor of the results. Realizing it would be tough enough to tell the story once, I asked the financial director to come with me to her office. I did not want to have to repeat the story. I intended to remain strong and composed, but it was impossible to hold back tears as I relayed the doctor's report.

"We want you to know our agency will be there for you," she comforted, "We will work with whatever schedule you have. We have always been very good about that. You can work around your treatment schedule. But for now, why don't you pick up your things and go home this afternoon?"

I thanked them for understanding and went back to my desk. I wanted to finish the job I had been working on before I left. There would be enough disruption at the office with my absence next week. Before I left, the owner stopped by my desk to offer some words of encouragement. My eyes brimmed with tears. I could not talk now.

"I need to get out of this office," I thought. "I need to get out of here before I completely lose my composure. I need to be alone in my car to let all this sink in. I just want to go home so I can digest all this." I looked at the homemade Valentine's Day card one of the travel agents had given me earlier. It was her tradition each year to make one for everyone in the office. I stared at the card, "Isn't it strange she should pick a lion on the front of mine?" It reminded me of I Peter 5:8-11 (3)

> Be calm but vigilant, because your enemy the devil is prowling around like a roaring lion, looking for someone to eat. Stand up to him, strong in faith and in the knowledge that your brothers all over the world are suffering the same things. You will have to suffer only for a little while.

Next, I recalled a story Tammy Faye Bakker shared in her book, *Run to the Roar.* (4) There was advice on fighting lions. As the title implied, when fighting these battles, we must run *toward* that which we fear. Avoiding it, or running in the opposite direction, is the worst possible path. "I need to *run to the roar*," I thought. "I have no other choice, nor do I have a great deal of control over the charted course before me. Instead, I find myself putting one foot before the other each day traveling down the unknown path as I battle cancer.

Monday morning, Art drove me to the hospital to check in. By 11:00 a.m., my biopsy was completed, and I was back in my room. The nurse informed me that they had an opening in the schedule and would be doing the second CT scan later in the evening. Having experienced one before, I was not as fearful when 6:30 arrived and they came to whisk me off to radiology. All went smoothly, and I felt no discomfort. I was thankful to mentally mark off one more procedure completed.

On Tuesday morning, February 17, Dr. Gillette awakened me at 6:30 a.m. from a sound sleep. He had stopped by to let me know he planned to do his procedure later that evening. He also left instructions with the nurses to give me an IV to keep fluids in my kidney, but I could not be given food.

"How long do you think my kidney hasn't been functioning?" I asked, fully awake by this time.

"Probably six to eight months," he guessed.

"Six to eight months!" I gasped. And I didn't have a clue; at least nothing that stood out to draw my attention. I felt I had not been a good friend to my body; I had betrayed it in my quest to complete my college degree.

Dr. Gillette explained in detail the procedure he would be performing. "There is only a 50/50 chance that I can get the stent in," he warned.

My heart sank at the odds. After he left the room, I knew what my prayer needed to be. "Oh Lord, please help the doctor get the stent in. I pray that You will send an angel to open up the ureter, so it can go in smoothly." I could not bear the thought of any further complications.

There was little time to worry about it, as Dr. Schwert was due in my room to do the bone marrow tests at 8:00 a.m. I was not looking forward to more needles. "Maybe I should get used to the idea," I thought. Moments later, he arrived with a technician from the lab and explained that first he would deaden the surrounding area and then place needles on both sides of the bone on the backside of my upper hip; first one, then the other, and then he would withdraw the needle containing samples from the bone marrow to send for the tests.

Following his instructions, I lay down on the bed with my face buried in my pillow. I felt no real pain, but I could feel pressure and hear the tugging on my bone. After a few minutes, he stopped, and I heard him tell the lab technician the end of the needle had broken off in me, and sent her to find a "tool" he could use to pull out the broken needle. While she was away on her errand, he explained this was the first time that the needle had broken off. That information was not comforting, and I grew very anxious. He still had one more hip to do! The technician returned with some kind of tool she had found on a nurse's tray and the doctor retrieved the needle's point.

Proceeding to deaden the tissue on my other hip, I continued to be very tense, wanting the whole ordeal to end. Perhaps sensing my state of mind, this time before inserting the needle, he told me to let him know if I felt pain and he would withdraw the needle and redirect it again. That thought was even more troubling, further increasing my stress. When I began to feel some pressure, I was quick to speak up. When he pulled the needle out, however, the specimen was lost, and it took three more times before he was satisfied that he had a sufficient sample for the necessary lab work. By then I was lying face down in a cold sweat. "Just get this done," I thought, annoyed by this time. "I am quickly running out of courage."

While the whole procedure took only a half hour, the process had drained my energy, both physically and emotionally. The doctor and the lab technician left the room after instructing me to lie still for a while. Thankful to be done with that procedure, I turned my mind to the next. I had the rest of the day to think about Dr. Gillette's task. I needed a day to pray. Right now, I knew I needed a spiritual boost.

Pastor Helman arrived just after Art left. He visited with me for a while and then prayed with me. Before leaving, he told me he had just come from a Bible study with Pastor Romberg, a mutual friend and retired Lutheran pastor, who knew our family well. When he had told him about my health condition, Pastor Romberg said he would visit me at the hospital later that day. Shortly after he left, my friend Donna came into my room and sat down to visit.

In the middle of our conversation, an attractive woman with long, flowing hair came into my room pulling a large harp. I'm looking for Bonnie Newhouse," she announced smiling broadly. She looked familiar, but I could not recall where I had seen her. Later, I remembered she was the nurse practitioner, who had been at Dr. Ward's side when I first heard the results of the ultrasound.

"I'm Bonnie Newhouse," I told her, still gazing at the harp.

"Would you like me to play the harp for you?" she asked. "You know, music is great therapy. "She pulled up a chair and positioned the harp in front of her.

"I . . . I guess so," I said reluctantly. The truth was I really did not want to listen to harp music but how could I tell her "No" without appearing rude and ungrateful? I felt as though we were a captive audience. "I know she means well," I thought, tears now streaming down my face. "But I don't feel comfortable with all this. It is just a little close to heaven for me—people sitting around listening to lovely harp music. I know I've got cancer, but I'd like to think I'm not going to die. I glanced over at my friend, "I wonder what Donna thinks about all this? Does she think this is a strange thing to be happening here?" If she was annoyed, she did not let on.

The pretty woman continued to gracefully, strum her harp while I sat on my bed crying. She played several beautiful melodies and intermittently watched me. Seeing me cry must have given her the impression I felt my situation was hopeless. Sensing her music therapy apparently was not having the soothing effect she expected, she finally stopped strumming and began to ask some questions about my health.

"The urologist is going to try to place a stent in my right ureter later tonight," I told her. "He said there was only a 50/50 chance that the procedure will be successful."

"Well, you must think positively," she said determinedly. "You need to visualize that stent sliding easily through your ureter." She stressed the importance of changing my thought pattern to positive thoughts. "By doing so," she explained, "you can have a positive effect on the outcome of the doctor's procedure."

After she left, I realized maybe that was why God sent her to me even though I did not welcome the intrusion. It was imperative to the day's success that I focus on the positive, not the negative. He wanted me to take a more active role in my healing. I must take charge and not be passive. Regardless of the odds the doctor gave me, I must begin right now, right this minute, to focus positively on the next procedure and believe that he would succeed in getting the stent in. I had all day to pray about it—all day to act positively. "Maybe there was more of a reason for this whole episode than to just make me depressed," I surmised at last.

After Donna left, Mother came in with my sister Barbara. Soon after, Art's sister arrived. Before they left, Pastor Romberg arrived as well.

"Would you like me to pray and anoint you with oil before I leave?" He asked.

"Yes, I'd like that." I told him eagerly. I was especially grateful that he had the courage and boldness to anoint me with oil. To my knowledge, it was not often practiced in our Lutheran denomination, yet I knew it was biblically sound and a custom in the early church. I remembered James 5:14–16 (5)

> Is anyone among you sick? Let him call for the elders of the church, and let them pray over him, anointing him with oil in the name of the Lord. And the prayer of faith will save the sick, and the Lord will raise him up. And if he has committed sins, he will be forgiven. Confess your trespasses to one another, and pray for one another, that you may be healed. The effective, fervent prayer of a righteous man avails much. (NKJV)

Healing was what I needed. Yes, healing was my goal. Pastor Romberg was another messenger from the Lord. The Lord was paving the way for the stent to slide easily into my ureter. With the anointing of oil, I could feel my faith being renewed replacing *fear* within my body.

Art came to visit after everyone else had left, and decided to stay until I returned from the operating room. I knew he was getting tired, but I was thankful for his support. I knew I would be Dr. Gillette's last patient for the day and was well aware that he had been in my room at 6:30 in the morning. "Oh Lord," I prayed, "Give Dr. Gillette the energy he needs to do this even though he must be tired." I added, "Thank you that I will be anesthetized for this procedure. I really don't want to know all the details."

It seemed as if no time had lapsed before I was awake and back in my room. Art had already spoken with the doctor. "The operation was successful," he said grinning. "Dr. Gillette was able to get the stent in! He said to tell you that he'll be in to talk to you first thing in the morning."

I got up early the next morning, and had finished my devotions before the doctors made their rounds. Dr. Gillette reiterated what Art had told me. "It might need to be replaced in three months if it's still needed."

"What about my kidney?" I asked, "Will it be able to function?"

"It should work at 80–90 percent of its capacity." He said, hopefully.

I breathed a sigh of relief to know there was hope for the damaged kidney. I was thankful. With that behind me, my mind turned to lesser problems. I had not eaten since Monday night, and I was hungry. I knew it would take some primping in the bathroom to get myself looking presentable.

"I'll take my shower after breakfast," I told the nurse who then turned her attention to the woman in the bed beside mine. With the help of several nurse aids, they finally were able to get her in the chair. One of the aids stayed and helped feed her. For the first time since my arrival, I focused my attention on her. I glanced over at the pitiful sight. She had brain cancer and had no hair. I knew she was depressed.

"I would be, too, if I were her," I reckoned, "She's so depressed she actually seemed to enjoy that harp music yesterday. I know I should speak words of encouragement—something—but somehow, I don't have it in me." Although I felt guilty about my selfish attitude and lack of compassion, I did my best to ignore her. In fact, I had to admit, seeing her laying there depressed me as the same question hammered my thoughts. "I wonder if the day will come when I will be in her situation."

Dr. Schwert came in later and released me to go home. "Call my office this afternoon and schedule an appointment for next week. By then, all the test results will be back, and we'll be able to decide on a treatment plan."

On Tuesday, February 24, Art met me at Dr. Schwert's office to go over the test results. After examining me briefly, he pulled up a stool and sat down. Just as he suspected, I have Non-Hodgkin's Lymphoma. "It's incurable," he dropped into the conversation, "You don't cure it; you manage it like diabetes." The conversation with the doctor reminded me of the "bad news letters" we learned to write in my business communications class in college. The bone marrow test was puzzling in that one side showed positive, the other side negative. Art and I sat there stunned. We could not believe the words we were hearing.

Dr. Schwert went on to explain that the cancer would go into remission and then reappear. Then you fight it again with drugs. After a while, your body will be unable to fight it because of the immune system's inability to create white blood cells. I could muster few questions; I was speechless. Art had the courage to ask the doctor how long we were talking about.

"Four to twelve years."

"Aren't there any success stories?" I questioned, looking for some word of hope. The doctor gave little encouragement. I still could not quite believe this was happening to me.

After dropping the bombshell, the doctor shifted the discussion to treatment. He offered us a choice. "You can do six months of chemotherapy, using four drugs. It will knock the socks off both you and the cancer, but the side effects will be harsh. Your other option is to do chemotherapy for twelve months, with two drugs. It will take longer to go into remission but the end result is no different. This will be a more gentle approach." He went on to explain I would still lose some of my hair. It would be thin enough to need a wig but not as fast. The other side effects would be less invasive; I may not be nauseated or fatigued and, maybe I could still work some.

The doctor left us alone in the room to discuss our options while he went to schedule the first chemotherapy appointment. When he returned, we told him our decision. The second option would best fit our situation. That way, we could have some normalcy in the family during treatment. Plan B's first appointment would be Wednesday March 4 at 9:30 a.m. Art should plan to accompany me in case I experienced side effects.

When we left the doctor's office, Art went on to the group session he co-led, and I went home. How thankful I was that Mom was there to share my news. After explaining it all to her, Pastor Helman called. "He's about the only one I am up to talking with," I told her.

"Do I have your permission to share this with the congregation?" he asked when I finished.

"Yes, you can tell them. We need all the prayers we can get."

The next day, Ash Wednesday, God spoke to my heart in my devotional, (6) based on II Corinthians 4:16–18:

> Therefore, I do not lose heart. Even though my outward
> man is perishing, yet my inward man is being renewed day
> by day. For our light affliction, which is but for a moment,

is working for me a far more exceeding and eternal weight of glory, *while I look not at the things which are seen, but at the things which are not seen. For the things which are seen are temporary, but the things which are not seen are eternal.*

I noted the date and wrote: "I got the diagnosis yesterday. I must walk in faith."

In fact, the whole day's devotion spoke deeply to my heart.

I will look to the Lord; I will wait for the God of my salvation; my God will hear me. (Micah 7:7)

Blessed be the Lord, because He has heard the voice of my supplications! The Lord is my strength and my shield; My heart trusted in Him, and I am helped; Therefore my heart greatly rejoices, and with my song I will praise Him. (Psalm 28:6–7)

I again dated 2/25/98 and wrote in the margin, "Here lies my hope!"

That same day, Pastor Helman mailed the following letter to the congregation (7)

FEAST OF VICTORY LUTHERAN CHURCH
4400 Mt. Hope Road • P. O. Box 298 • Acme, MI 49610 • (616) 938-1070

February 25, 1998

Dear Sisters and Brothers of the Savior,

I am writing you to make sure that I am communicating with each of you- that no one is omitted through a broken phone chain. I need to share news with you about Bonnie Newhouse, and I have Bonnie's permission.

Tuesday, February 24th, Bonnie and Art had a Dr's appointment where they were told that Bonnie has a lymphoma that is medically incurable. Through chemo-therapy treatments there can be periods of remission but no cure. People with this type of cancer can live for several years if the remissions occur and if no others organs/systems are invaded.

We now know what is medically possible and impossible. We also know that "with God all things are possible." (Matt. 19:26)

As Bonnie's sisters and brothers in Christ, we are called to be people of prayer and people of compassion. We pray for healing; we pray for a miracle. We offer ourselves, our time, our energy, our love for Bonnie, Art, and their children.

We will keep you posted as to how we might be most helpful to the Newhouse family. For now we ask you to pray, lifting Bonnie to the feet of Christ. Remember her on Wednesday, March 4th, as she begins chemotherapy at her Dr's office.

Let us come together as God's people and offer God's support, taking turns holding each other up in the name of Christ.

God bless you all as you pray.

In Him ... together,

Jim Helman
Pastor

Pastor Jim Helman's Letter

Chapter 22

WARFARE IN THE VALLEY

"A time for healing"
Ecclesiastes 3:3 (JB)

Thrust to the front line, we prepared for the battle of my life. It was not only our immediate family that took on our battle, but everyone close to us joined in the spiritual warfare. Throughout the ordeal, my prayer was, "Lord, You know my needs this day. You have promised to supply them—no matter what they are. I am counting on your provision. (Phil. 4:19 JB) (1) The interesting thing about God's provision was, the help each one gave and the weapon they used were directly related to their God-given spiritual gifts. People, whose spiritual gifts included the gift of intercessory prayer, joined in the effort and prayed for us and my healing daily. They also added my name to prayer chains first in Traverse City and then other Michigan cities and elsewhere so that other prayer warriors could also pray for me.

The day after I came home from the hospital, knowing my mind was in a whirlwind, God sent someone gifted with organizational skills. He sent my sister Barbara from Charlevoix to help in whatever way I needed. My pressing need was to "run to the roar" by going to the wig shop before my hair fell out so I could match my hair color and style. I had been warned the chemotherapy treatment would cause some hair loss, probably enough to need a wig.

Barbara also offered to come over a day each week to help with the cleaning, laundry, and meal preparation. "If I do that," she told me, "then you can save your energy for working. That way when you get home, you can relax and know things are in order."

Mother lent her support by coming to stay with the family during the week, when Art was working. Her presence in our home helped provide stability for the children, whose lives had turned upside down. She also served as secretary and was able to field telephone calls when we were not up to talking. Most important, she served as my loving nurse, insisting I rest as much as possible and preserve my energy so that my body could aid in its own healing.

Despite mental and spiritual preparation, I was apprehensive when we arrived at the doctor's office for my first chemotherapy treatment. It is one thing to read about someone else's experience but quite another to submit yourself to it. Perhaps the most frightening aspect was deliberately allowing chemicals to drip slowly into my body; drugs powerful enough to kill the disease within me and yet not kill healthy cells. For me, it was as though I had two authorities in two different worlds. One was the medical world: tests, statistics, and lymphoma research; the other was the Holy Spirit whispering, "Trust God!"

The battle raged on two fronts. The first was mental — in the mind. I knew the battle raging in my mind had to be first. The key to my victory over cancer was faith. Faith was my new name. I needed faith; I needed to believe in the *unseen* power of God. I must remember my God, who knows all about me and cares for me, is watching over me. Ultimately, He is the One in control, not only in control of me, but my doctors, and my treatment. I must continually remind myself of His faithful presence in this experience.

Second, in the physical realm, choosing to focus my attention on God's words of encouragement, especially while my body was undergoing chemotherapy, helped me to stay centered on God. That way instead of being emotionally, drained of energy, my spirit was renewed. My sister-in-law, Lynette sent me, *Devotional Classics,* (2) a wonderful collection of devotions and selected readings by some of the greatest devotional writers. Reading them during my treatment nourished my mind and my soul.

My daily Bible reading, private prayers, and my daily devotional, also ministered to me. The devotional on March 9 (3) seemed to express my being, pulling my life together in one verse. I made a note in the margin—My Funeral Passage:

> By grace I have been saved through faith, and that not of myself; it is the gift of God, not of works, lest anyone should boast. For I am His workmanship, created in Christ Jesus for good works which God prepared beforehand that I should walk in them. (Ephesians 2:8–9)

I heard God again speaking to me in two verses on March 15 (4) :

> The Lord is my light and my salvation;
> Whom shall I fear?
> The Lord is the strength of my life
> of whom shall I be afraid? (Psalm 27:1)

> But to you who fear My name
> The Sun of Righteousness shall arise
> with healing in His wings. (Malachi 4:2)

On Wednesday, March 25, Pastor Helman held a congregational healing service as part of the Lenten service. He explained the three large candles placed on the altar symbolized relationships, health, and faith. Those wishing to receive the laying on of hands and anointing were instructed to come to the altar and take a candle before standing or kneeling at the communion rail. After he laid hands and quietly prayed with you, parishioners were to light their candle from the large candle that represented their prayer concern before returning to their seat.

I took a candle and knelt at the altar, one of the first to get up. Art followed and knelt beside me. After Pastor Jim's laying of hands, anointing, and prayer, we lit the health candle before returning to our seats. I was amazed at the stream of parishioners that followed. Randomly, one by one, people went forth as God led them. "Praise God for this positive response to this service," I thought. I knew

Pastor Helman had stepped out in faith, not knowing how the congregation might respond to his first healing service.

As was arranged, I continued working at the travel agency part time. Rather than return to my original position in one department, I worked in several departments. I chose to work Tuesday, Wednesday, and Thursday from nine until four. Thus, I could send Traci off to elementary school and be home when she returned. Scheduling my chemo treatments for early Friday morning left me four days to recover from any negative side effects. Having laboratory work done on Mondays assured me that I would not knowingly expose myself to germs at the office the remainder of the week, if the blood work showed my white counts to be down.

It was good to be busy, and most of the time I felt quite well. When I was at work and not having treatments, it was easy to forget I was a cancer patient. However, every Monday I was reminded when I had to have a blood draw at Dr. Schwert's office. Whenever I had my treatment or a doctor's appointment, the reality was undeniable. During those times, thoughts of cancer enveloped my mind, bombarding me with negative thoughts.

Art had his own battles. Rarely a day went by, when someone at his office did not inquire about me. They were genuinely concerned and interested, yet afterward it was difficult for him to lay it aside and concentrate on his work. I knew the children were all dealing with much the same in their lives, but most conversations about our feelings were one-on-one as the need arose or a situation presented itself. We never knew when a chance meeting or conversation with someone would trigger those intense emotions, which lay so close to the surface. It was not always possible to conceal them. Sometimes they just erupted.

One such occasion occurred on Saturday, April 4, after dropping Matthew and his friend off at the movie theater. I stopped at the drugstore to mail some letters on the way home. Planning to go to the grocery store next door, I had left my grocery list on the car seat. As I walked out of the drugstore, I met a friend I had not seen since college. It was not a good day to see an old friend. All day I had been fighting back tears.

"Hi Bonnie, how's it going?" she asked, "Did you find a job?"

"Yes, I found a job, but . . . I have cancer," I blurted out as tears streamed down my cheeks.

She hugged me in disbelief, now crying herself, "How can it be?" she said sympathetically. "We're supposed to start enjoying life now that we're in our fifties. The kids are off to college. But look what's happened! We both go back to college to get our degrees. My marriage fell apart, and you have cancer!"

She, too, was having a bad day. She had to go back on antidepressants to cope. I told her I was worried about losing my hair as now is the time it is likely to start thinning. The thought of losing my hair was frightening. Hoping to encourage me, she shared a story she had just read—a positive, upbeat story about a cancer patient. I was too upset to offer much encouragement for her situation. The words did not come, and I could scarcely talk. We hugged one another and then parted ways.

I jumped into my van and closed the door to the outside world. I looked at the grocery list sitting on the car seat. There was no possible way I could go into the grocery store now. I could not bear to see or talk to another soul. "Art will have to do it," I told myself. "He'll have to leave early to pick the boys up from the theater, too. I'm not going out anywhere else today!" Still crying, I arrived home. Between sobs, I shared with Art the conversation with my friend. He gave me a hug and left to do the errands.

I knew the imminent reality of losing my hair was weighing heavily on my spirit. "Oh Lord," I prayed, "I know I have a wig. I know I will get through this. But Lord, I have children at home, and I know how scary it is to see women with no hair. I remember how I felt the first time I saw a bald woman. Lord, I pray for a miracle. I pray that despite what the books say, I will not lose my hair."

Later, I noticed Traci stayed downstairs to watch television most of the evening. When she did come up for a snack, she was quiet. "I wonder if she's just tired from her birthday party or overheard me crying?" I said to Art. "If she did, she's probably upset and scared." The wheels in my mind rewound to the time I was her age. My mother was the tower of my strength. I was troubled whenever she was sick, for any reason. I could not imagine what it must be like being Traci's age and dealing with a mother battling cancer.

289

One day in May, I heard the notes of a familiar song flowing through the house. Instantly I stopped to listen. The music was coming from Traci's room. She had been playing her keyboard more since "turn off the television week" at school. Wanting to encourage her, I had gladly purchased new batteries for her instrument when she had asked. She had played many songs but never this one. This song she was playing from memory. Then, I remembered the song: "I Was There to Hear Your Borning Cry." (5) Occasionally sung at our contemporary church service, I could never sing all the verses without crying, even before my illness.

The words had special meaning to me; as if they were written just for me! Two or three years before, I had decided I wanted it sung at my funeral. In fact, to assure my wishes would be followed, I had written "Sing at Bonnie's funeral" in bold large letters with a black marker at the top of the page in my ELCA Women's Worship Resource Book. (6) I had carefully hidden the only copy of the book in my file downstairs, where I also kept my birth certificate. I knew Traci had never seen it.

"Mom," she said, "Can you help me with the notes?"

"Sure, Honey," I reluctantly answered, heading downstairs to retrieve the songbook. Struggling to fight back tears, I tried to hum the notes for her. I would not have discussed the importance of the song to me, had I been able to erase my writing at the top of the page. I did not want to discourage her from learning it, but hearing it upset me greatly. When she finished, I told her I didn't want it left lying around where someone else in the family could read what I had written, and would keep it in a secret hiding place. I was certain it would upset Dad if he saw my note.

The next day, after Traci and I returned from shopping, she turned on the keyboard to perfect "Borning Cry." "Mom," she said winking at me, her dark eyes dancing, "You'll need to get that book out again."

When she began to practice with the book in front of her, she hesitated then spoke. "Maybe I can play it at your funeral—that is, if I ever learn it."

On the verge of tears, I answered, "Maybe you can, Honey." All the while thinking, "Honey, I don't think you realize just how difficult that might be for you."

Again, I fought back tears. Traci repeated the song until she had memorized all but one part. Finally, she asked for my help. This meant I had to sing the words myself to carry the tune. Tears flowed until I could barely see the page. I struggled to conceal them so she would not know how difficult it was for me to hear it, let alone sing it. A week or so later, she decided to master it on her viola. I was thankful when she tired of practicing the song and turned her attention to something else. Returning the songbook to its hiding place, I noticed the black writing at the top now read, "Sing at Bonnie's funeral & *Traci's*."

I wondered if God was sending me a message through our twelve-year-old daughter. Maybe I would not survive this cancer; maybe I should be preparing to die instead. I wanted to have faith. I knew I needed a positive attitude. But, what if it was my time to die?

On May 10, Mother's Day, I wondered if this would be my last Mother's Day celebrated on earth with my family. With all the happenings of the past few months, I could not be sure. "How strange," I thought. "May 10 of last year I was proudly sitting in my cap and gown at my graduation service from Ferris State University. Who would have guessed one year later would find me battling cancer? Who would have thought I might be facing death? What happened to the future that once looked so bright? What happened to the wonderful vacation I had planned for the kids on spring break? Working at a travel agency had opened up new opportunities for travel to exciting places. We had not taken a family vacation since our trip to Washington, DC before I had returned to college. I had promised the kids, it would be worth the wait."

With our spiritual gifts class in Sunday school ending, Pastor asked for volunteers to talk about the results of their spiritual gift inventory. When Art volunteered to do his in two weeks, eager to share my experience, I raised my hand and offered to do mine the same week. Having delved into this topic years ago at seminary, I had already experienced and moved beyond the discovery stage of gifts into the next stages.

I had known about the gift of writing since I first delved into the subject at seminary. This spiritual gifts class, (7) however, expanded my knowledge. Before taking the gift inventory, we had studied each of the gifts Paul named in Corinthians quite extensively. After we understood the attributes of each gift, we had been required to take a spiritual gifts inventory. This exercise revealed God's blessing of several other dominant gifts. I was fascinated with the new information because I saw how intricately they worked together to accomplish God's work.

Enlightened and encouraged, I was anxious to share with the class how God had brought it together in my life. Using my experience on school committees as an example, I explained how God led me to join the junior-high parent advisory committee when Danielle was in junior high and how He had answered after I "threw out a fleece." It was not until eighteen months later I realized why God wanted me involved. He knew there was a complex problem to solve, and He had given me the gifts to be a part of the solution. He had sent me to the front lines of the battle.

I told the class how God had faithfully guided me, step-by-step, and showed me I was not working alone. He had others in position as well, using their gifts and talents. Often, they would provide information or the leads to acquiring it. They listened as I explained the process. I spent hours following leads, researching the issues, gathering information, and attending meetings before documenting the reasons why an alternate plan would be best for reconfiguring the buildings of Traverse City Area Public Schools (TCAPS). First, writing forum articles to raise public awareness, followed by another presenting my findings. The article, published in the *Traverse City Record-Eagle,* had created a fury and planted doubt in the minds of community leaders. Then I had to follow it up by personally delivering the message at community meetings.

All work concluded with the hiring of an out-of-state consulting firm whose findings echoed the ones I had presented. In the end, the school district did change their plans and the configurations for the new schools. The new schools had been built just as recommended: three new elementary schools, one new junior high school, and a new senior high school. Needed renovations to the old senior-high and junior-high schools were still under construction. How rewarding to be a part of God's plan.

When I finished my presentation to the spiritual gifts class, the atmosphere filled with excitement and expectancy, as each one began to visualize beyond the first step of identifying their gifts. Other presentations uncovered a variety of other gifts that had been identified. I knew our congregation was in for many exciting future experiences in the months and years to come. I praised God for allowing me to witness His spiritual renewal in our congregation.

Later, after listening to Charles Stanley's series of tapes on the Motivational Gifts (8), I realized with each gift comes weaknesses that, unless they are shored up in the life of the Christian, Satan will use to discredit the person or cause them to tie up their gifts and return them to the closet. With the gift comes the ability to stash it, misuse it, or use it to God's glory. Any Christian can be used by the enemy and in the flesh misuse the gifts. By the time I learned this teaching I could already see the enemy's tactics at work among us.

The door of my closet, filled with stashed gifts, was about to be thrust open. At the end of June, another CT scan done to review the progress in my cancer treatment, revealed the chemotherapy treatments, thus far, were ineffective. Dr. Schwert decided to start me on another regime of drugs. This time I would go to the outpatient clinic at the hospital where the oncology nurses could monitor me and be able to react immediately if the drugs caused serious side effects.

I was not extremely tired after my first treatment, but when I went to the doctor's office on Monday for my usual lab work, my white count was down. It was not low enough to cause concern or prevent me from working. On Tuesday, I worked my regular hours. On Wednesday night, my sister, Marion and her roommate, visiting from Virginia, joined us for dinner. After they left, I felt extremely tired and had the chills so I took a hot shower to warm up. I spent most of Thursday on my feet at work while filing. By the time I arrived home, once again, I was extremely fatigued and felt chilled.

By Friday, I felt as though I had the flu, but I had to take Traci to the eye doctor for a scheduled appointment in the morning. After checking Traci in, I told the receptionist I was not feeling well and would wait in the car. When finished, she could get me to come back in to sign the necessary insurance paperwork and make further arrangements.

Returning home, I immediately curled up on the sofa to rest.

"Mom," Traci urged, "Why don't you take your temperature?"

"That's a good idea, Honey. I hadn't even thought of doing that." I took my temperature, and it was 102 degrees. Alarmed, I remembered to look in the handbook they had given me at the hospital. My high temperature and chills were danger signals to watch for. I instructed Traci to call Dad at work and tell him what was happening. He quickly left the office, came home, and called the doctor.

"Bring her to the emergency room," the doctor ordered, "I'll meet you there."

Before the doctor arrived, the emergency room staff took and sent blood to the lab and examined me. The high temperature indicated infection somewhere in my body. The lab work showed my white count dangerously low. Dr. Schwert came to my bedside.

"You know," he said sternly, "If you would have stayed home and tried to tough it out, it could have been fatal!"

I fought tears, wondering why I had been so neglectful of my condition. Why hadn't I looked over the handbook? Had I done that, I would have realized the chills I had been experiencing since Wednesday were serious symptoms. I felt as if I was a small child, being scolded by a parent.

"What happens now?" Art asked.

"We'll have to admit her. She's neutropenic, and we're going to have to carefully monitor her condition. We'll give her shots to bring up her white blood count and try to find out where the infection is." Then he turned to me, "You'll be in isolation. Make sure that anyone who visits your room; including the medical staff, washes their hands when they come in. Don't be hesitant about reminding them."

Hearing all this frightened me. Had I not read all the brochures, warning there might be times when the white count would go down after a chemo treatment? In my case, however, my guard had been down because the symptoms occurred a week later. Hadn't I had my lab work done on Monday and received no special instructions from the nurse?

Dr. Schwert was not on call that weekend, leaving me in the care of another oncologist. He also secured the services of an infectious disease specialist, Dr. LeFebvre, to treat the infection and make the decisions in that regard. The antibiotic to treat the infection caused further problems because my kidney could not process the medication. Dr. LeFebvre considered putting me on a dialysis machine when my creatine level shot up to 7.8.

Even though I was taking medication to reduce the fever, it continued to rise. Dr. Schwert had left instructions for them to place me on a cold pad, if necessary to bring down my fever. When I learned what they were referring to, I wanted to escape! I felt as though I was being tortured! It felt like lying on a sheet of ice. This was suffering I had never known. As I lay there suffering, I remembered the suffering of Jesus on the Cross. He was not able to escape His suffering, either. Was I sharing in Christ's suffering as the Apostle Paul once referred to in Scripture? Was this a refining fire to glorify God?

The cold pad was used for a minimum of an hour or longer, twice. One time, I called Art to come to the hospital at ten o'clock in the evening and stay by my side. The second time, my brothers were in town to visit me. Seeing my distress, my younger brother Rich took my feet in his hands and massaged them to offer some kind of comfort. When he tired, my older brother Wayne relieved him. Serving as a focal point to distract me, similar to the focal point used in Lamaze childbirth classes, their gentle massage was the only thing that made the experience bearable. For an hour and a half, I prayed for my temperature to come down to an acceptable level so I could get off that miserable thing!

When my temperature returned to nearly normal and my white blood count came up, I still had to contend with the high level of creatine in my blood, not filtered out by my kidney. Every day, the nurses would take and send blood samples to the lab, and every morning I would wait for the doctors to make their rounds and give me the reports of my progress. I felt as if I was a prisoner and every day begged to go home. It looked as if I might go home at the end of the first week but learned I could not. The swelling in my body indicated my kidney was still not functioning properly. I needed to be near medical staff where my creatine level could be closely monitored. I was nauseous much of the time and took medicine to allow my stomach to settle so I could eat and keep the food down. I could not stand the thought of eating the hospital food because I had no appetite. Why was it that when I ordered food from the menu that I usually liked, looked so unappetizing when I removed the lid? Yet, if I did not eat, I would not regain my strength. Only then, did I realize an appetite was a gift of God. I took it for granted until it was taken away.

This time during my hospital stay, I had ample time to communicate with God, and He used the time to teach me. First, I learned with God, there is no pretending. The lessons are real! There are no dress rehearsals. He does not pretend that I may not live to see tomorrow. He asks the questions: "What would you do if you knew you were going to die? What items would rise to the top of your 'to-do' list?" I thought about it. All alone with only the basic essentials in my hospital room: my bed, my Bible, and a few devotional books, I meditated on God's message to me.

I needed to get my "house" in order. First, there was the will. That had been on my "to-do" list for months. Drawing up a will was imperative and no longer postponed. Regardless of the expense, it must be prepared. It was only fair to my husband and my family to be certain that there would be a smooth business transition. There was no excuse for delaying these matters, no matter what expenses would need to be paid. Finances needed to be in order to protect our assets. Second, I must begin at once to organize my home so that files and records could easily be located by someone other than me. Insurance policies and other documents needed to be clearly labeled in the files.

"What other unfinished business remained in my life? What needed to be completed before I passed into eternity?" God reminded me about the manuscript that lay on the shelf unfinished for the past ten years. "What about the vow I made years ago? Had He not instructed me to write it? Didn't He remind me about it every time I read Psalm 56:12?" (9)

> I must fulfill the vows I made you, God;
> I shall pay you my thank offerings,
> for You have rescued me from Death
> to walk in the presence of God
> in the light of the living."

Every time I had read that scripture, the Holy Spirit had convicted me. The margin in my Bible recorded God's message to me each time I read the verses:

"11/13/88—I got my word processor two days ago. I need to finish my manuscript."

"5/1/91—It is two and a half years since I got my word processor and my manuscript lies yet unfinished."

"11/16/88—So I shall always sing of your name, fulfilling the vows I have taken, day after day (Psalm 61:8)." (10)

For all these years, God had been patient with me, not calling me to account. Now, there was no question in my mind; He was speaking sternly to me now. There could be no more excuses and no more wallowing in self-pity because the publisher's words had been harsh. I must believe with all my heart that if God gave me the direction in the first place, and trusted me with the experiences, He would also complete what He began.

God brought to mind once again the scripture that spoke to my heart on March 9—the scripture I noted would be my funeral passage: Ephesians 2: 8–9: (11)

By grace I have been saved through faith, and that not of myself,
it is the gift of God, not of works, lest anyone should boast.
For I am His workmanship, created in Christ Jesus for good works
which God prepared beforehand that I should walk in them.

Then it became clear. This work, this testimony of my walk with Him, was God's work not mine. He gave me the gifts. How humbling to realize that He even prepared the work beforehand. He gave me the rich experiences. My part was the walk. All of my experiences were prepared beforehand that I should walk in them. He would see that it was complete because it was really His work. I was only the vessel, the clay pot in the His Hand.

I also recalled the scripture in my devotional on January 25, 1998: Paul's letter to the Hebrews 12: 5–6, 11–13: (12)

My son, do not despise the chastening of the Lord, Nor
be discouraged when you are rebuked by Him: For whom

the Lord loves He chastens, And scourges every son whom He receives; Now no chastening seems to be joyful for the present, but painful; nevertheless, afterward it yields the peaceable fruit of righteousness to those who have been trained by it. Therefore strengthen the hands which hang down, and the feeble knees, and make straight paths for your feet, so that what is lame may not be dislocated, but rather be healed.

After two weeks, the doctor finally released me. Treatments would not resume until my body was stronger. Before I left the hospital, Art learned how to give me daily injections of Procrit to keep my white blood count up. I knew then that I could not continue working. How could I pay attention to getting well if I could not rest when I was tired? After all, they paid me to work. I was tired of dealing with my cancer in the public view. Now, I only wanted to go home to be alone with my family and put all my energies into getting well. I sent a letter to the travel agency requesting a leave of absence until my health improved. Somehow, we would manage financially.

During my hospital stay, my family had become gravely concerned about my future. Fearing my health might worsen by their December wedding date, Danielle and her fiancé Rodney discussed with us the idea of downsizing the lovely church wedding they had been planning for months and moving up the wedding date.

"Maybe we should have a summer wedding instead," Danielle suggested, "We could have a smaller wedding—in our backyard."

"Absolutely not," I vehemently objected, "Your wedding will be exactly as you have planned. We will trust God!"

By September, the doctor felt I had recovered enough to resume my treatments. Hoping to avert a relapse, he reduced the dosage of Fludarabine, which seemed to be more manageable for my body. Remembering my vow, I retrieved the unfinished manuscript from a file and began to set aside time each day to write. As soon as I took the first step of obedience, the Holy Spirit quickly rekindled my spirit and reenergized the work. The ten years on the shelf seemed only a slight pause as the wheels of my mind rolled back to the season and chapter I was working on. The process of recalling God's faithfulness to me in the past served as encouragement for the present trials. God also brought back to my memory the scripture spoken so clearly to my heart on January 4. In Habakkuk 3:2: (13), it says, ". . . . O Lord, revive Your work in the midst of the years! In the midst of the years make it known."

These reminders of God's past faithfulness, helped shore me up for the disappointing news we received when we visited the oncologist in October. Well into the new treatment schedule, we were hopeful there would be a noticeable change in the tumor size. Pressing down on the outside of my abdomen, Dr. Schwert measured it. Comparing these measurements with the previous one, there had not been any reduction on the one side and the other side appeared to be even larger. His expression told us he shared our frustration at the lack of positive results. He ordered a CT scan before my next treatment.

When I went to the hospital for the next treatment, my spirits were low, and it was an effort to concentrate on the devotional reading and remain positive. It was depressing to be in that environment every day for a week, seeing people with cancer, listening to talk about cancer and tumors and blood draws and needles. I could not wait for the infusion to be over and walk out the door. How thankful I was that Traci had two basketball games later that afternoon. Watching her play provided a welcome diversion from cancer. There, I would be like any other parent, caught up in the actions of life.

On October 23, Art had an afternoon appointment with Pastor Helman. Later that night he revealed the reason for the appointment and shared a strange experience he had had in church a few weeks before.

"I was sitting in church one Sunday. You weren't there because your white counts were down. During the service, it seemed as though God was very real and present in the sanctuary. There was an overwhelming feeling of love and the presence of God. It was the most wonderful feeling. I didn't want to leave. I didn't hear any voice or anything, yet it seemed very clear that God was speaking to me.

'I know how much you love Bonnie and will miss her, but it is time now that she comes to be with Me.'

"The message upset me so much that I wanted to just get out of there but couldn't because Matt and Traci were with me. Even stranger, when the service ended that Sunday, Pastor Jim announced to the congregation that he had felt an unusual Presence of the Lord in the sanctuary. He didn't know if anyone else had felt the Presence as he had."

"Why didn't you tell me?" I questioned, both astonished and hurt that he had kept this experience from me for almost three weeks.

"I didn't want to tell you because I was afraid it would upset you. But I couldn't stand bottling it up any longer. I had to talk to someone, so I called Pastor Jim.

"Well," I said, shaking my head emphatically. "I believe God was present, but I don't believe it was His voice you heard. It just doesn't sound like something a loving God would say. Nor does it sound like the way He would say it. I . . . I think the devil was also in the room trying to ruin the experience for you. I just cannot believe it was God."

Art stared at me with a puzzled look.

"What did Pastor Jim say when you told him?"

"He seemed to think the experience was really from God because He, too, felt God's presence in the sanctuary that day. But, he also said that flies in the face of his certain belief that you will be healed."

Art seemed somewhat relieved to have shared the experience but remained skeptical and unconvinced about our interpretation. Later, I read the experience as he recorded it in his journal:

That sense of Him telling me that, kept coming back over and over. As I would look at the window above the altar, it seemed that He was *there*, somehow. Not in the physical sense, but His presence was very *real*. The unusual thing about it all was also the overwhelming sense of His love. I got the distinct feeling that He was "telling" me this out of a great love, not out of any sense of retribution or evilness or anger, but a *great sense of His love* . . . . It was almost like God was saying that He has shared Bonnie with me for the past thirty some years, and now it's His turn to have her.

Troubled by his experience in church, and unwilling to accept the notion that he could do nothing, Art prepared for our November doctor's appointment by taking an offensive posture. If Dr. Schwert's plan was not working for me, maybe it was time to get another opinion. Researching online, he learned that Dr. Mark S. Kaminski at University of Michigan Comprehensive Cancer Center was working

with a new experimental drug called Bexxar that was very promising for treating Non-Hodgkin's Lymphoma. The doctor's name was
familiar. Art recalled receiving an email several months ago from
Pete, a friend whose wife had my type of cancer and had been treated
by Dr. Kaminski. Maybe we should consult him? Yet, how would
we tell Dr. Schwert? What would he say? Art sent an email to Pete,
seeking his advice and received the following:

> Art, I don't blame you for being concerned. This is
> not a dress rehearsal, and both of you need to have
> the utmost confidence that Bonnie is getting the best
> there is to offer. More than likely she is, but you need
> to *know that*. You asked when is the time to get a
> second opinion, and I believe the best time is when-
> ever you want one.

We looked for an opportunity to discuss Art's research when we
met with Dr. Schwert on November 9 to learn the results of the prior
week's CT scan.

"The CT scan showed no reduction in the tumor," he told us,
"In addition, there are two new cancerous sites farther down your
abdomen. It looks like the chemotherapy isn't working, so there's
no reason to continue with it."

Art and I looked at one another in disbelief. Not only had the
tumor not reduced, but two more sites had appeared. I felt as though
I had a runaway disease taking over my body. I wanted to have faith
and wanted to be positive, but at some point, this takeover had to
stop. This invasion has to halt!

"Maybe I'm not going to get well, after all," I thought, "Maybe
it *was* God speaking to Art, after all. Maybe, I had interpreted Art's
experience all wrong, and he had been right." Then I was reminded of
a vision; or dream I had had a number of years before. It had occurred
when life was going smoothly. It was only one scene, just a snapshot
of Matthew standing beside me at Art's funeral as a grown man. For
all these years, I had believed it was a message from the Lord that
Art would precede me in death. While the dream had troubled Art, it
had given me comfort over the years when Art was traveling in bad

weather, or someone was sick, because it was years into the future for Matthew was still a young child. Matthew would be a grown man. "Had I been mistaken in my interpretation of that dream for all these years, as well?"

Dr. Schwert seemed at his wit's end. My cancer had not responded as he had expected. Nor had it responded as other patients with the same type of cancer. In fact, he had checked with a few other specialists to see if they would take on my case. Two had responded negatively, one favorably. Dr. Mark Kaminski at University of Michigan Hospital had agreed to see me and review my case. Possibly he could get me in the new clinical study with Bexxar. If we decided to take that avenue, he would have his office schedule an appointment for me as soon as possible. Hope! At last, we had hope that something might work out.

A week later Patti, a member of our congregation, called one morning to tell me she'd had a strange dream, a dream about me.

"About *me*?" I questioned.

"Yes. In my dream there was a private healing service for you at church," she began cautiously, "You and Art were sitting in the middle of a small group of people. They were praying over you and laying on hands."

"Do you remember who was in the group?" I asked, excitedly.

"Oh yes! I was there, Pastor Jim and Sherri (his wife), Barb and Craig, Sharron, Lori, Paula, and Paul."

My spirit stirred hearing the names. There was a common thread among them. As far as I could recall from our spiritual gifts class, all of them had the spiritual gift of intercessory prayer.

"I don't know what to do about the dream. What do you think?"

"Well, I think we should be obedient to the Lord. If this is something God has shown you, we need to do it. Call Pastor Jim. He'll know what to do."

I believed God was testing us. Would we be obedient, even though a private healing service such as this was not a common occurrence in our church? It was not the first time God led us out of our comfort zone. Had not He called our congregation to a day of fasting earlier in the year? Pastor Jim had taken that bold step of faith then and led the congregation down a new path, whether or not some of the members were familiar with fasting. My thoughts trailed back to the excitement and flurry of anticipation among those who had never experienced the spiritual closeness of God during a fast.

It was not long before Pastor Jim called. He felt impressed we were to do a healing service before Art and I left for Ann Arbor. Since our departure date was unknown, he felt it important that we proceed on the earliest possible date. "Do you think it should be a private service or part of a larger church service?" he asked.

"I think it should be private, with the people present who were named by Patti as being in her dream," I said, beginning to catch a glimpse of God's plan. "It seems God wants each of them to be a part."

"I agree," he said enthusiastically. "I'll call each of them to see when will be the best time. Do you have a preference?"

"I'll have to check with Art," I said excitedly. "I'll let you know."

The private healing service took place on Thursday November 19. It happened to be Art's birthday. Most of the people God called to be present had never attended a private healing service such as this. All but one of the people Patti saw in her dream felt honored that God would call them to such an important gathering. The missing person had left the congregation several months before and would not be attending. Pastor put two chairs side-by-side in the middle of his office and instructed the group to form a circle around us and lay their hands on our heads. He would begin with prayer, and each person could pray or read scripture, as led by the Lord.

"I don't know what will happen here tonight or the reason God has called us together," he told the group, "It could be one of three things—or perhaps all three. Bonnie will be healed, to strengthen her and Art for what is to come, or for whatever God is doing with each of us here."

There was an awesome air of expectancy in the room. I felt it had as much to do with Art and encouragement for him, as for my healing. The past months had been extremely emotionally draining on him. Whenever there had been a crisis for me, he had dealt with it. But, when the crisis was over, he often had a migraine headache requiring medication. It was humbling to realize God knew the depth of our needs was so great that He would give Patti a special message to call this group of people together, this small group named by Him to pray and lay hands on us. It was humbling to be on the receiving end, to be prayed for, and not pray myself. It was not long before our emotions gave way to soft tears. I did not feel any burning sensation, indicating that God had instantly zapped me with a miraculous healing as I might have expected. Yet I knew without a doubt, God had called this gathering. Afterward, we shared a cake someone had brought for Art's birthday.

The Sunday after the healing service, a member of our congregation who had not been present at the healing service, took me aside after church and told me about a dream she'd had about me. I listened intently as Mary recalled her dream.

> I walked into the church and it was filled with water swirling around. You were standing by the altar, dressed in a satin wedding gown with a long train. It looked beautiful, and the dress was so dazzling white — so brightly illuminated — that I could no longer look at it because it was so bright. She covered her face and eyes when she recalled the dazzling white dress and continued. "You were talking to the Light — Jesus. He appeared as a bright light. While at first you looked normal, your hands started turning brighter and brighter. I looked up at the cross and could see the bright light directed at you.

Completely caught off guard, I was speechless. Giving Mary a quick hug, I exited the church, carefully avoiding all conversations except for a brief word with Pastor Jim who was standing in the rear of the sanctuary shaking hands with the parishioners.

"Mary had a dream," I said quietly. "I asked her to tell you about it to see how you interpret it. Call me after you talk to her."

By the time I got to the car, I had dissolved into tears. How thankful I was that neither Matt nor Traci had come with us. Seeing me crying, there was no way I could avoid telling Art about Mary's dream.

"The only way I could look like that — illuminated, shining brightly, is in heaven," I told him, "Maybe you were right after all. Maybe I *am* going to die. Maybe God was speaking to you that day in church and not the devil as I had at first thought."

Seeming to agree with my interpretation, Art was visibly upset. I continued to cry, and we both became very quiet, both upset, and wondering what to make of the future. Although I had attempted to conceal my true feelings from Mary, I must have been unconvincing because she called me in the afternoon. She hoped she had not upset me and usually didn't tell people when she had a dream like that. But for some reason, she felt led to tell me.

"How did you interpret the dream?" I asked, having recovered from the initial shock and feeling more at ease discussing the matter away from other parishioners. Now, I wanted to hear every detail she could recall. I also did not want to discourage her from sharing her dreams; after all, if this was God's message to her, she was required to be obedient.

"I sensed God was holding you and telling you He loved you," she said quietly.

The following Sunday, Mary handed me a letter detailing more about her dream:

> When I walked into our church, and it was filled with water going around like a whirlpool, I was scared. But, then I saw something in the water. It looked like a piece of driftwood. I wanted to get it out. It reminded me of the story of Noah's Ark. God came with the rain and ended the world and started a new world . . . "Come to me all you who are weary and carry heavy burdens and I will give you rest." (Matt 11:28) . . . Taking turns holding each other up in the name of Jesus, we seek to use our spiritual gifts. And this is where you come into my dream. You have the gift of wisdom and discernment I have been drawn to you because of your gifts, I believe. The bright light so strong has always meant God's presence to me ever since I was a little girl. Please forgive me if I have caused a discomfort to you or your family. I do believe God holds you close to Him. I believe He was holding your hands and talking to you.

After reading and rereading Mary's letter, I carefully tucked it into my box with other letters and greeting cards received from friends after learning I had cancer. I sensed this was not an ordinary letter. These words from deep within her heart were a treasure. Mary was usually shy, quiet, and not outgoing. There was an angelic countenance about her and her eyes sparkled.

On Monday, my mind was still preoccupied with the dream. If God was sending me these strong messages, I'd better listen up and heed the warning. If I am going to die, I no longer can procrastinate about drawing up a will. Hadn't God spoken so clearly about it when I was in the hospital? Didn't He tell me to "get my house in order?" He had even gone so far as to send Theresa, a friend whose husband also was battling cancer to question me about a will. During our conversation, she had given me the name of her attorney who had set up a living trust for them, instead of a will. His name was familiar and I knew his wife. Somehow, that would make the task easier. I was ready to take the next step but how would Art feel about it?

Later that evening, I raised the subject. "Well," I began slowly, "If Mary's dream means what we think, then we should move ahead with our will. What do you think?"

"Yes," he answered resolutely and without hesitation. There was a sense of relief in his voice.

The attorney agreed to meet with us on December 11, the week before our scheduled appointment in Ann Arbor with Dr. Kaminski. The timing was perfect. It would not interfere with Danielle's December 5 wedding and before Christmas. In the meantime, I would have no additional treatments to cause my white blood counts to be down, making me susceptible to germs. I did not want my illness to overshadow or dampen anyone's spirits for the wedding celebration. This was a joyous time—time to focus on my responsibilities as mother of the bride.

Once again, help arrived to do those tasks I was not able to do. Her friends helped her with the wedding planning. Art's cousin Sarah, also gifted with organizational skills, brought her mop bucket of cleaning supplies to help get our home ready for special out-of-town guests. Those special guests included Danielle's birthparents, their spouses, and their extended families from California and Colorado. Danielle had been reunited with them at the age of twenty-one and remained in communication with them.

Mother came to stay with the children, while Art and I made the trip to Ann Arbor to see Dr. Kaminski. Except for the music on the car radio, there was little conversation. With negative thoughts swirling about in my mind, I fought tears the entire trip. Even though this first appointment was simply a consultation, the realization that my serious health problems necessitated the trip caused my fears to resurface. The truth was, neither of us really knew what would happen next. The tumor had not been reduced by any treatments so far, and two more sites had been revealed by the CT scan. Dr. Kaminski might be using a new drug on me.

Art had researched the new drug, Bexxar, and had printed pages of information from the Internet. It was an experimental drug, used in clinical studies. The outlook looked positive, yet there were some side effects for some people. Not every participant in the clinical study found it successful. Questions fluttered about in my mind. What if I experienced side effects? If I did join the study, would I be away from home at Christmastime? What if I could not participate in the Bexxar clinical study?

I was concerned the will was not finished. Although we had met with the attorney the previous week, it was not complete. Before our next appointment, we had to fill out the seven-page questionnaire that included financial questions, an inventory of our belongings, and questions about executors of the living trust we were setting up. It was not simply a matter of filling in the blanks. I knew it would require several days, if not weeks, to get all the paperwork together. I would have to trust God to give us time to do what needed to be done.

After reviewing my records and analyzing the pictures, Dr. Kaminski told us he did not want to involve me in the clinical studies at this time because the tumor was too large. When he saw our disappointment, he explained his main concern. If the main tumor continued to block my right kidney and he gave me a drug with a radioactive tag the kidney could not process, I might be faced with more trouble with an overdose of radiation to the kidney. However, he believed there was a good chance that a lower dose of radiation might effectively reduce the tumor and not harm surrounding tissue and organs. He expressed utmost confidence in both the Traverse City facilities and doctors for administering the proposed treatment. He planned to present my case before the University of Michigan's lymphoma doctors at their next scheduled meeting later in the week and would seek their input about his treatment plan.

We were discouraged as we drove home. We were skeptical about undergoing radiation treatments because initially Dr. Schwert had been opposed to the idea. He thought it too risky as it could harm the surrounding tissue and organs, as well as being fearful that future problems might result from the scar tissue. What would he think of this second opinion and the proposed treatment plan?

Dr. Kaminski's meeting with the lymphoma doctors confirmed his opinion as to the best treatment plan for me. Had Dr. Schwert had any misgivings about the second opinion and proposed treatment plan, he did not let on. I sensed he felt some measure of relief to share the responsibility for my treatment with other doctors. He arranged for treatments to begin after the first of the year with a radiologist at the Biederman Cancer Center in Traverse City. We gladly put all worries on the shelf until after Christmas. Writing Christmas notes to out-of-town family and friends, who knew nothing of my health concerns, allowed them to join others who were praying for me—for us.

By February 12, I had finished radiation treatments and met with Dr. Schwert to learn the results.

"You've done a lot better than most people receiving radiation," he said smiling. "You haven't lost weight or been real sick or had other problems."

"I've had a lot of people praying for me." I grinned, "Family and friends . . . I believe God was working."

He nodded and then changed the subject like he always did when I interjected something spiritual into our discussions. "The tumor is less than half the size it was," he said after measuring me and looking at the results of my latest CT scan, "We'll do another scan in six weeks as it may take that long to see the final results of the radiation treatment."

"Is it all right now to color my hair and go to the dentist?" I asked hopefully. It had been a year since I had colored my hair and had my teeth cleaned, adhering to the rules in the cancer booklets.

You can do both," he encouraged. "We won't do any more treatments until the CT scan comes back.

"What then?" Art chimed in.

"Well, I hope the tumor will be small enough so we can use the new drug, Bexxar. I will contact Dr. Kaminski with the results to see if she will qualify for the clinical study. That is my hope."

It was a relief not to have any treatments for the next six weeks and to live an almost-normal life. Although I had been forewarned the effects of the radiation might still cause extreme fatigue, I did not experience any negative side effects. I continued to work on my manuscript a few hours during the afternoon while the kids were at school, and each day I worked on some project organizing our home.

On March 26, we met with the doctor to learn the results of the latest CT scan. This time the scan showed no more reduction of the tumor than the previous 40 percent. However, rather than be in the shape of a softball, it had changed in its configuration and was now flatter. In fact, upon first examining me, the doctor could not feel it at all. He told us that he would get in touch with Dr. Kaminski to talk about a treatment plan.

On Good Friday, April 2, Dr. Schwert called to say he had heard from Dr. Kaminiski. The Bexxar study was now closed so that was no longer an option. He had also raised concern about the stent being in my right ureter, and suggested when the urologist replaced the stent in the next few weeks, he do some testing to see if the tumor was still pressing against it. Hopefully he could remove the old stent and not replace it. There would be another study coming to the University of Michigan in a month or so. Possibly, I would be a candidate for it.

After our telephone conversation with Dr. Schwert and hearing the disappointing news I would not be able to participate in the Bexxar study as we had hoped, Art and I were numb. The fact that medically nothing would be happening to further try to reduce the tumors was upsetting. What were we going to do? There was no certain action plan for us to look forward to in the future. It was troubling having to wait another month even to see the doctor. Until then, the only thing scheduled was the procedure with the urologist to replace the stent.

By Saturday, I had decided despite the bad news, I felt physically well enough to return to work. Regardless of the status of the cancer or when future treatments would be or what they might entail, I would call the travel agency and tell them I was ready to return to work on a part-time basis. I was apprehensive about the change again but felt it was the thing to do.

Instead of welcoming my call, I was informed there were no positions open for me in the accounting department. I hung up the telephone in disbelief. I thought a job would be waiting for me. They had told me they would work with me during my illness. I had written a letter last July, requesting a leave of absence until my health improved. I was devastated. I never imagined a job would not be waiting for me there. If not there, who would hire me, knowing I was a cancer patient? I tried not to cry around the children, but Art found me sobbing on the bed later that evening. By then, we were both so deflated, we had nothing more to say to one another about the events of the past week. We were both depressed.

Negative thoughts once again bombarded me. Do these obstacles mean that I am not going to get well? Is that the reason why I was not able to be in the study? Is that why I could not return to work? Is that why You wanted me to get my house in order so that it would be orderly when I left it behind? I thought about our two children still at home. I hated to have them grow up without a mother. A mother is not the same as a dad. I was the one who tucked them in bed each night and listened to their problems. Art did not usually know what was going on in the depths of their world. He was not aware their hearts were breaking from a disappointment. Usually, he was preoccupied with his own world of clients and troubles at the office.

"Lord," I prayed the next morning during devotions, "Please give me time to raise these children. Please don't take me until they are through school. I am needed right here. It wasn't my idea to be a mother so late in life. That was Your idea. I never dreamed when I asked for babies that I wouldn't live to see them grow up. I can't believe that You want me in heaven now, when I haven't finished the job You gave me down here."

The battle now was fighting off the barrage of negative thoughts and feelings. Do I pursue my scheduled dentist appointments, to talk to the periodontist and get a new crown as if I have a future or put it all off? Why should I waste money getting the dental work done if I'm not going to live? I looked in the mirror at my hair. I knew I would need it trimmed and colored if I went to work, even a temporary job at Manpower. Then, I remembered the scripture that taught about the importance of *living ready*. I needed to be ready and as healthy looking as I could possibly be. I went to the bedroom and found my little address book with my hairdresser's telephone number.

"Lisa, this is Bonnie Newhouse. I need my hair trimmed and colored. Can you fit me in sometime this week?"

Two hours later, Lisa was standing at my front door with bag in hand. I still did not know what the future would hold. I only knew that whatever took place, I was ready. God, who loves me and knows all about me and my family, knows what the future holds. There is nothing in my future that He does not know. Regardless of what others might think, I know all of this is not a surprise to Him. Did not the psalmist say in Psalm 139:16(14):

> You had scrutinized my every action,
> All were recorded in your book,
> my days listed and determined,
> even before the first of them occurred.

That was seventeen years ago. This year, August 2016, when I had a CT scan, the tests revealed kidney disease on the original damaged right kidney and the left kidney. This time my oncologist referred me to the University of Michigan Hospital, due to the complications of my case. I am again uncertain about the future, but I am ready for what is in store. The will is complete, the children have grown up and the book *Carved on the Palm of His Hand* is finished.

CHAPTER 23

IN THE TRENCHES

"A time for peace"
Ecclesiastes 3:8 (JB)

I had been applying for a full time job since August 2003, and by October, I had gone for at least five job interviews, while fighting discouragement. On October 18, I read the Prayers of Thanksgiving in my devotional: "I will look to the Lord. I will wait for the God of my salvation; my God will hear me" (Micah 7:7). (1) In the margin, I wrote, 'I am waiting!'

On Saturday December 6, I saw the ad in the local newspaper: "Non-profit organization seeking a bookkeeper/information referral coordinator. Must have excellent communication, organizational, and computer skills. Looking for an individual who works well with public and takes initiative in problem solving. Full time. Person with a disability preferred."

"It's as though the ad is directed to me!" I explained to Art as he sat down at the breakfast table. No sooner had I finished reading the ad to him, Danielle called.

"Mom, I found the perfect job for you!"

"I know, Honey, I saw it, too. I was just reading it to Dad. It's as though it has my name on it! Can you believe they even want someone with a disability?"

That same day I responded to the advertisement:

"I have a bachelor's degree in accounting from Ferris State University and have worked both in private business and public accounting. I also have considerable experience while working on parent and advisory committees for the Traverse City Area Public schools. Writing as a hobby has developed my communication skills and most recently led to volunteer grant research for the Traverse Junior Symphony Orchestras. I believe the attached reference letter from my business communications instructor at Northwestern Michigan College demonstrates my ability to be a positive influence in the workplace and a valuable asset to you."

I paused for a few minutes before going on. I did not normally include the next sentence in my letter to a potential employer. "I have actively been seeking employment since August, after having been on disability during my treatment for Non-Hodgkin's Lymphoma. Now in a good remission, my doctors have determined that I may return to the workplace."

After driving to the post office to mail my letter, I drove by the office where I hoped to work on my way home. It was a small office, situated next door to an insurance company about six miles from our house. Since the office was on a main travel route to town, in the days that followed, each time I drove by I would look for action at the office. Seldom did I see any cars parked in front. As the wait for a response continued, I became discouraged. I had been so certain that job was mine.

Finally, the second week in January I received a call to come in for an interview with the executive director. Another staff member sat in on the interview, taking notes. I was confident in my capabilities and was able to answer the questions posed to me and left the office encouraged. Several more weeks passed, when I received a phone call from the executive director, thanking me for coming in for the interview and informing me that someone else had been selected for the position. I thanked him for calling rather than sending me a letter and hung up the phone. I was puzzled as I had been so sure this job would be mine. I had been so sure, that for two months I had pursued no other jobs. Now, I was back to square one.

The scripture reading in my devotional on January 23, 2004 spoke to my heart:

I would have lost heart, unless I had believed that I would
see the goodness of the Lord in the land of the living. Wait
on the Lord; be of good courage and He shall strengthen
your heart; wait I say on the Lord. (Psalm 27:13–14) (2)

After two more days, I captured my anxious thoughts and wrote
in the margin of my devotional, "I continue to wait!"

Three days later Jim, the executive director, called me about references for the job at Northern Michigan Alliance for Independent Living. Soon after, he called back again to offer me the position and explained the person he had selected had taken another position, and I had been the second choice.

Although the office was small, the Center for Independent Living (CIL) was actually part of a larger network, not only in Michigan but also across the United States. The Mission was to help people with disabilities of all ages and all types of disabilities. To understand what that mission entailed, part of my orientation required an on-line Independent Living Philosophy course. I welcomed the opportunity to learn more because, unlike most of the staff, I had little knowledge of the disability movement or training in social work.

I learned the earliest CIL was in Berkeley, California in 1972 and later in Boston, and Houston. Six years later, the passage of Federal Legislation, Title VII of the Rehabilitation Act provided funding to establish independent living centers in every state. These centers differed from other service organizations because they were mandated to be governed by a majority of people with disabilities: both their boards and employees. In the search for employees to fill open positions, they seek qualified people with disabilities to fill management and service delivery positions.

Northern Michigan Alliance for Independent Living (NMAIL) was a developing Center for Independent Living with a staff of only four, so everyone had multiple responsibilities. When Jim needed someone to serve on the State Disability Network Work Group for Long-Term Care, he asked me. There were monthly conference calls to attend and occasionally a state-wide meeting in Lansing. The chair of our committee also served on the Governor's Long-Term Care Committee, so I had access to some of the latest developments in the nation in the area of long-term care. In the first several years, I wrote two forum articles for the local newspaper, informing readers about the changes on the horizon for seniors as the baby boomers reached retirement. Having been born the month World War II ended, I identified with the baby-boomers and found the subject most interesting.

I decided to take some copies of my latest published article, when I attended a statewide conference in April 2006, hoping some of the attendees would find the information of interest. Later that morning, the Metro-Detroit Marketing Manager for *AgeWise Magazine* stopped by my booth, looking for sponsors to advertise in his magazine. I knew our agency did not have funds available to advertise, but I did see an opportunity for statewide exposure of my recently published piece. So we exchanged my article for one of his business cards. Turning to leave, he mentioned that the Magazine's editor was also attending the conference. Later, he returned to introduce her to me.

After lunch, I looked across the room and saw some conference attendees I knew from another agency in Traverse City and briefly left my booth to go visit them. While talking to them, I noticed the Editor of *AgeWise Magazine* walking by scanning the crowd, looking for someone she planned to ask to write an article for her magazine. Suddenly, she turned to me. "Would you be interested in writing a piece about the mystery of Castle Farms?"

"Yes, I'm interested," I shot back without hesitation. "When is the deadline?"

"I need it the first part of July," She answered. "I'd like some pictures to go with the piece."

It wasn't until later the following weekend when I had time to think more about my commitment that *fear* slowly crept in. "What in the world was I thinking?" I groaned to Art. "I've never written an article like this before." The only time I had ever been to Castle Farms was to attend a Willie Nelson concert in August of 1983, and I knew very little about the mystery surrounding it.

I went downstairs to the computer that weekend and began to fervently research my topic. The following week, I visited the library and checked out several books. Little by little, I devoured all the information I could find and began taking notes and piecing the story together. Once I began to delve into my subject, I found it not to be a laborious task but extremely fascinating. The mystery surrounding

Castle Farms involved the teenage son of the owner of Castle Farms. It came to be known as, the trial of the century (20th) in Chicago, and the story occupied the front pages of newspapers across the nation and around the world the entire summer of 1924. On trial, Richard Loeb and his best friend Nathan Leopold, Jr. were accused of kidnapping and murdering fourteen-year-old Bobbie Franks. The defense attorney was the famed Clarence Darrow.

Once I had completed the article, I had to find suitable photos. What an adventure to race home from the office on my lunch hour to contact the archives of the New York Times and Chicago Tribune for permission to publish the photos. I visited the Historical Society in nearby Charlevoix to obtain a 1924 period picture of Castle Farms. How exciting for me, when it all came together and the fall 2006 issue of *AgeWise Magazine* arrived at our home with my article on page 30. My compensation included complimentary copies of the magazine, which I promptly signed, shared with my co-workers, and sent off to family and friends around the country.

I kept in touch with the magazine's editor and, the following May, met her for coffee while attending an annual conference in Lansing. I told her about the book manuscript I had been laboring over for more than thirty years during our conversation. The following year, I took her a copy of my manuscript for review. She found it interesting and offered to take a serious look at chapter 1. Upon its return, I could scarcely see past the red lines and comments.

"I guess I'll redo the rest before agreeing to any more editing," I told my friend Judith, who shared my vision of the finished manuscript. The manuscript would stay on the shelf until I could focus on it without other distractions. I chose to concentrate on the other areas of my job, and I did not write any more articles. In addition to being the accountant, my responsibilities had grown to office manager and the agency's name had changed to Disability Network/Northern Michigan (DN/NM). We had grown from covering five counties to covering seventeen—the top third of Michigan's Lower Peninsula.

As I reflected on my daily routine at the office and looked at the population we served, I smiled. God hadn't made a mistake in placing me where he had. If believers truly are His hands and feet, why wouldn't I be here? All around me were the very people Jesus surrounded himself with when He walked the earth—the disabled, the blind, the deaf, and those suffering with any number of physical and mental disabilities. At first, I noticed the disability; however, in no time I looked past the disability and saw the person whose need brought them to our office. Every day, I had the opportunity to serve by listening and giving hope for the situation and encouragement for the journey.

One of our core services was the role of advocate, and I learned that could mean an even deeper involvement with an individual for a longer period. It reminded me of the old western movies from childhood. Sometimes two cowboys would meet on a trail at some point and travel quite a distance, side by side. The longer you traveled with someone, the better acquainted you became. I thought a lot about the concept. The Bible talks about the Holy Spirit being our Advocate and praying for us when we do not have the words to pray for ourselves. Jesus spoke of the Advocate He would be sending (John 15:26) (3): "When the Advocate comes, whom I shall send to you from the Father, the Spirit of truth who issues from the Father, he will be my witness."

Roget's Thesaurus offers even more explanations: close friend, supporter, and defender. Yet, I have never seen the word described as enabler, thus the delicate balance, guided by the Holy Spirit. What a privilege to serve in that capacity relying on Him to guide each step. What a blessing to have someone in the role as an advocate.

Another lesson God taught me in the trenches was an appreciation for Art's unique ministry, working for Community Mental Health. Not until I began to have contact with individuals with mental health disabilities and witnessed the battles they faced in society did I begin to understand. God had given him that gift to understand. He had a heart for them and the struggles they faced and was able to be an effective advocate with sincere compassion for those who suffered with depression, bipolar disorder, or other mental illnesses. Not everyone had that gift. It was a special calling.

As Art retired as operations manager from Northern Lakes Community Mental Health in 2010, after serving there almost twenty-five years, our life began to take on significant changes. While there, he had supervised emergency services, outpatient services, and the Assertive Community Treatment Program. During his tenure, he had developed the mental health program for both Grand Traverse and Leelanau County jails. After retirement, he did maintain a small private practice at The Maple Clinic, primarily working with sex offenders, another group often ostracized by society.

Perhaps scheduling his long-needed knee replacement surgery the month he retired complicated the transition for both of us. During his weeks of recuperation, he spent hours on the couch in the living room. When he was able to get around more, he immediately began to take charge of his new surroundings. His first project was to paint the four walls in the living room. Next, he decided to redo our small galley kitchen, which had always been my domain. Had he stopped with painting the kitchen, I may have understood. But when he subtly began to reorganize the contents, I bristled!

After years of working with the public and managing teams at Community Mental Health, he found it quite an adjustment to adapt to his new routine. Our roles reversed, Art was home managing the household, cooking the meals, and grocery shopping, while I left each day to interact with the public and carry out my responsibilities at the office. Before long, I realized how thankful I was to still be working and escape during the workday. One day, I came home to find my favorite cutting board in the garage and a new one in its place. Other things that he did not use were stored away and moved to a box in the basement. When I was home on the weekends or vacation and had more time to spend in the kitchen, I would be furious to discover some utensil I had always used now displaced.

Another source of disagreement was the home computer, which until now, we shared. He did not like my style of disorganization and little by little set out to reorganize our files. I did not mind when he was organizing his files, but when it came to the desktop, or finding one of my files, I would be furious when I could not find it. We had more arguments that first year than we had had the previous ten years! The saving grace for me was the reprieve of escaping to my job each day. It was not too long before he got me my own laptop computer for Christmas.

Once I recognized my anger on the surface, God revealed to me a deeper level of anger. That level required forgiveness. This emotional layer took longer to wade through. Slowly, issues surfaced I needed to address. I carried memories of all the years, home raising children, doing domestic duties, taking the back seat to all of Art's fans and co-workers. I was angry about all the years, when Art's attention and energy focused on other people—first in the church and then in his job at mental health. I harbored resentment for all the years when only remnants remained for family.

The kids were thrilled to get all this new attention from Dad and soaked it up like sponges. Without exception, all called home during the week to talk to Dad and share the events of their lives. The reacquainting period was mutual with the children. By the time I got home from work, he would do his best to relay the conversations and the news. Then later, when everyone got a cell phone, it was not only calls; it was text messages. Feeling left out of their lives, I realized the need to make more of an effort to connect with them even though working.

Fortunately, God bridged the void in Art's life due to a crisis in our congregation. We had joined Bethlehem Lutheran Church—an ELCA congregation like our former congregation, but much larger, enabling us to successfully fade into anonymity. In fact, we took it a step further and attended the Saturday evening service attended by less than fifty parishioners. Church attendance was our only participation in the congregational life.

We did not get involved in the usual church controversy when the pastor retired, and the congregation called a married couple to serve as pastors. Weary of congregational turmoil, we both lacked the emotional energy to join the fray. In the end, the couple left and took a percentage of the congregation with them to start a new congregation.

With a divided congregation, the Synod decided to call an intentional interim pastor to help in the healing process. When no one seemed willing to take on the task, one pastor sent a letter to the district office offering his services. Although officially retired, he was ready to take on the challenge. He and his wife had previously visited our congregation and had family in the area. When we learned the name, we looked at each other in disbelief. Dan had graduated from the same seminary as Art—only two years ahead and worked at the same CPA firm that I had during our seminary years.

Later, we learned that Dan and Mary Lou had left the Missouri Synod during the same turbulent time in the synod. The last congregation he served was in Alpena on the eastern side of Michigan. Although their paths had never crossed at seminary, and I had minimal contact with him at work, we had traveled similar paths since leaving the seminary. Dan proved to be a very dynamic preacher, and God's healing message to the congregation was delivered every week. When he went on vacation or was sick, he did not hesitate to ask Art to fill in. Dan served our congregation for two years before ill health caused him to resign.

During the months of the pastoral search, Art was one of the four retired pastors, all members of Bethlehem, who served on the rotation. Retired from his job at Community Mental Health, once again he was thoroughly enjoying preparing sermons and serving in that capacity. It was wonderful to see him delving into scripture and bringing an inspirational message to the congregation. I could see it helped him defuse from his years serving in the mental health community and the daily problems he faced. It helped him make the transition and bridge the gap between the two worlds.

We learned of the fortieth anniversary of Art's seminary class indirectly from another of Art's classmates. We had stayed in touch with Bruce and Ann over the years via Christmas cards.

"Are you going to the class reunion?" Bruce asked.

"I didn't get an invitation," Art responded, "I haven't heard from the seminary in years."

"The reunion is May 17 and 18 in Fort Wayne, Indiana. I'll give them your email address," he said in closing.

"Thanks for letting me know. I'll talk to Bonnie and get back to you," Art promised.

"I'll go only if there are no hassles or arguments about religious controversies," I told him when he called me at work about the upcoming reunion. "I think our best witness will be our actions. If some of them still think we are heretics for leaving the Missouri Synod, they can hear our witness and see what paths God has led us on before making the final judgment!" Agreeing, Art began making all arrangements and registering our attendance.

Our participation proved healing for us. Along with all of his seminary classmates, Art received an Award of Achievement in recognition of having served forty years in the Holy Ministry. God proved larger than the synodical divisions, which had divided us since graduation. The work of the Holy Spirit continued in the lives of the seminarians, regardless of where they had served. It reminded me of Paul's experience, when he and Barnabas clashed over the issue of taking John Mark with them on their missionary journey (Acts 15:39–40). (4) The result was Barnabas sailed off to Cyprus with Mark while Paul chose Silas for his traveling companion and went in the direction of Syria, Cilicia, Derbe, and then on to Lystra where he met the disciple Timothy for the first time.

As I look back on the seasons of my life, I notice some seasons repeat: seasons of loved ones being born and seasons of loved ones dying. There were also more scatterings of people. No one was more surprised than I, when six months before I retired from Disability Network/Northern Michigan, other staff members also left the agency. By the time I left, Jim faced a 90 percent turnover of full-time staff. I told him I likened it to "a perfect storm." First was Lisa, our volunteer coordinator finishing her master's degree and going to another agency in town; next was Annie, our resource development manager who needed a new challenge and moved out of state. Then Phil, our disability guide specialist, took a new job with a sister CIL downstate to be nearer family. Some were complete surprises to me; others were not. By far the biggest shock was when Renee, our information and assistance and quality assurance manager, passed away the day before I officially retired, after spending the month in ICU with an infection. She was only thirty-nine years old, married and the mother of three children, ages 20, 13, and 3.

Renee and I had worked closely together, and her office was right behind mine. Sometimes we would talk about our walk with the Lord and would share our experiences. She had great faith. The scene etched in my memory is the first day I met her, arriving at our office to attend a staff meeting. The beautiful young woman with long, dark hair and a lovely smile, fashionably dressed in bright colors, pretty scarf around her neck, briskly moved her wheelchair to the conference table. Renee was feisty and unforgettable to all who knew her.

She had completed her master's degree in social work during her tenure at DN/NM and as a requirement for one of her classes, had interviewed my mother in her ninetieth year and written a paper about her life and experiences.

Until the last day, I had hoped and believed for a miracle for Renee, praying for God's complete healing. Maybe in the healing process, God might even heal her paralysis of nearly fifteen years. But that was not to be. I recalled several things that occurred over the last few months and tried to understand the meaning. The first was the beautiful clump of roses that grew up on the side of the office beside where Renee parked her van. I could see the rosebush from my work window and had been watching the unusual flower growing since July. When all the buds had blossomed, I noticed although they were on the same stem, the first bud to blossom was a light pink while the remainder on the stem were a darker shade of pink.

Both Renee and I had been so fascinated at the unusual bouquet of blossoms, we had taken pictures on our cell phones. By the time all the darker buds had fully blossomed, the pink one in the center had already begun to wither, so I decided to cut the stem off and put it in a vase on Renee's desk. She had leaned over to smell the fragrance, and counted the roses commenting that the roses signified each of the office staff. Wanting to preserve it, she had sprayed hair spray on the petals. We were both dismayed when, rather than preserve it, the petals fell all over her desk and on the floor. So I gathered all the rose petals and put them in the vase on her desk to still enjoy the fragrance.

September came, and Renee was admitted to the hospital with an infection after Labor Day. About the middle of September, I noticed that the clump of roses was growing back on the same stem and when the buds had blossomed, they had blossomed exactly like the bouquet I had cut off! I had been intrigued at that unusual circumstance. Renee was in critical condition on September 17, the twenty-fifth anniversary of the Americans with Disabilities Act (ADA), and most of the office staff had gone to Lansing for the State celebration. I planned to go visit her at the hospital even though she was in critical condition and in a coma.

During my devotions, I had felt impressed to take to Renee a little treasure I had been carrying in my change purse for the past seventeen years. It was a small, oval artifact given to me by a member of our congregation, when I was in the middle of my battle with cancer. He had carried it for many years as he was raised Catholic, and said I should keep it until I felt led to pass it to someone else. I had taken it out and made a copy of it before passing it on. There was a picture on the front of the face of a young woman with a pink rose below. The inscription on the back read: *Soil from the Grave of Marie Rose Ferron Known as Little Rose Stigmatized Ecstatic 1902–1936.*

Not being Catholic, I really did not know what its significance had been to me all those seventeen years or what it might mean to Renee. I only knew I needed to get it to her. For some reason, it belonged with her. She had been raised Catholic, so it seemed logical that she should have it in her time of crisis.

The next day, those who had traveled to the ADA celebration were back in the office. Marte presented me with two pins—three puzzle pieces glued to the back of a pin. They had been a craft project handed out by a group affiliated with another downstate CIL. She said one was for me, the other for Renee. I put Renee's on her desk, thinking it symbolized my connection to her. We were puzzle pieces of each other's lives. It was not the first time a puzzle symbolized such a connection. I recalled another time I felt so connected to someone else's puzzle was when I met my two half-sisters in 1976, thirty-nine years before.

As I reflect on my journey, I see the similarities and patterns God allows in each of our lives. The paths may vary, but the patterns remain. Sometimes, God will separate us for a time from close friends. Sometimes we drift apart and go down separate paths, never to reconnect. Other times, we find our paths cross again and once more connect. With some, the bonding is so close in the connecting, it may seem no time has passed even though we may have aged and raised our families during our years apart. In this, God's blessing is powerful. The blessing is even greater when He allows reconnection in a marriage.

I looked back on God's faithfulness over the years when we celebrated our fiftieth wedding anniversary in 2015. I remembered my fearfulness prior to sending out our wedding invitations in 1965, as I faced the reality of my decision to commit to spending an entire lifetime with one person. I had prayed fervently for God's guidance in proceeding with our wedding plans.

Then in 1971, when God clearly spoke, "I don't will for you to be unhappy. I love you. I care for you. Don't wait for Art to change himself and become the same person who once needed you. Don't count on that happening. He won't even be able to help you solve your problem. He's in an entirely different place than you. Only I can help you. You must begin at once, listening and trusting that still, inner voice you have come to recognize as Mine. You must be fully prepared to act whether or not Art understands. The root of your unhappiness is idolatry. You have gradually elevated Art to a pedestal, the same pedestal on which many others place their husbands. He has become the center of your life.

Your depression is directly related to your preoccupation with him, his importance, and his activities. As a result, you now find yourself in the dangerous dilemma Jesus warned about: serving two masters. Your husband has become an idol in your life, and you must take immediate steps to put him back in his proper place of importance. You must take your eyes off your husband and look only to Jesus. Your dependency on Art must be transferred to Him where it rightly belongs. It is necessary for you to arrive at a place in your spiritual life where you can say and mean: Jesus is the center of your life. He will totally care for you, filling any needs you have. You must arrive at a place where you can truthfully say, 'I can get along without Art if that is required of me.'"

I remember my response to God's words: "But Lord, that's such a drastic measure. To consciously push my husband out of my mind sounds so cold, so cruel. It doesn't sound like something a wife should be doing. What will happen to our relationship? What will happen to our marriage?"

God's words are forever etched in my memory: "You will just have to trust Me and have faith in My guidance. Because of the extreme to which you have gone, it is necessary to revert to an extreme to correct your path. When I know you are safely able to return to a more middle ground, I, myself will bring it about. You must believe I know what is best for both you and your marriage."

Truly, He is the potter and I am the clay. *"I am His workmanship, created in Christ Jesus for good works, which God prepared beforehand that I should walk in them"* (Ephesians 2:9). (5)

The potter knew what He purposed for this piece of clay, how He wanted to use me, and what tools would be required to mold me into that vessel for His own purpose. Sometimes the tool was heavy and came close to breaking me. Sometimes the fire was so hot, it seemed to consume me. Yet, the Father knew exactly the process that would mold me to match the vision He always had for me and for my life. The process continues. He has fulfilled His promise to me. He has *Carved Me on the Palm of His Hand* and I have fulfilled my promise to Him. The vow I made more than forty years ago has been finished.

In reading my devotional for May 2 titled "The Passion of Patience" in *My Utmost for His Highest* (6), Oswald Chambers refers to Habakkuk 2:3: "Though it tarry, Wait for it." He wrote:

> Patience is not indifference; patience conveys the idea of an immensely strong rock withstanding all onslaughts. The vision of God is the source of patience, because it imparts a moral inspiration . . . You always know when the vision is of God because of the inspiration that comes with it; things come with largeness and tonic to the life because everything is energized by God . . . 'Though it tarry wait for it.' The proof that we have the vision is that we are reaching out for more than we have grasped.

Once again, my thoughts reverted to my confirmation verse, chosen by Rev. Woldt for me and read as he laid hands on my head at the altar of Christ Lutheran Church in Lansing, Michigan, at the age of 14:

> Wait on the Lord;
> Be of good courage,
> And He shall strengthen your heart;
> Wait, I say, on the Lord! (Psalm 27:14) (7)

This same verse was also the verse in my devotions on May 10, 1997, the day I graduated from Ferris State University, at the age of fifty-one. Waiting on the Lord has been the theme of my life—I would wait for childbirth, wait thirty years to graduate from college, and wait forty-four years to finish the book He had directed me to write. God has been faithful through it all. I praise His name!

CHAPTER 24

UNFINISHED BUSINESS
VIET NAM REVISITED

"A time for healing"
Ecclesiastes 3:3 (JB)

*T*hree days before Christmas 2001, Art's brother, Tom called to tell him he had responded to an offer by Ginko's in Lansing. They would scan pictures of deceased Viet Nam War veterans and post them beside their names on the Virtual Wall (www.thevirtual-wall.org). Since Tom did not have an Internet connection at his house to check it out, he wanted Art to go online to investigate.

Hurrying downstairs, Art pulled up Bernard's site on the World Wide Web. The picture of Bernard was there along with a remembrance, posted on Thursday October 4, 2001. It read:

> Doc Newhouse, I remember you well, and think of
> you often."
> Relationship: "We served together"

George had posted his name and email address at the site. A name! At last, a name of someone who knew Bernard when he was in Viet Nam!

Quickly Art typed an email to George, explaining Bernard was his brother, and he had been searching for thirty-three years, hoping to find someone who might have served with him in Viet Nam.

Within a few hours, Art received a response:

> So glad to hear from you. You wonder sometimes if people will ever see what you wrote on those remembrances. The time I spent with your brother was on my second tour of duty in Viet Nam. I do remember him very well. I was with him when he was killed. If I can help you in any way regarding information, and so on, please feel free to call me or email or write. I would be glad to answer any questions you may have. Your brother has been in my mind all these years as well.

Listed at the bottom was his home address and telephone number. After printing out the email for me to read, Art hurried upstairs. Tears welled up in my eyes as I read the words: "I was with him when he was killed."

The tape of our lives rewound to another Saturday—nearly thirty-four years before—to the day the family had been notified that Bernard, a Navy corpsman, had been killed the previous Sunday, April 21, 1968.

"I think we should send him a dozen white roses," I said, choking back tears. Maybe Art would think the idea a bit presumptuous; I only knew the idea had come as a sudden flash—a directive from God.

"That's a great idea!"

"Let's call the florist right now." I said excitedly. "We have his address. Maybe they can deliver them yet this afternoon!"

Art reached for the telephone book and called.

". . . a dozen white roses . . . Yes, an arrangement. The message on the card should read:

'God Bless you—Doc Newhouse's Family'"

"Hopefully the flowers can be delivered today," he relayed joyfully. "If not, they'll be delivered on Monday, Christmas Eve Day."

Later that evening, Art checked our email and found a message from George:

I don't know what to say! Thank you so much for the roses. My wife and daughter saw them first and couldn't get over how beautiful they were. From your e-mail and the flowers, of course, I can tell just how much Ben meant to you . . . We tried to call you, but I found your telephone number isn't listed. We tried to call when we received the flowers. There are so many things I would like to tell you about Ben and his experiences in Viet Nam, including other people who knew him that I have been in contact with. . . . Once again, my family and I are overwhelmed by such a gift, especially at this time of year.

God Bless You—George

Art's reply thanked him for the communication and the offer to share additional information about Bernard. He also explained to revisit Viet Nam after all these years was overwhelming, and he was not quite ready. George replied he understood and to let him know when he was ready.

It was strange, and seemed as though we were living in two different time periods—thirty-four years apart. Physically we were a middle-age couple with four children, a son-in-law, and three grandchildren, going through the motions of the present, going to church on Sunday, and last-minute Christmas preparations. Emotionally, we were reliving the tragic event of nearly thirty-four years ago as two college students in our early twenties with no children, grieving over the loss of a brother. The rest of the family did not fit in that picture. I longed to be alone with my thoughts and to cry if I wanted. I sensed Art felt the same way because periodically each of us would well up with tears and choke them back as much as possible.

On Christmas Eve Day, we checked our email and found four pictures from George. The first was one of George and another Marine in Viet Nam in December of 1967—the month before Bernard arrived. The second picture, taken by Bernard just after his arrival in January 1968, showed ten Marines in his new unit. The last pictures were recent, taken in July 2001 when the surviving members of the Marine

Unit held a reunion in Washington, DC. One showed George and two others standing in front of the Viet Nam Memorial Wall where Bernard's name is listed along with the others killed that day.

"Let's call him!" Art suggested.

"Yes! Do you mind if I pick up the other phone? I don't want to miss anything he says."

When no one answered, Art left a message and returned to gift-wrapping, while I continued making pies. It was nearly five o'clock on Christmas Eve when the phone rang. For the next hour, we listened intently as George told us of the events surrounding Bernard's death.

"I have to start at the beginning of that day," he began slowly. "It was Sunday morning, April 21, 1968. We had been occupying a hill for the past two months when the order came that we were to evacuate and relocate to another hill near Ke Sahn. The guys began gathering up all the supplies and ammunition, making a huge pile — about ten feet by eight feet. The Lieutenant was standing on top of the pile, giving directions. Suddenly, one of the guys threw a box of ordinance on the pile, without having diffused it. The whole pile exploded, instantly killing the Lieutenant and five other men."

"That was 9:00 in the morning. Now, with the Lieutenant and all the other officers dead, I was in charge of the platoon. Eventually we were evacuated out to the other location. Soon after we arrived there, we were ordered to retrieve the bodies of some Marines who had been overrun the day before on another hill."

"Twenty of us in the platoon, including your brother, started up the hill. When we got to the top, it was bare grass with the exception of two stumps. No sooner had we reached the top that we started taking on heavy enemy fire. I sent them off scattering in twos, telling them to dig holes for cover. You see, we had little shovels."

"Your brother was the first to be killed. I was looking right at Ben when I saw a mortar round coming in and make a direct hit on him and the other guy who was digging in with him. The other guy was badly injured but survived. He died last year of cancer."

"I was about twenty feet away from your brother and was wounded as well. The shelling lasted from 1:00 that afternoon until 9:00 the next morning without any let up. Guys were getting hit all night, and there was nothing I, or anyone else, could do as we were all pinned down. Ben was the only corpsman, and he had been carrying all the medical supplies."

George paused a moment before going on. "We listened to guys dying all night long. Out of the twenty of us, only five survived. That was the most terrible day I have ever experienced . . ."

Art and I continued to listen, spellbound, as George recounted the horrific day. He, too, had been injured and medically evacuated to a hospital. That was to be the last day on the battlefield for him, ending his second tour of duty in Viet Nam.

Our hearts went out to him, realizing how much suffering he and the others had experienced that fateful day. We wanted to reach out through space and hug him. Perhaps that was the reason for the white roses, something tangible—a token to express our love and appreciation for being there when we couldn't. Before we got off the phone, George's wife, Patty asked to speak to us.

"Do you know what white roses signify?" she asked.

"No, we only knew they were supposed to be white."

"They symbolize eternal love—I raise roses, so I know a little about them. In the arrangement you sent, one of the roses stands a little higher. It's as though it represents your brother."

After we hung up the phone, we realized George was our Christmas miracle. His story was a Christmas gift to us from God—a gift of healing that few could understand. We praised God that George had taken a leap of faith when he had posted that remembrance. By doing so, he was risking the opening up of a deep and painful wound for himself and his family.

"Why, God? Why now?" we asked.

Something Art told me gave me a clue. He didn't recall when his morning routine had changed. But for some time, each day when he arrived at work an hour early, he went to the Viet Nam Memorial site on the World Wide Web where each day's casualties of the War were listed by day of the year. Each day he prayed for the families of each one. Could it be those prayers offered had unleashed the new miracle we were living? My mind flashed back to the story of Job. His circumstances turned around when at last he was able to pray for his friends (Job 42:10).

For the next six months, we continued to exchange emails and occasionally a phone call. One thing was certain. We knew we must arrange a meeting with George and his wife Patty. There was so much more to share, more to talk about face to face. That meeting would take place on July 4, 2002 when they would visit us in Traverse City. Bernard's twin sister would also have an opportunity to meet and talk with them. As we exchanged memories of our loved one, we realized the weekend was really a celebration of life—Bernard's life—just thirty-four years late!

By July 4, 2005, George would publish his own book: *Born in the '40s, Raised in the '50s, Died in the '60s.*

Art and Bonnie's wedding picture

Art and Bonnie 50th Anniversary

Benjamin and Family

Danielle and Family

Matthew and Claudia

Traci

END NOTES

Introduction
1. Stowell, Joseph M., *The Weight of Your Words*, Moody Press, p. 123, Chicago, Illinois, 1998.

Chapter 1
1. Peale, Norman Vincent, *The Power of Positive Thinking*. Englewood Cliffs, N.J.: Prentice-Hall, Inc., 1952. p.3.

2. Ibid.

Chapter 6
1. Price, Eugenia, *Woman To Woman,* Grand Rapids, Michigan: Zondervan Publishing House, 1959.

Chapter 9
1. Peale, Norman Vincent, *The Power of Positive Thinking*. Englewood Cliffs, N.J.: Prentice-Hall, Inc., 1952.

2. Ibid.

Chapter 10
1. Marshall, Catherine, *Beyond Ourselves*, New York, N.Y.: McGraw-Hill, 1961.

2. II Corinthians 12:7–10 (JB).

Chapter 11
1. O'Connor, Elizabeth, *Eighth Day of Creation,* Waco, Texas: Word Books, 1971.

Chapter 12
1. Ephesians 6:10–17 (JB).

Chapter 14
1. *Missouri in Perspective,* Document, ELIM Tracts, 12015 Manchester, St. Louis, MO 63131.

Chapter 15
1. I Corinthians 12.

2. Frost, Dr. Robert C., *Aglow with the Spirit.* Northridge, Calif.; Voice Publications, 1965.

3. Acts 1:4–5.

4. Carothers, Merlin R., *Prison to Praise.* Plainfield, N.J.: Logos International, 1970.

5. Carothers, Merlin R., *Power in Praise.* Plainfield, N.J.: Logos International, 1972.

6. Newhouse, Rev. Arthur M., *The Redeemer Tidings,* Denver.

7. Preus, President J.A.O., *Letter to the Members of the Boards of Directors* of the Atlantic, California-Nevada, Colorado, Eastern, English, New England, and Northwest Districts of the Lutheran Church—Missouri Synod, Saint Louis, Missouri, February 5, 1976.

8. Letter to Members of Redeemer Lutheran Church, Denver, Colorado, November 15, 1976.

9. Culver, Virginia, "Another Lutheran Pastor Quits," *The Denver Post,* November 22, 1976.

10. Newhouse, Rev. Arthur M., Letter to the Members of Redeemer, Denver, Colorado. November 21, 1976

Chapter 16
1. Isaiah 61:1.

2. Isaiah 66:2.

3. Jeremiah 27:12.

4. Jeremiah 29:11.

5. Mumford, Bob, *The Purpose of Temptation,* Old Tappan, New Jersey: Fleming H. Revell Company, 1973.

6. Ibid, p. 43.

7. Ibid, p. 69.

8. Ibid, pp. 76–77.

9. Ibid, p. 131 (I Corinthians 10:13)

10. Phil 4:8.

11. Jeremiah 30:3.

Chapter 17
1. John 16:24

2. Roberts, Oral, *Believe In a Miracle* Tulsa, Oklahoma. Oral Roberts Evangelistic Assoc., Inc. 1977.

3. Luke 23:43 (JB).

4. Revelation 11.

5. Micah 5:3.

6. Habakkuk 2:1–4.

Chapter 18
1. Newhouse, Bonnie, "Ex-hostage Tells of Ordeal," *Traverse City Record-Eagle,* June 12,1981.

2. John 14:31.

3. John 16:32.

4. Hebrews 11:1.

5. Chambers, Oswald, *My Utmost For His Highest,* Barbour Publishing, Uhrichsville, Ohio 1963.

6. Frost, Gerhard E., *The Color of the Night,* Minneapolis, MN. Augsburg Publishing House, 1977.

7. I Samuel 1:10–11.

8. Moya, Mimi, "Concerned Women Chapter Forming," *Traverse City Record-Eagle,* Nov.18, 1985.

9. Roush, Matthew," A Few Good Words For the Anti-Porn Movement," *Traverse City Record-Eagle;* Oct. 1985

10. Newhouse, Bonnie, "The Link Between Pornography and Crime," *Traverse City Record-Eagle*; December 9, 1985.

Chapter 19
1. Newhouse, Bonnie, "More Should be Told About Firing of Hospital Chief," *Traverse City Record-Eagle;* October 5, 1987.

2. Newhouse, Bonnie, "Ninth Graders Shouldn't Be Put in High School," *Traverse City Record-Eagle;* April 27, 1988.

3. Towner, Nicki, "Questions Warranted," *Traverse City Record-Eagle,* May 16, 1988.

4. Norton, Mike, "Election Forum Offers Surprises," *Traverse City Record-Eagle,* July 20, 1988.

5. Newhouse, Bonnie, "An Alternative to the T.C. Middle School Plan," *Traverse City Record-Eagle,* September 2,1988.

6. Matthew 18:20 7. Norton, Karen, "Oxender Resigns as TC School Chief," *Traverse City Record-Eagle,* November 22, 1988.

8. Norton, Mike, "Chamber Hires School Curriculum Consultant," *Traverse Record-Eagle,* February 2,1989.

9. Norton, Mike, "Trust between Schools, Public Urged," *Traverse City Record-Eagle,* March 8, 1989.

10. Finley, Lorraine, "T.C. School Millage Bond issue Ok'd" *Traverse City Record-Eagle,* June 13, 1989

Chapter 20
1. Iserbyt, Charlotte T., "Reading: The Civil-Rights Issue of the '90s," *The Camden Herald,* July 6, 1989.

2. Letter from Ron Cowden, Principal T.C Senior High School.

3. Newhouse, Bonnie, "New School Assessment Test Program Generates Concern," *Traverse City Record-Eagle;* March 8, 1990.

4. "Letter to the editor," *Traverse City Record-Eagle,* May 6, 1990.

5. Personal Notes from telephone call to Matt's teacher, October,1990 Traverse City, Michigan.

6. Newhouse, Bonnie, "Letter to DAC Members," January 7, 1991, Traverse City, Michigan.

7. Stanton, Anne, "Area Students Outperform State Average in MEAP Tests," *Traverse City Record-Eagle,* February 8, 1990.

8. Stanton, Anne, "Traverse City Students Score Low in Essential Skills' Reading Test," Ibid.

9. Newhouse, Bonnie. Personal notes from an in-service meeting. Speaker: Dr. George Sherman, Michigan State University, Traverse City, Michigan February 22, 1991.

10. Newhouse, Bonnie, "Basic Reading Essential," *Traverse City Record-Eagle,* March 28, 1991.

11. Notes from meeting with Pat Dolanski, Grand Traverse Dyslexia Association

12. *U.S. Senate Republican Policy Committee Report on Illiteracy* September 13, 1989.

13. Blumenfeld, Samuel, "One Third Become Disabled," *The Blumenfeld Education Letter,* Vol. IV, No. 9 (Letter #37).

14. *Turning Points, Preparing American Youth for the 21st Century, Carnegie Council on Adolescent Development,* Washington, DC, 1989

15. Caldemeyer, Cecile, "The Trust Me Express," July, 1989, p. 13. Originally the qoute is by Hooks, Vandlyn. "Educational Reform: The Political Agenda for Restructuring Education," p. 3.

16. Newhouse, Bonnie, "Opt Your Kids Out of Michigan Model," *Traverse City Record-Eagle,* November 25, 1990.

17. Perloff, James, *The Shadows of Power, The Council on Foreign Relations and the American Decline,* 1988 pp. 105–6.

18. Ibid., p. 218.

19. Ibid., p. 219.

20. Snow, John Howland and Shafer, The Honorable Paul W., *The Turning of the Tides,* Long House Publishing, pp. 63 & 67, 1953.

21. Newhouse, Bonnie, "Parents Must Help Plan Our Children's Future Education," *Traverse City Record-Eagle,* March 18, 1992.

22. "Progress Reports," ASCD High School Futures Planning Consortium III, Park Place Hotel, Traverse City, Michigan, August, 1991.

23. Newhouse, Bonnie, "Sound the Alarm, Freedom Issues for the 21st Century," *Free World Research Journal,* Vol. 1 No. 1, Spring 1994.

24. Stanton, Anne." Diplomas at Stake with New Exam," *Traverse City Record-Eagle,* April 19, 1993, 1A.

25. Iserbyt, Charlotte, *The Deliberate Dumbing Down of America,* Conscience Press, Ravenna, Ohio, 1999.

26. Taber, Tiffany "HOMEROOM," Blog. US Department of Education *The Critical Voice of Parents in Education* 6/29/2015.

Chapter 21
1. Hebrews 11:1 (JB).

2. Habakkuk 3:2, (Paraphrased).
   Boa, Kenneth & Anders, Max; *Drawing Near,* Thomas Nelson, Inc. Publishing, Nashville, Tenn. 1987 (Reprinted by Concerned Women for America, 1989 as *Strength for the Coming Days*) (p.199).

3. I Peter 5:8–11.

4. Bakker, Tammy Faye, *Run to the Roar,* New Leaf Press, Inc. 1980, Harrison, Arkansas, p.16

5. James 5:14–16.

6. Boa, Kenneth & Anders, Max; *Drawing Near* (p. 259), Ibid.
   II Corinthians 4:16–18, Micah 7:7, Psalm 28:6,7 (Paraphrased),

7. Pastor Jim Helman's Letter to the Congregation 2/25/1998.

Chapter 22
1. Phil 4:19.

2. Foster, Richard J. and Smith, James Bryan (eds), *Devotional Classics* HarperSanFrancisco, A Division of HarperCollins Publishers Copyright 1993 by RENOVARE, Inc.

3. Ephesians 2:8–9; Boa, Kenneth and Anders, Max; *Drawing Near* (p. 189).

4. Ibid, Psalm 27:1; Malachi 4:2 p. 213.

5. Ylvisaker, John, *I Was There To Hear Your Borning Cry,* Women of the Evangelical Lutheran Church in America Worship Resource Book, Minneapolis, Minnesota, Augsburg Publishing House, 1987.

6. Ibid.

7. Haugk, Kenneth C., *Haugk Spiritual Gifts Inventory,* St. Louis, Missouri, Tebunah Ministries, 1998.

8. Stanley, Charles, *Motivational Gifts,* Charles Stanley Ministries, 2000.

9. Psalm 56:12.

10. Psalm 61:8.

11. Ephesians 2, 8–9.

12. Hebrews 12:5–6, 11–13, (Paraphrased).
    Boa, Kenneth and Anders, Max; *Drawing Near,* p. 265.

13. Habakkuk 3:2, Ibid. p. 199.

14. Psalm 139:16.

Chapter 23
1. Micah 7:7
   Boa, Kenneth and Anders, Max; *Drawing Near* p. 259, Ibid.

2. Psalm 27:13 and 14
   Boa, Kenneth and Anders, Max; *Drawing Near* p. 268, Ibid.

3. John 15:26.

4. Acts 15:39–40.

5. Ephesians 2:9.

6. Chambers,Oswald; *My Utmost For His Highest* Uhrichsville, Ohio,
   Barbour Publishing, Inc. 1963. (May 2) The Passion of Patience
   Habakkuk 2:3.

7. Psalm 27:14.

Appendix D
1. In the Missouri Synod, Who Are the Conservatives, *Missouri
   in Perspective Document Reprint ELIM Tracts*, St.Louis,
   MO 63131 p.2

2. Ibid p.2-3

3. Ibid p.3

4. Ibid p.3

5. Ibid p.3

6. Ibid p.3

7. Ibid p.3-4

8. Ibid p.4

9. Ibid p.4

10. Ibid p.4

11. Ibid p.4

12. Ibid p.4

13. *Voice of Triumph, Vol. III No. 5, May 1977* Portland, Oregon. Report Adopted by Commission on Theology and Church Relations Lutheran Church Missouri Synod

14. The Meaning of the Movement: The Lutheran Charismatic Renewal, July, 1973, *The Charismatic Movement in the Lutheran Church in America*, a Pastoral Perspective, Board of Publications, Lutheran Curch in America, 1974

15. *A Statement of Scriptural and Confessional Principles, Study Edition*, p.31, J.A.O. Preus, St. Louis, Missouri 1972

16. *Faithful To Our Calling, Faithful To Our Lord–Part I, A Witness To Our Faith*, A Joint Statement and Discussion of Issues p.37 The Faculty of Concordia Seminary, St. Louis, MO

17. *A Statement of Scriptural and Confessional Principles, Study Edition*, Mission of the Church, Part III p.15 J.A.O. Preus, St. Louis, Missouri 1972

18. *Faithful To Our Calling, Faithful To Our Lord–Part I, A Witness To Our Faith,* A Joint Statement and Discussion of Issues p.33 The Faculty of Concordia Seminary, St. Louis, MO

19. *A Statement of Scriptural and Confessional Principles, Study Edition,* Mission of the Church, Part III p.39 J.A.O. Preus, St. Louis, Missouri 1972

20. Historical-Critical Methodology, *Missouri in Perspective Document Reprint ELIM Tracts*, St. Louis, MO 63131

Appendix E
1. Tietjen, Dr. John H., *FACT FINDING OR FAULT FINDING? An Analysis of President J.A.O. Preus' Investigation of Concordia Seminary,* St. Louis, Missouri, September, 1972. p.2

2. Ibid., p.3

3. Tietjen, Dr. John H., *Memoirs in Exile* Augsburg Fortress Press, 1990 p.107.

4. Ibid., p.110.

5. Tietjen, Dr. John H., *Letter to all Pastors in the Lutheran Church—Missouri Synod,* St. Louis, Missouri, September, 1972.

6. Culver, Virginia, "Lutheran Delegates Open Heresy Trial," *The Denver Post,* July 12, 1973.

7. Culver, Virginia, "Heresy Now 'False Doctrine'" *The Denver Post,* July 13, 1973.

8. Letter drafted by ELIM Board of Directors sent to all members of The Lutheran Church—Missouri Synod, St. Louis, Missouri, September 25, 1973.

9. Letter sent to Congregations in the Colorado District by Colo. District President Dr. Waldemar Meyer and 3 District Vice Presidents (Arnold Obermeier, Walter A. Enge, and N.E. Hattendorf) Aurora, Colorado, February 13, 1974.

10. Letter sent to the Pastors in the Colorado District by Colo. District President Dr. Waldemar Meyer, Aurora, Colorado, April 10, 1974.

11. "LCMS Presidents Fail to Solve Issue of Seminex Ordinations," *The Lutheran Church—Missouri Synod Weekly News Update* #19, St. Louis, Missouri, May 7, 1975, p. 3.

12. Colorado Laymen's Newsletter (Convocation Issue) Number 17, Denver, Colorado, October, 1975.

13. *TOGETHER IN MISSION,* Volume 2, Number 4, St. Louis, Missouri, September, 1975, p. 8.

14. Roth, Rev. Samuel J., Ibid. pp. 9–11.

15. "Clusters," *MISSOURI IN PERSPECTIVE* Reprint, St. Louis, MO August 1975.

APPENDIX A

ART'S JOURNEY

I suppose, as it is with most people who graduate from seminary, I was eager to begin my ministry as an ordained pastor. Bonnie and I had endured the hardships and joys of three years of seminary campus life and one year of vicarage, as well as three months of Clinical Pastoral Education (CPE) at Fort Logan Mental Health Center in Denver. While I was doing my CPE at Fort Logan, during the last three months of my vicarage, I got a phone call from my brother, informing me that our dad had just died in a vehicle accident. Following the death of our youngest brother in Viet Nam just two and a half years earlier, it seemed as though the bottom had dropped out again. Being in the Clinical Pastoral Education program was a great help in beginning to deal with the grief of two great losses in such a short time.

Returning to the seminary for my last year, following my dad's death was difficult. It took some time before I was emotionally ready to tackle the academics of my senior year. I wandered aimlessly through my studies for several months but finally, with Bonnie's support and direct urging, I began to get back on track.

One of the important things I learned on Vicarage was that it was okay to struggle with Scripture, faith, and my role as a Christian, as well as getting a whole new perspective regarding ecumenism. Upon returning to the seminary for the last year, I was not only struggling with elements of my faith but also the efficacy and the importance of baptism. Thinking my Romans' professor would be able to help me sort this out, I went to him, and shared with him that I was having difficulty with the concept of baptism.

He said, "Mr. Newhouse, Do you want to graduate from this seminary?"

"Of course," I replied.

"Then you had better believe it," he stated emphatically. End of discussion!

His response was a bit less than helpful. Looking back, this was most likely one of the first indications that I might have conflict with the LC—MS mindset in the future. From then on, my approach was, "cooperate and graduate" and work out the rest later.

Finally the day came, we all had been waiting for: Call Day. We had been eagerly awaiting the Call Service, when I would find out where I would be starting my formal ministry as pastor. My name was announced, and I was informed I would be returning to the church at which I had completed my Vicarage: Redeemer Lutheran Church, Denver Colorado.

It was with excitement, as well as trepidation that Bonnie and I began our journey, not simply as husband and wife, but now as pastor and pastor's wife. We were excited and somewhat naïve. As I firmly believed the Lord whom I served was an inclusive God, rather than an exclusive God, I gradually discovered this belief was about to be challenged by the Synod. There were hints during my last year in the seminary that my firm belief in God's inclusion of all Christians in His grace might prove to be an issue as I started my official ministry within the LC—MS. However, I felt confident it would not be an issue at the church to which I had been called. As I had served my Vicarage at Redeemer, I knew the senior pastor was more open to associating with other denominations and Christian organizations than were the more conservative pastors in the LC—MS.

As time passed during my time at Redeemer in Denver, however, it became increasingly more evident to me that the LC—MS was gradually becoming less and less open to any informal affiliation or participation with other Christian denominations or their clergy, even including other Lutheran denominations. It seemed that "Law" was more important than "Gospel," and an internal struggle was beginning to manifest itself. I was involved in several ecumenical endeavors, which seemed to me to be part of what practicing faith was all about.

As part of the senior pastor's and my belief that the Lord Jesus died for *all* people, we made the decision that all Christians were welcome to participate in the Lord's Supper. This was in contrast to the stance of the LC—MS, which allowed only LC—MS members to partake of communion in LC—MS churches. Although this did not meet with immediate opposition at Redeemer, it eventually did become an issue with the leaders of our congregation as the controversy within the synod moved to local congregations.

The impact of decisions and edicts from the Synod office began to trickle down to the local congregations, resulting in a fostering of divisiveness, anger, accusations, and controversy within the local congregations. Redeemer was not immune to the growing dissension, and individuals within the congregation began to align themselves with whichever "side" they thought was "right."

Members became increasingly suspicious of the pastors as well as fellow members of the congregation. The so-called "moderate" pastors within the synod began to feel the need for something, which would bring them together as a unit, in order to respond to the crisis within the synod. Thus, an organization called ELIM (Evangelical Lutherans in Mission) was born. One purpose of ELIM was to attempt to move the Synod officials into dialogue in an effort to resolve our differences. The senior pastor and I were not alone in having difficulty with the increasing pressure from the Synod administration to refrain from what they considered "unauthorized fellowship." There was a national response growing among many LC—MS pastors in opposition to the extreme exclusive practice of our Christian faith demanded by the Synod officials.

In February of 1974, about 600 students and forty-five faculty members exited from the St. Louis Seminary campus. This began what was became known as Seminex, or seminary in exile. Classes continued off campus with the now-fired former faculty. Soon, ELIM focused on the effect this would have on the call process of the Seminex graduates.

Meanwhile the LC—MS Anaheim Convention in 1975 met and passed what became the turning point with regard to ELIM membership, as it declared the activity of ELIM as schismatic. The result was to force those of us affiliated with ELIM to make a choice between ELIM and LC—MS.

The Synod's response was to condemn ELIM as being "outside the Lutheran Confessions" and eventually required all pastors to reaffirm their loyalty to the LC—MS. The result was to force those of us affiliated with ELIM to make a choice between ELIM and LC—MS. That same decision would eventually make its way to the individual congregations.

I would have to make a decision. After much prayer and discussion, I decided I could not sign a reaffirmation of loyalty to the LC—MS. I was loyal to my Savior, not a denomination named LC—MS; especially one that seemed to be operating outside the very things our Savior stood for: compassion, love, understanding, and forgiveness, which were being replaced by false accusations, fostering of dissension, judgment, and self-righteousness.

Following the formation of ELIM, members believed a more formal association was necessary. Therefore, the AELC (Association of Evangelical Lutheran Churches) formed, and years later, the constituting convention was held. This brought together the ALC (American Lutheran Church), the LCA (Lutheran Church in America), and the AELC (Association of Evangelical Lutheran Churches) into one body called the ELCA (Evangelical Lutheran Church in America). (The constituting convention of the ELCA was to begin April 30, 1987, and I would be privileged to attend the AELC convention in Michigan as a voting delegate and participate in the vote to unite the AELC, ALC, and LCA into the one body of the ELCA. My joy was overwhelming.)

In the Denver area, not only was our congregation affected, but also the local community. There were articles in the Denver newspapers giving blow-by-blow accounts of many of the accusations of teaching false doctrine as the Synod claimed, as well as judgments and innuendos against moderate pastors and congregations. We held several meetings at the church in an attempt to inform members of issues in the current controversy, as well as to dispel the many false accusations, which were being circulated. We had hoped to be able to initiate a healing process, but it soon became apparent the divisions were growing and any healing would be extremely difficult, if not impossible.

One particular day I was in a local pharmacy to pick up a prescription. While waiting for it to be filled, a woman recognized me from an article in one of the Denver papers. She glared at me and in a very stern voice, while shaking her finger at me, said, "You're one of those pastors who don't believe in the Virgin Birth!"

Not only was I shocked at such an accusation, I also was not one to shrink from an accusation and responded, "I do, too."

Angrily, she came back, "You're lying, I know you don't!"

Realizing this was a no win, situation, I simply said, "Okay, whatever, but I'll pray for you." She left in a huff.

I did not fully realize the toll this controversy was taking, not only on me, but on my family as well. It was an all-consuming situation. I faced it at church, at meetings, in the community, and at home with a myriad of phone calls. Sleep was a luxury that seemed to arrive only at 3:00 or 4:00 a.m. Headaches were my daily companions. I was ignoring Bonnie and the children. Occasionally, I would have muscle spasms, which took me to the floor in pain. It seemed as though everywhere I went, the "Synodical War" was a topic of conversation.

I did not realize how all-encompassing this was until one evening during a party at another minister's home. I was in the usual Synodical conversation with Rev. Art Schroeder at whose home we were gathered. Art was a very gentle, wise, and faithful pastor. After he had allowed me to grumble and complain for a while, he finally put his hand on my shoulder and in a gentle voice gave me possibly the best pastoral advice I have ever gotten. He said, "Art, when this is all over, what are you going to have to complain about?" The 2 x 4 had hit the mule right between the eyes. God had given him the courage to tell me exactly what I needed to hear. He was absolutely correct.

After we moved from the Denver area in August of 1977, Art and I remained in contact through Christmas letters, but it was not until about the summer of 2010, he called and we reconnected in person. He was vacationing at a lake near our home in Traverse City,

Michigan. Bonnie and I then visited him at the cottage where he was staying with a friend of his. By then, in his '90s and still as compassionate and caring as ever, He did not remember his statement to me, but every time we have an opportunity to talk or meet, I thank him for his tough words, which were delivered with kindness and love.

Finally, after much turmoil within the congregation, the president of Redeemer congregation called a special congregational meeting on November 21, 1976 to vote whether to remain a member of the LC—MS or join the AELC. The vote was in favor of remaining affiliated with the LC—MS. It was now clear I had a very difficult decision ahead of me.

As time went on, it became clearer and clearer the divisions within our congregation were so great, and the distrust of both pastors so intense, that resignation may have been the only course of action. Finally, in November of 1976, I turned in my resignation as assistant pastor of Redeemer Lutheran Church. This was one of the most heart-wrenching and difficult faith-based decisions I have ever had to make. However, to do otherwise would have only continued the hurt and divisions festering in the congregation. With two small children, we were now without an income to pay a mortgage, car payments, and other general expenses. Amazingly, I didn't feel any sense of panic. This decision had been made with much prayer and trust in my Lord. Even though we didn't know what the future would bring, we were confident our Lord would walk with us through it.

Hardly a week had passed before a group of about 100 former Redeemer members called a meeting to discuss forming another congregation in affiliation with the AELC. We met in one of the member's home, and the initial meeting to form what was to become Peace with Joy Lutheran Church began. As we were discussing a myriad of possibilities for a name for the new congregation, I commented that I felt an enormous peace and joy of not having to face the daily anxiety regarding the crisis and controversy within the LC—MS. At that moment, it was suggested we name the new congregation Peace with Joy Lutheran Church.

Through much discussion, the new church body elected to call me as their full-time pastor and the former senior pastor of Redeemer, who had also resigned, to be the part-time pastor. Eventually, we met in a local community center for Sunday services with about 100 to 150 members of the new church. We were associated with the evolving national church body of the AELC (Association of Evangelical Lutheran Church).

For several years, my oldest brother, a psychiatrist, had been talking to me about coming into private practice with him in Traverse City, Michigan. I did not have an advanced degree in the mental health field and needed to move in that direction. I soon enrolled in the Masters of Psychology program at the University of Northern Colorado (UNC). Classes were held three days a week, enabling me to go to school and maintain my responsibilities as Pastor of Peace with Joy church. Finally, in August 1977, I completed my studies at UNC, and we planned our move to Traverse City, Michigan. We left Denver, Colorado in August of 1977 to embark on a new journey of faith.

Arriving in Traverse City, Michigan, we purchased a home with no current income and I began building a private practice in counseling, which I maintained for several years. In 1985, I accepted a position at what is now Northern Lakes Community Mental Health, where I eventually supervised several departments. I retired in 2010 after about twenty-five years of service. I currently continue to maintain a small private practice and occasionally conduct services at Bethlehem Lutheran Church where we attend services. God has ways of turning lemons into lemonade, and although I had left the parish ministry, He positioned me in a place where a ministry began with the mentally ill. I have been extremely privileged to work with those folks who, through no fault of their own, have had great burdens to bear because of mental illness. Even with the pain in this journey, God has continued to triumph and His grace to be shared.

APPENDIX B

The Phone Call

*M*y twenty-one-year-old brother Bernard was deployed to Viet Nam as a Navy corpsman in January of 1968. The day before he left, he came to visit us at our apartment, and later the two of us went out to play some pool. We reminisced and cautiously avoided any discussions of him possibly being wounded or killed in action. We all knew the mortality rate for corpsmen was about 80 percent, but we did not speak of it. It was as though if we avoided talking about it; it could not happen. Returning from our pool games, he returned to the farm in St. Johns to spend time with our mom and dad before leaving for San Diego.

The next morning, we met him at the Capitol City Airport in Lansing, Michigan, where he was to start his journey overseas; first to San Diego, California, then on to Saigon, South Viet Nam. Several of our family members were there to send him off, and we were all reserved in our farewells. None of us wanted to think this might be the last time we would see him alive. I so wanted to give him a huge hug but held back as we were all very, stoic. Again, it seemed as if we didn't acknowledge he was heading into harm's way, believing he would be okay and back home after his tour was completed. That missed hug continues to be one of my biggest regrets ever! Bonnie and I had scraped together $10.00 or $20.00 and put it in an envelope along with a note. We asked him not to open until he was airborne.

355

In the note, we assured him we would be praying for him and were sure God would be watching over him.

As the weeks passed, we were continually sending him "care packages" and letters. We prayed for his safety every night as we went to bed. Above my study desk, I had a map of Viet Nam and tried to keep up with where he was through the letters he sent to us. We anxiously awaited his letters and breathed a sigh of relief when we received a letter from him as it meant we had confirmation he was still okay.

Meanwhile, on the university campus there were numerous protests against the Viet Nam War. It was difficult to travel to my classes around campus while running into various groups of students protesting the war. I wanted to scream at the protestors because it seemed as though they were protesting against my own brother. I was proud of Bernard, and I wanted to somehow let them know that while they were protesting, my brother was putting his life on the line every single day. I kept my anger to myself and tried to think about the day he would return home.

The week of 21 April, Bonnie and I had gathered several items, and packaged them in a "care package" that we mailed to Bernard. We knew not only did he appreciate getting these packages, but also that he shared the contents with others, as it was a sort of unspoken decision that whoever got packages from home would share. On Saturday morning, 20 April, 1968, I hurried to the mailbox to see if we had gotten a letter from Bernard, as it had been a couple of weeks since we had heard from him. To my great relief there was a letter awaiting us. "Thank God, he's okay," I thought, as I brought the letter back to our apartment.

The last week in April 1968 was a busy one for Bonnie and me as I was attending Michigan State University as a full-time student in my senior year. We lived in Spartan Village, a housing complex on campus for married students. I was putting in extra hours with our next-door neighbor Israel Lindenfeld, a PhD math major, who had agreed to tutor me in German in exchange for me teaching him how to drive so he could pass his driver's test. Israel was born in Germany, fluent in the German language, and a good friend. Prior to coming to the United States, he had served in the Israeli army as a math instructor. Bonnie was working full time at a CPA firm in

Lansing as a bookkeeper. Our hours together, when we did not have other obligations, were few and far between.

On Saturday morning 27 April, 1968, we woke up about 7:00 a.m. but as it was a Saturday, we decided to just roll over and catch up on some much-needed sleep. About half an hour later, our phone rang, but we decided to let it ring, thinking if it was important who-ever was calling would call back.

About an hour later, the phone rang again. I answered it to the voice of my older brother, Tom. "Bernard's been killed!" he said.

Stunned, it felt as though my whole body exploded at his words, and my entire insides, torn out. I was numb. I was in shock. I had no words.

As our parents lived on a farm in St. Johns, which was about twenty miles south of Lansing, I told Tom we would drive right over there and meet him there. Our oldest brother Bob, a medical doctor, was a captain in the army stationed in Germany with his family, and our sister Barbara, Bernard's twin, was with her husband in St. Louis, Missouri, where he was attending his last year in the seminary. Tom and I, along with our spouses, were the only siblings close to home.

I don't remember much about the drive to the farm other than an overwhelming sense of disbelief. We had no details of his death, and my imagination ran wild. How did he die? Was he alone? Did he die in some mud hole all by himself? How could this be when we had prayed so fervently every day that God would protect him?

Gathered together at the farm in grief and disbelief, we learned Bernard had been killed on 21 April while on patrol in Quang Tri Province, South Viet Nam, the day after we had gotten his last letter. The telegram delivered by the Department of the Navy provided only minimal information. It would be a week before his body would return home.

That week was the longest and most torturous time in my life! I had to return to my classes, and Bonnie had the week off from work, but my ability to concentrate on my studies had totally disappeared. Every time I saw someone in uniform, I would well up with tears. Passing by all the student demonstrations going on against the war was unbearable. There seemed to be no place for my anger to go but inward. I withdrew from Bonnie, the one person who could offer me support, as we awaited my brother's return and his funeral.

By the time the funeral was arranged, our oldest brother Bob and his family had returned from Germany, as well as our sister Barbara and her husband from St, Louis, Mo. The funeral home environment was surreal. Of course, friends and relatives gathered, attempting to offer their condolences as best they could. But all I saw was my little brother lying so still in his casket in his Navy uniform. His twin sister Barbara could not bring herself to go to the funeral home, as she said she wanted to remember him as he was before he left for Viet Nam.

Bernard's body was accompanied by a young man from the Navy, who stood quietly by as the rest of the visitors wandered and mingled with each other. Among the flowers was one particularly exotic and beautiful arrangement. In the group of people who had gathered was a man whom none of us knew. He appeared to be taking Bernard's death especially hard. At some point, he and I began to talk. He felt terrible at Bernard's loss. It seems he had promised Bernard he would include him on a mountain-climbing expedition in Washington State, but due to lack of funds at the last minute, had excluded him from the group. He expressed his great sorrow and remorse over having excluded him from the expedition. He said he had special ordered the flowers from Hawaii in remembrance of Bernard. My heart went out to him as with me; his regrets could not be remedied.

As most of the people who attended the visitation were aware, I was intending to enroll in the Lutheran seminary in Springfield, Illinois at the end of the current school year. I felt a need to put on a front and attempt to help others with their grief. In retrospect, I think this was another way of my attempting to deny the reality of Bernard's death. The more I could think I was helping others, the less I would have to deal with my own grief and guilt.

That all came crashing down when someone came up to me and, in an effort to be helpful, said, "Just remember, all things work together for good to those who love God." Inside I was enraged! I wanted to slap him and tell him "What the hell do you know about anything working together for those who love God?" At that moment, I did not love God. I was angry with Him for allowing my best friend, my little brother, to die! I had believed with all my heart,

God would keep him safe. Over and over, we had prayed to Him. But I stuffed my feelings and thanked him for his concern; after all, I was to become a minister and must understand these things.

While Bernard was at Great Lakes Naval Base in Chicago, he had met a young woman who was also in the Navy. He and Janie had become a serious couple, and we had gotten to know her through Bernard's communication with us while he was in training. She had gotten leave in order to attend Bernard's funeral and was considered a part of our family. She had placed a bouquet of Shasta daisies in his casket as a token of her love for him as she said they were his favorite flowers.

The day of his funeral, the church was full. As St. Johns was a rather small town, there were people at the funeral service from Bernard's high-school class, former teachers, friends, as well as relatives and family. Father Banninga of St. John's Episcopal Church conducted the service and read a couple of the poems Bernard had written. The poems were prophetic in that Bernard seemed to have a premonition he would not survive his tour in Viet Nam. Each word struck like a lightning bolt into my very being. It sounded as though he was at peace with whatever happened to him, yet I was far from it.

The trip to Deepdale Cemetery in Lansing for the burial was one of the longest twenty-mile trips I have ever taken. It was putting finality on the fact that Bernard was dead, and I would not be seeing him ever again. I would never again be able to share time with him. I would never again be able to have the closeness we had shared throughout our lifetime. We would never again be able to share mutual adventures. All that had been yanked away from me, and I was angry, hurt, and depressed. My faith had taken a major hit, and I didn't have a clue how to fix it. I was not sure I wanted to at that point.

We arrived at the cemetery and gathered at the grave. I don't recall much of that graveside service except the military honor guard who were present were very respectful and caring as they shared with us the loss of a brother as well. The gun salute followed by the playing of taps also seemed to drill another hole deeper into my heart, a solemn reminder that it was finished.

Following family gatherings after the funeral, the obligations and responsibility of returning to classes was difficult. As my life went on, feelings of guilt, anger, and frustration mixed. I had to push forward with my classes in order to graduate to be able to enter the seminary at the end of the year.

Toward the end of fall term 1968, I received permission from the university to take my final exams early, as classes at Concordia Theological Seminary in Springfield, Illinois were to begin prior to MSU's term end. I lacked only four credits for graduation, but I was able to take my final German class at the seminary for transfer credit, so I graduated with a Bachelor of Arts from MSU in 1969.

Bonnie and I had rented an apartment across from the seminary in Springfield, sight unseen, while we were still at MSU and arrived to a rundown, dilapidated building which housed a pool hall on the lower level and two apartments on the second floor. It was to be our future home. We shared the apartment with hundreds of silverfish and cock-roaches, which was a new and unwelcome experience for both of us.

As I struggled with Greek class, I also struggled with the fact of Bernard's death. However, as time went on, my studies required so much of my mental energy that his death was relegated to the remote parts of my mind. The only conscious effect was that I no longer felt confident in praying for anyone's safety. My thinking was, "It doesn't do any good anyway, so why even ask God to protect anyone?"

My first two years at seminary, followed by a year of vicarage, Clinical Pastoral Education in Denver, Colorado, and my final year of studies at the seminary were all haunted to one degree or another by the loss of my brother. April 21 was always an emotional day as I felt his loss more than ever, but our lives went on. I was called to serve as assistant pastor at Redeemer Lutheran Church in Denver, Colorado, where I had done my vicarage and somehow put his death on a back burner, or so I thought.

Throughout the following years, it became more and more an obsession to learn exactly what had taken place the day he was killed. I needed some closure and information seemed to be the answer. That came to some degree with the unexpected contact with my brother's sergeant, who was with him when he was killed. George has since become a close friend, and we communicate with each other on a regular basis. Still, the fact that I missed him so much was at times, overwhelming.

His loss was, for me, a huge faith issue, and I prayed constantly for God to take away my pain and provide me with some peace. In my mind, I knew he was with his Savior in heaven, but my heart still ached at his loss. There were times when I did feel at peace, but there were other times, when the thought of his loss was overwhelming.

A couple of years ago as a substitute pastor at our church, I preached a sermon based on John 20:19–31 entitled, "Faith, Doubts, and Grace." The point of that sermon was that even though we are faithful Christians, we may still struggle with our doubts and with the tension between our day-to-day living and our faith. I shared with the congregation my faith struggle over my brother's untimely death. I told them that throughout this long, struggling journey, I had begun to understand the journey God's people went through as they wandered through the wilderness for forty years.

They had to learn God had not abandoned them but, rather, had much to teach them about faith, grace, and His love. They had to learn to trust Him, even in the darkest moments. What I had to learn was that understanding God's decisions is not faith for we may never understand while we walk this earth. God is interested in trust— trust in Him.

The lesson continues to this day, and there are still moments of sadness over the loss of my brother. He was an important part of my life for which I am truly thankful, and I still miss him greatly. However, underneath it all is the faith that God is in charge as he says to me, "Come unto me all who are weary and burdened, and I will give you rest. Take my yoke upon you and learn from me, for I am gentle and humble in heart, and you will find rest for your souls."

Chronology of Events—Missouri Synod Schism

05/19/1969 John H. Tietjen elected president at Concordia Seminary (CS), St. Louis, MO

07/12/1969 A. O. Preus elected president of the Lutheran Church—Missouri Synod (LCMS)

09/09/1970 Preus appoints a Fact-Finding Committee (FFC) to investigate the CS faculty

09/01/1972 Preus issues report condemning numerous CS faculty members for teaching false doctrine

09/08/1972 Tietjen issues *Fact-Finding or Fault-Finding* to counter the Preus Report

07/10/1973 LCMS New Orleans convention affirms adopted doctrinal statements as binding

07/11/1973 New Orleans convention adopts "A Statement of Scriptural and Confessional Principles"

07/12/1973 New Orleans convention condemns CS faculty for teaching false doctrine

08/28/1973 Conference Evangelical Lutheranism organizes (ELIM)

01/20/1974 Concordia Seminary Board of Control suspends Tietjen as president

01/21/1974 Concordia Seminary student body announces moratorium on classes

01/21/1974 CS faculty announces that it considers the faculty to be suspended

02/19/1974 Students decide to join faculty in resuming seminary education "in exile" (Seminex)

02/20/1974 Classes of CS Seminary in Exile begin at St. Louis University and Eden Theological Seminary (A United Church of Christ Seminary)

05/24/1974 First class graduates from Seminex

08/26/1974 Second ELIM Assembly held in Chicago

06/29/1975 Missouri District official Oscar Gerken clears Tietjen of charges of false doctrine

07/04/11/75 LCMS Anaheim convention condemns ELIM and censures eight district presidents for ordaining Seminex graduates and authorizes their removal from office by Preus

08/13/1975 Third ELIM Assembly authorizes formation of a new association

08/1976 CCM ruled congregations, pastors, and teachers could not be affiliated with AELC

04/02/1976 Preus removes four district presidents from office

12/3/1975–4/1976 Assoc. of Evangelical Lutheran Churches (AELC) is organized with five constituent synods

4/14–16/1978 AELC issues "A Call for Lutheran Union"

08/29/1986 ALC, AELC, LCA conventions agree to form the Evangelical Lutheran Church in America (ELCA)

APPENDIX D

Issue of Controversy	Authoritarian Conservative	Individual-Responsibility Conservative
1. Way to resolve theological differences of opinion within the Synod	Provided by the highest authorities in the Synod, especially by the synodical conventions and the synodical president (1)	Solutions should be found through the study of the Scriptures and free discussion with all opinions considered. Stress the Scriptural promise that the Holy Spirit will lead Christians into all truth. (2)
2. Approach to overseas mission activity	Leaders of a "parent" church have the obligation to supervise overseas mission churches so that the practices of the overseas groups conform to the policies of the "parent," especially in the area of cooperation with other Christian denominations in the proclamation of the Gospel, worship, and Christian ministry. (3)	Members of overseas "sister" churches having heard and believed the Gospel should be encouraged to cooperate with other Christians in accord with the dictates of their own consciences and the best stewardship of resources. (4)
3. Question of whether pastoral candidates from Seminex should participate in interviews for placement, ordination, and calls at the seminary they left in protest	They should because LC—MS administrators have so decided and thus everything else is sheer disobedience to authority. They must be certified by LC—MS, Concordia Seminary Faculty in order to be placed, ordained, or installed. (5)	Submitting to interviews may be a matter of conscience for a candidate. He should be free to decide after examining his own conscience in the light of the Gospel. (6)

4. Question of the effective power of the Gospel to motivate Christians to be led by the Holy Spirit	Fear that under the banner of "freedom of the Gospel" Christians will wander into all manner of sin and error. Thus, they believe that rules and regulations must continually be enforced to prevent this. (7)	Believe that the Gospel has such a transforming effect in the lives of Christians that they should be encouraged to evaluate all rules and make all decisions in light of the will of God expressed throughout Scriptures. (8)
5. Current debate of the "Third Use" of God's Law in the lives of Christians	See Christian freedom as an excuse for freewheeling, nonconformist behavior, which must be curbed. (9)	See this freedom as the blessed result of the restored relationship between God and His people wrought by Christ and announced in the Gospel. (10)
6. How firm is the dividing line between the authoritarian and individual-responsibility approaches	No firm line—both approaches share many common values: a. importance of tradition b. unchangeable character of God's moral law c. the need for self-discipline d. dependence on God to vindicate righteousness and punish evil e. some who take an authoritarian approach on most issues may take an individual-responsibility approach on another. (11)	No firm line—both approaches share many common values a. importance of tradition b. unchangeable character of God's moral law c. the need for self-discipline d. dependence on God to vindicate righteousness and punish evil e. some who take an individual-responsibility approach on most issues may take an authoritarian approach on another. (12)

7. Current renewal concerning the Baptism in the Holy Spirit and the use of the spiritual gifts	The most serious doctrinal problem of this movement is its tendency to claim direct spiritual illumination apart from the Word—a malady that may have its origin in a loss of confidence in the divine efficacy of the Word. Pastors who propagate neo-Pentecostal doctrine in Lutheran congregations often divide the church, thereby giving offense to their flocks . . . They must take seriously the possibility of coming under church discipline. (13)	Where it is authentic, that is, where it bears good fruit, the charismatic experience must be understood within the scope of the life of the Church. There is no cause for Lutheran pastors or people to suggest either explicitly or implicitly that one cannot be charismatic and remain Lutheran in good standing. In ALC churches, using the gifts of the spirit of healing and prayer were even encouraged and supported. (14)
8. Inerrancy of Scripture	With Luther, we confess that "God's Word cannot err" (LC, IV, 57). We therefore believe, teach, and confess that since the Holy Scriptures are the Word of God, they contain no errors or contradictions but that they are in all their parts and words the infallible truth. We hold that the opinion that Scripture contains errors is a violation of the sola scriptura principle, for it rests upon the acceptance of some norm or criterion of truth above the Scriptures. We recognize that there are apparent contradictions or discrepancies and problems, which arise because of uncertainty over the original text. (15)	The reliability or "inerrancy" of the Scriptures cannot be determined by the twentieth-century standards of factuality. Nor do the Scriptures link the work of the Holy Spirit with this kind of "inerrancy." The purpose of the Spirit imparted by our Lord is to lead us into the whole truth about what God was doing in Jesus Christ, that we might be redeemed, and He may be glorified. In disclosing that Truth, God does not err, and in achieving that purpose, the Spirit is active in the Word that does not lead us astray; to that the Spirit within us bears witness. (16)

9. Mission Affirmation	We believe and confess that the primary mission of the church is to make disciples of every nation through the preaching of the Gospel and the administration of the Sacraments. Other necessary activities of the church, such as ministering to men's physical needs, are to serve the church's primary mission and its goal that men will believe and confess Jesus Christ as their Lord and Savior. (17)	Those who follow in the steps of our Lord are called to confront the gainsayers of our time with the truth, to heal the lepers and lame of our day while we speak God's message of forgiveness, to be ready to share our wealth with the hungry of the world while we proclaim the Gospel, and to share our power with those oppressed while we announce the message of Christ the Liberator. (18)
10. Ordination of women	No	Yes
11. Ecumenism, including fellowship, communion with other believers including other Lutherans in America: ALC and LCA	No	Yes
12. The issue of the status of doctrinal statements adopted at Synod conventions. Are they binding and equal to the Lutheran confessions?	Yes	No

| 13. Use of the Historical Critical Method in Interpreting Scripture | No. Since God is the Lord of history, and has revealed Himself by acts in history and has in the person of His Son actually entered into man's history, we acknowledge that the historical framework in which the Gospel message is set in Scripture is an essential part of the Word. Furthermore, we recognize that the inspired Scriptures are historical documents written in various times, places, and circumstances. We therefore believe that the Scriptures invite historical investigation and are to be taken seriously as historical documents. We affirm, however, that the Christian interpreter of Scripture cannot adopt, uncritically, the presupposition and canons of the secular historian, but that he will be guided in his use of historical techniques by the presuppositions of his faith in the Lord of history, who reveals Himself in Holy Scripture as the one who creates, sustains, and even enters our history in order to lead it to His end. (19) | Yes. Contemporary biblical scholars believe that, to be understood fully and properly, the Scriptures must be understood in the context of the historical situation in which they were written. These scholars note that, then as now, God's people were affected by contemporary forms of language, worship, and understanding of the nature of the world. These influences naturally shaped the work of the scriptural writers as they attempted to communicate the Word of God to their contemporaries. Thus, historical-critical methodology provides tools that help scholars understand better the historical setting of the biblical writings in order to help them more fully understand and relate the message of the Scriptures today. (20) |

APPENDIX E

EVENTS LEADING TO LC—MS SCHISM 1969–1975

*I*n 1969, two leaders had emerged to the forefront of the developing controversy: Dr. John H. Tietjen, president of Concordia Seminary in St. Louis, Missouri, and Dr. Jacob A. O. Preus, former president of Concordia Seminary in Springfield, Illinois, newly elected president of the Lutheran Church—Missouri Synod. A few months after his election, Preus met with Tietjen and told him that he considered his election to be a mandate to clean house doctrinally in the Synod and especially at the St. Louis Seminary. He further stated that it was his intention to bring the seminary into line with the traditional doctrinal position of the Synod. (1)

Preus appointed a fact-finding committee in September 1970 to investigate the doctrinal positions of the St. Louis faculty. Six months later, he distributed his "Statement of Scriptural and Confessional Principles" and a letter to all congregations, pastors, and teachers in the Synod. The letter explained that he prepared the statement for use by the Seminary's Board of Control in identifying areas, which need further attention in terms of the Synod's doctrinal position. (2)

The fact-finding committee completed their faculty interviews in March 1971 and submitted their report to President Preus in June, 1971. Preus turned them over to Concordia Seminary's Board of Control for review the next month.

By June 1972, the Seminary's Board of Control had finished their task and reported:

> A basic issue lies at the root of the issues . . . and comes to the surface again and again no matter what the topic of discussion may be. From one perspective, the issue is not doctrine but method. How does a Lutheran theologian carry out the task of interpreting the Scriptures? Looked at from another perspective, the issue is very much doctrinal. It is the question of the proper relation between the Scriptures and the Gospel in the task of Scripture interpretation. Finally, they summarized their findings. "In its careful review of the Fact Finding Committee report and in the interviews and discussions held with faculty members, the board to this date has found no false doctrine among the members of the seminary faculty. Though unsubstantiated accusations against the faculty as a whole, and individual members continue to be made, the board has not been required to deal with any formal charge of false doctrine. (3)

In September of 1972, Preus issued his 160-page "Blue Book" report, contradicting the Board of Control's progress report and condemning numerous and unnamed faculty for teaching false doctrine. In the concluding section, he explained why he as president of the Synod was exempt from following the procedures to be followed when dealing with your "brother" as outlined in Matthew 18, demanding the Seminary's Board of Control deal with Tietjen's failure to exercise the supervision of the doctrine of the faculty. (4)

A week later, Tietjen issued his official response to the Blue Book—a thirty-five-page document titled "FACT FINDING OR FAULT FINDING—An Analysis of President J.A.O. Preus's Investigation of Concordia Seminary," which he mailed to all clergy in the Synod. In the introduction, Tietjen addressed his concerns, both about the committee and the interview process, saying many people in the Synod viewed the committee as a "stacked deck" from the beginning. "The Fact Finding Committee Report claims to present a profile of the doctrinal position of the faculty of Concordia Seminary, St. Louis. Its claim is false. The Report is in fact a distortion and misrepresentation of what faculty members believe, teach, and confess. "(5)

Every time the clergy gathered for any social function, the controversy was the main topic of discussion. Not only was the controversy being discussed in Lutheran circles, it was being reported on in secular newspapers and news magazines across the country. *The New York Times, Detroit Free Press, Washington Post, Chicago Tribune, Chicago Sun-Times, Cincinnati Post, Milwaukee Journal, Minneapolis Tribune, Minneapolis Star, Toledo Blade, St. Louis Post Dispatch, St. Louis Globe-Democrat, Evansville Press, Hartford Courant, Newsweek* and *Times Magazines,* and *The Denver Post* all carried stories.

I recalled the previous July 1973, during the Synod's Convention in New Orleans, when I read the headline on the religious section of *The Denver Post:* "Lutheran Delegates Open Heresy Trial." Reading the highlights of the week-long convention attended by 2,000 visitors in addition to the 1,100 voting delegates by religion reporter Virginia Culver, helped to draw me out of my complacency.

> A heresy trial with 1,100 judges began here Thursday morning as delegates to the convention of the Lutheran Church—Missouri Synod (LC—MS) considered charges brought against faculty at one of the church's seminaries. Delegates heard a resolution Wednesday night charging that the faculty of Concordia Seminary, St. Louis, MO had supported false doctrine teaching. (6)

The following day, she reported:

> Delegates to the LC—MS convention approved a resolution Thursday that charged many professors at a church-owned seminary with teaching of false doctrine. The action means that as many as 45 professors

could lose their jobs at Concordia Seminary, St. Louis. More than 400 persons protested the resolution by filing quietly to the secretary's desk where they left their names. The president of the seminary, Dr. John Tietjen and faculty members, repeatedly have denied the charges, but the issue has continued to be the focus of this convention. (7)

The voting results on the various resolutions by the delegates revealed a polarized Synod. With no middle ground, convention delegates were forced to choose one camp or the other. The conservatives supported Preus, and the moderates were sympathetic to Tietjen and the faculty majority.

Within a month, an opposition group formed called Evangelical Lutherans in Mission (ELIM) held their first convention in Chicago, attended by more than 800 from all parts of the country. The ELIM board of directors summarized the mood of the participants in a letter to all Synod members:

> The suspension of Dr. John Tietjen from his office as president of the St. Louis Seminary (now delayed because of constitutional questions), coming barely three days after he was charged with false doctrine, is a vivid illustration of the crisis of legalism we face. At least four other synodical school faculty members face a similar fate now, and more actions are in the offing ... We cannot simply because we detest controversy, sit back and do nothing, in hope that it will all go away. Those who have been reluctant to speak out before will have to make their voice heard now. (8)

Tietjen's suspension from office in January 1974 had resulted in a mass exodus of a majority of the professors and over half the student body who then formed a "Seminary in Exile." Known as "Seminex," classes were split between two locations in St. Louis: St. Louis University School of Divinity run by the Jesuits and Eden Seminary, a United Church of Christ School.

In February 1974, Colorado District President, Reverend Waldemar Meyer, and three Colorado District Vice Presidents had sent a letter to all congregations in the Colorado District, expressing their concern about the crisis that was confronting the Synod and the St. Louis Seminary:

> We believe that the purposes, for which God has called us as His people, are being hindered by political processes in our Synod and the District. We wish that we could agree with the synodical president, who says, 'The issue always has been and continues to be basically doctrinal.' We do not deny that there are doctrinal issues as there always have been in the history of the Church. We believe that those issues can be resolved through brotherly discussion under the Word of God and the Lutheran Confessions. We are seeking to create a forum in the Colorado District where issues can be discussed and where we can discover to a greater degree the unity that is ours in Christ. Such discussions have not always taken place in our Church in recent months. Instead, there have been public denunciations of pastors and professors without proof, suspensions and terminations of ministry without consultation with those accused and terminated, and blanket condemnations of unnamed persons. Such procedures do not even meet the world's standards for fairness, to say nothing of the directions of our Lord in His Word. We believe that such procedures make our church an object of ridicule before the world and hinder our mission. (9)

In the next letter from the district president in late April, Rev. Meyer stated that the Council of Presidents would soon be meeting to wrestle with the issue of placement of graduates from the Seminary in Exile since the Commission on Constitutional Matters has ruled that these graduates "cannot be eligible for placement in the ministry of the LC—MS." (11). The Colorado District Board of Directors,